CW00972333

Affair of State

A Biography of the
8th Duke and Duchess of Devonshire

Henry Vane

PETER OWEN
LONDON AND CHESTER SPRINGS

PETER OWEN PUBLISHERS
73 Kenway Road, London SW5 ORE
First published in Great Britain 2004
by Peter Owen Publishers
© Henry Vane, 2004
All rights reserved.
No part of this publication may be reproduced
in any form or by any means without the prior
permission of the publishers.
A catalogue record for this book is available
from the British Library.
ISBN 0 7206 1233 0
Printed and bound in Spain by Graficás Diaz Tuduri

ACKNOWLEDGEMENTS

I WOULD LIKE to express my thanks to the Duke of Devonshire for access to the papers of the Cavendish family at Chatsworth, to Mr Charles Noble, the Keeper of the Devonshire Collection, for his very kind help in the research stage and in the search for illustrations, to the Duke of Devonshire and the Chatsworth Settlement Trustees for permission to reproduce photographs and portraits from Chatsworth and to Lord Cavendish of Furness for permission to reproduce the portrait of Lord Frederick Cavendish from Holker Hall. I am particularly indebted to Mr Alan Akeroyd for providing free of charge the Kimbolton photograph from the Huntingdon Record Office.

CONTENTS

ILLUSTRATIONS
between pages 144 and 145

INTRODUCTION

THE STORY OF Lord Hartington's thirty-year affair with the Duchess of Manchester, and their subsequent marriage as Duke and Duchess of Devonshire, has long been known to historians of the period, but no book on the personal life of either of them has ever been written. Louise von Alten, the 'Double Duchess', has had no biography at all, in spite of her legendary beauty and the dictatorship she held for half a century over a large section of English society. The letters to her published by A.L. Kennedy in *My Dear Duchess* (1956) illuminated a very few years of her life; of the remaining collection much was unfortunately lost when a writer who was working on it at home suddenly died; the residue is now at Chatsworth.

Hartington – the 8th Duke of Devonshire – may be thought to have been better served, since two lives of him were published in 1904 and 1911; but they are almost wholly concerned with his political career. Unusually for a figure of his prominence, he then escaped the interest of any later historian until 1994, when Patrick Jackson published *The Last of the Whigs*; but this, too, is a political biography. The private Hartington is therefore hardly known and that especially because he was a man who made very different impressions on the public and on his close friends. He was a figure about whom anecdotes accumulated, and these were progressively distorted according to what people supposed to be his character. One of my prime tasks has been to track these anecdotes to their original version and to discard the inauthentic. It is typical of the man that hitherto the story of his first affair, with the famous courtesan Skittles, has been known only in a form that was almost complete fabrication. Now, however, the complete series of Hartington's letters to Skittles has become available and the genuine story can be told.

Hartington epitomized the kind of aristocrat his contemporaries most admired: a sportsman, personally casual but born to a splendid historic fortune, without ambition for himself but raised to the forefront of politics by family tradition. After becoming a Cabinet minister at thirty-two and leader of his party at forty-one, he was three times offered the premiership, which he refused. He seems to typify the kind of career that Victorian England laid easily at the feet of its well-born leaders. Recent historians have revised the underestimation he formerly suffered and have discovered more political ability and less pre-ordained privilege in this stately progress.

Louise Alten, for her part, exemplifies another vanished feature, the role of the political hostess. The part she played in Hartington's career even while she was his mistress gives a special twist to this function, and her more conventional ascendancy as Duchess of Devonshire, when she was said to be the most powerful person outside the government, shows the influence that could be wielded by women in a political system from which they were formally excluded.

The three political biographies of Hartington leave little need for covering the same ground. I have therefore felt free to treat politics with a broad brush, only to the extent that they affected the lives of the two main characters. Those who are looking for miniatures are referred to the three works cited.

A word of explanation is required for the use of names in this book: 'Louise' for the Duchess of Manchester/Devonshire is at the opposite end of the scale of formality from 'Lady Frederick' for Hartington's sister-in-law; but I have chosen them both for brevity and recognizability. Both criteria are defeated in the case of the Duke of Devonshire, who went through three names in the course of his life, and the only solution was to use the one by which he was known in each period.

1
Louise von Alten

THE SCENE IS Hanover; the date is 5 June 1851. King Ernest Augustus is celebrating his eightieth birthday. As Duke of Cumberland and the eldest surviving uncle of Queen Victoria, he inherited the Hanoverian throne when she became Queen of England, in accordance with the German law limiting the succession to males. The Hanoverians were glad to have their own king again, and they are now celebrating his birthday with great demonstrations of joy. The whole town is garlanded with flowers; there have been military tattoos, processions and firework displays; and now a sequence of *tableaux vivants* is being paraded past the King. One of them consists of a single figure, a gloriously blonde nineteen-year-old, Louise von Alten; she is sitting in a huge shell of mother-of-pearl, with a bouquet of roses in her hand, a vision of freshness and beauty.

King Ernest is probably too blind to see Louise very well, but he knows exactly who she is. The Altens are long-time favourites at the Hanoverian Court. Louise's great-uncle was the kingdom's most distinguished soldier when Ernest came to the throne. He had served under Wellington in the Peninsula while Hanover was under Napoleonic occupation and commanded the Hanoverian contingent at Waterloo. He then returned to his liberated country and continued his services to its Governor, Adolphus Duke of Cambridge, the youngest son of George III, who gave him the title of Count and made him Minister for War and Foreign Affairs. When his elder brother died in 1820, General von Alten took over the responsibilities of the head of the family. His young nephew, Victor, was advanced in the royal service; in 1829 he married Hermine Schmincke, whose father had been a minister of the neighbouring Landgrave of Hesse-Cassel. They had four daughters and one son: the eldest was Helene; the second, Louise, was born on 15 January 1832; and she was followed by Carl, Julie and Baldine.

The Altens belonged to the oldest nobility of Hanover, with a pedigree stretching back to the twelfth century. Their *Schloss* of Wilkenburg was one of those rustic and roomy German country houses which suggest that their architects were more practised in the designing of barns. Their town house had a fine garden on the banks of the Leine, its attractions being so superior to those of the royal palace that, before Louise and the other children had had many years to run around in it, their father sold it to the King to give him somewhere in town where he could stretch his legs.

At the Court of Hanover English connections were highly prized, and those of the Altens were better than most. General von Alten was a Knight of the Bath and represented Hanover at the coronation of Queen Victoria. The children were brought up to speak English under the care of an English governess, Miss Cuthbert, who used to refer to Louise as 'the Beauty'. The youngest child but one, Julie, described the evenings they would spend sewing while Miss Cuthbert read English history to them; and we may guess that Louise shared her sister's preference for the nights when their parents had guests and the children were allowed downstairs to play cards with the grown-ups.

Of their mother, Hermine von Alten, who is to be seen in a portrait of 1830 looking as if butter would not melt in her mouth, we are told that before King Ernest's arrival in 1837 she had been the mistress of the royal Governor, the Duke of Cambridge. Lady Augusta Fane, writing in 1926, stated that she had borne him four children before being passed on to Victor von Alten. In that form at least the story is absurd.* Hermine was only twenty-three when she married Victor von Alten and had lived at Cassel until her marriage. She was not a courtesan but a noblewoman, who would have waited until she was respectably married before beginning an affair. Certainly the Duke of Cambridge was known for his enjoyment of his subjects' company, and the Countess was a popular lady at Court. Nevertheless, Louise von Alten was too like her father for any informed person to believe that royal blood ran illicitly in her veins.

Julie gives a glimpse in her memoirs of the Altens' country life at Wilkenburg when she recalls the day that a gypsy woman came by and read the girls' palms. She foretold – rightly – that they would all live their lives abroad, but

---

*In 1909 Wilfrid Scawen Blunt accepted from Skittles an even more preposterous version, that Louise was the illegitimate daughter of 'the King of Hanover' and his coachman's wife.

when she came to Louise she exclaimed that here was a true child of Fortune; she would marry a foreigner like her sisters and would seldom be ill and always lucky.

It was shortly after her appearance before Ernest Augustus that Louise began turning this promise into fact. Three or four months after the King's birthday the Altens decided to spend the winter on the Riviera, taking all their children with them. It was a scene where their high-spirited, amusing and lovely second daughter would be sure to catch many eyes. At the opera one night in Nice she was spotted across the crowded house by a young English aristocrat, Viscount Mandeville, who was looking for a bride. The news reached Francis Cavendish, a man-about-town in London, in January 1852; 'I hear from Nice that Mandeville [eldest son of the 6th Duke of Manchester] is much in love there with a young and beautiful Hanoverian, Countess Louise d'Alten, and means to marry her.' The Altens showed no sign of thwarting his wish. Even if the suitor was less than thrilling, the heir to an English dukedom was not to be sniffed at. Lord Mandeville was a stringy young man of twenty-nine, had recently retired from ten years' service in the Guards and was a Tory Member of Parliament. Louise von Alten was ambitious and adventurous, and the prospect of becoming an English duchess could not be unwelcome. The engagement was announced; Miss Cuthbert was delighted that 'the Beauty' had had the good taste to choose an Englishman; the Altens went to Paris to buy Louise's trousseau; and the wedding ceremonies were planned for July in Hanover.

A few days before the wedding the Altens held a great ball at Wilkenburg. A marquee was set up in the garden and hung with lamps and flowers until it looked like a huge ballroom. Troops of Lord Mandeville's relations came from England, and there were over a hundred guests, Louise danced all night in a rose-coloured gown, 'herself like a rose in the bloom of her youth' in the eyes of her admiring sister Julie. Then the family's state coach with their footmen in liveries adorned the progress of the Altens and their guests to Hanover, where the marriage ceremony was held in duplicate on 22 July in the palace chapel and immediately afterwards at the British embassy. Louise's three sisters were her bridesmaids in blue Parisian confections, the two youngest thrilled to be in their first long dresses.

The same afternoon Lord Mandeville and his wife set off for a honeymoon in the Tyrol. But the wedding breakfast had gone on too long; they reached their first stop, Brunswick, very late, and the inn they found had only one wretchedly furnished room to offer. The innkeeper was distraught at having nothing better for the young couple and sent to the ducal palace for two huge beds, a table and some chairs, enabling the merry bride to amuse her friends afterwards with accounts of how she spent her wedding night amid the pomp of the reigning Duke of Brunswick.

From their arrival in England that August we have glimpses of the stir that Louise's beauty made in the circles to which she was introduced. At a party given by Lord Ravensworth in Northumberland she made such an impression ('a perfect Juno of a bride') on a neighbouring squire, William Charlton, that the event figures in the memoirs of his wife written forty years later, even though she herself was in Paris at the time. In November Francis Cavendish met them in London and noted: 'She is very pretty and will be a "beauty" next season. Considering she is Hanoverian, she speaks English very well.'

Cavendish did not mean that Louise was about to progress from prettiness to beauty; his comment reflects a social convention of the time. One of the commonest remarks of those who wrote their memoirs in the early twentieth century was on the decline of feminine beauty since the high Victorian age. We may be sceptical of this complaint, but it seems peculiar to this generation, and the critics include Margot Asquith, who was neither a *laudatrix temporis acti* nor herself a faded beauty with an interest in slighting her successors. The unflattering black-and-white photography of the period does nothing to substantiate the lament. What is certain is that the mid-Victorians had a cult of beauty; men paid homage to it like medieval troubadours; it formed one of the leading topics of discussion; with each new season the talk of the small circle of high society was of the latest dazzler to appear on the scene. This was the background to the admiration which Louise, from the moment of her introduction to English society in the season of 1853, commanded and continued to command for many years. Even in 1873 Princess Catherine Radziwill, meeting Louise when she was over forty, wrote: 'She struck me as the loveliest creature I had ever set my eyes upon. Indeed, I have only met in my whole existence three women who could be compared to her.'

Arriving in England, Louise found that she had married into one of the less ancient of the great families of the country. The Montagus, Dukes of Manchester, were descended from a Lord Chief Justice of James I, who, in the manner of his time, had used his office as a path to great wealth. He acquired the castle of Kimbolton, where Catherine of Aragon had been confined after her repudiation by Henry VIII, and was created Earl of Manchester in 1626.* His son, the 2nd Earl, was Parliament's leading general in the early stages of the Civil War, although after being edged out by Cromwell he avoided the association with the Commonwealth regime that would have proved disastrous at the Restoration. The 4th Earl, after supporting the Revolution and the Hanoverian succession, earned a dukedom from George I, but by the nineteenth century the Manchesters had turned their back on this Whig past and become staunch Conservatives.

A peculiarity of the dukedom of Manchester is that the heir is a mere Viscount by courtesy; the reason is that Duke's second title is Earl of Manchester, which would give the son the same name as the father, and to avoid this he uses the next title down. A Viscount Mandeville nevertheless has the same precedence as any other duke's eldest son, between marquesses and earls. By the aristocratic custom of the time the eldest son's courtesy title was used even in the family as if it were his Christian name. Louise's husband, whose baptismal name was William, was not unusual in going through three identities. Until 1843, when his grandfather died, he had been Lord Kimbolton and was called Kim by his family. As Louise had met him after that period she called him Mandy and continued to do so to the end of his life.

Her apprenticeship as an English aristocratic lady lasted only three years, for in August 1855 Mandeville's father died and he succeeded as the 7th Duke of Manchester. By now Louise had had time to discover that her husband's position was not as glittering as it had seemed to the twenty-year-old girl in Nice. The family's main residence was Kimbolton Castle in Huntingdonshire, a square courtyard house, not particularly large, rebuilt to a somewhat weak design by Vanbrugh and supporting its old name only by a row of battlements round the roof-line. Unlike the grandest English houses, which isolate themselves in miles of walled parkland, Kimbolton Castle is a short drive's length from its gates, which stand in the village street, and the surrounding park is flat and modest. The second residence was Tanderagee Castle in the north of Ireland. Nor did the Manchesters possess one of those historic town houses,

---

*The family had no connection with Manchester or anywhere near it. Looking around for a title, their gaze tripped on Godmanchester, near Kimbolton, and they chose the name of the most similar-sounding large town, which had not yet acquired its smoky connotations of the nineteenth century.

bearing the names of the families that owned them, which dominated the London scene. Their address was 1 Great Stanhope Street in Mayfair; a big, smart house but well short of a palace.

The Manchester estate in Huntingdonshire and Ireland amounted to 40,000 acres worth £40,000 a year. By ordinary standards it was a splendid fortune, but it did not place its owner in the first rank of magnates; he was outside the sixty or sixty-five with over 50,000 acres and £50,000 in income, let alone the dozen or so with over £100,000. The society which those great landowners composed in London left in the shade the provincial Court circles that Louise knew in Germany, and probably only in the imperial capital of Vienna was there anything to compare with them. Early in her reign Queen Victoria went to visit one of the greatest of her subjects, the Duke of Buccleuch, near Edinburgh. She went from the royal residence, Holyrood House, to the Duke's Dalkeith Palace, and on arriving she said: 'I come from my House to your Palace.' The story was often transposed to her visiting the Duke of Sutherland at Stafford House in London (absurdly enough, for Stafford House, although very grand, would have gone several times into Buckingham Palace); but the transference is significant, since it reflects the way in which the great aristocratic houses eclipsed the Court. Whereas in Vienna or Berlin a royal invitation was everything, an English socialite would be far more pleased with an invitation to one of the great ducal houses than to the rather dowdy royal household.

The political scene in the 1850s was set by the split over the repeal of the Corn Laws in 1846. The Conservative Prime Minister Robert Peel had been thrown over by his party and had left with most of his ministers. The Liberal–Peelite alliance became the key to British politics for the next twenty years, leaving the Tory squires as a powerless rump out of touch with the industrial age. They had lost not only their front bench but a large swathe of the great aristocracy, who had bowed to the will of the new political classes. Tory dukes were thin on the ground, and the Duke of Manchester with no exertion found himself one of the leading magnates of his party.

For want of anyone more active the Tory leadership had passed to the 14th Earl of Derby. As a dashing young Whig in the 1830s he had been called 'the Rupert of Debate' and was seen as the next leader of his party; but he clashed with Lord John Russell over disendowment of the Irish Church and crossed the floor of the House. He followed Prince Rupert's precedent of galloping as far as possible to the other side and became champion of the Tory diehards when they rejected Peelite free trade. The chore of leading a permanent minority party attracted him less than his interests in racing and in translating Homer. Off-hand and debonair, he was forced to devote a certain portion of his time to cultivating supporters such as the Duke of Manchester.

But if there was anything to make this sort of thing congenial, it was the new young Duchess from Germany. Lord Derby's un-Victorian temperament was responsive to feminine charms. He formed a flirtatious, teasing relation-ship with Louise, and she saw the opportunity to use this to crown her ambition. The prize she had her eyes on was the role of Mistress of the Robes to Queen Victoria; it was the highest Court post open to a lady and was a polit-ical appointment, conferred on the wife of a government supporter; its holder was always a duchess. So far in the Queen's reign the Mistresses of the Robes had been the Whig Duchess of Sutherland and the Tory Duchess of Buc-cleuch, whose husbands held two of the richest and grandest fortunes in the kingdom. To be placed on an equal footing with such social leaders would make Louise Manchester's position impregnable.

The story went round that one evening at dinner, as they joked over a glass of champagne, that Louise made Lord Derby promise that he would make her Mistress of the Robes the next time he returned to office. According to Sir Shane Leslie, she made him sign a written promise; which would suggest that there was more than a glass of champagne involved. It was a time of unstable political conditions, and Lord Derby might well be back in power again.

In the mean time Louise adapted herself to the role of a great political lady. She visited Ireland in the summer of 1856, when the Viceroy, Lord Carlisle, was 'much struck with the Duchess of Manchester's beauty and charming manners'. On her husband's estates at Tanderagee she carried out the duties expected of her position. In London she was also spreading her social influ-ence, and Disraeli writes in July 1857: 'We were at the Duchess of Manchester's on Friday night; a ball of very *haut ton*.' That autumn Louise and her husband went to Paris and were received by Napoleon III at Com-piegne. The British ambassador, Lord Cowley, was kept entertained by her descriptions of the pomposity of Count Walewski (an illegitimate son of Napoleon I and now Foreign Minister). Knowing how well her talk went down with the Foreign Secretary, Lord Clarendon, the ambassador wrote to him that he must get her to repeat these impressions when she returned home. Lord

Clarendon was interested in the gossip about Walewski's Italian Countess, who was the Emperor's mistress and could not abide the attention he was showing Louise. These French visits provided Louise with a store of anecdotes with which she amused her friends all her life; but there was also a deeper influence; for the pleasure-loving, gambling habits of the Napoleonic Court left a permanent impress on her tastes.

In February 1858 Lord Palmerston's government fell, and Lord Derby became Prime Minister for the second time. Within a few days the promise he had so frivolously made was redeemed with the same frivolity. 'My dear Duchess,' he wrote, 'The exquisite taste in dress which you displayed in your late present to me [evidently she had sent him a tie or something of the sort for Christmas] naturally points you out as the fittest person for the office of Mistress of the Robes.' If Louise accepted, Lord Derby would submit her name to the Queen, who would make the offer in a personal letter.

Louise had of course been presented soon after her marriage, but the Queen did not yet know her well. She described to her eldest daughter Louise's first appearance on 27 February: 'I have seen the Duchess of Manchester who was very smart and looked very pretty in a pink terry velvet mantelet or cloak trimmed with ermine, a pink bonnet and black velvet gown. She inquired much after you . . .' Princess Victoria had recently married the Crown Prince of Prussia, and such German connections were just up Louise's street, especially as her brother Carl was then in Prussian service in Berlin. In no time at all she had established herself as an immense success at Court. The duties of the Mistress of the Robes were to attend the Queen at some ceremonial functions, and she also spent a great deal of time in the royal company, without being permanently in waiting. The Duke of Manchester, on the other hand, was clearly going nowhere in politics. He held a minor Court appointment in Derby's first ministry of 1852, but it was not repeated. Such distinction as the House of Montagu was to win would have to be aimed at by Louise.

That summer, when the Queen went to see her daughter in Berlin, Lord Granville wrote to Louise Manchester: 'I hear that the Queen wrote to you from Germany a very amiable letter. I was never so sure of anything as your making HM's conquest. It must be confessed that you are irresistible for man, woman, and I should think beast. I can conceive, if it was not for your grande dame much-too-big-for-any-street-to-hold-me look, being passionately in love with you.' As Granville was the Whig leader in the House of Lords, we can see that Louise was not rationing her charms on any party lines.

A few weeks later the Manchesters themselves went on a visit to Hanover, and Louise's letters to the Queen give a hint of the conversational style that made her such an entertaining companion: 'Your Majesty would have been amused to hear General Wrangel tell at the top of his voice how delighted the soldiers were to see the Princess [Victoria] on horseback.' She goes on to describe how, at an officers' dinner, an English general who spoke not a word of German insisted on proposing the royal toast in that language from a piece of paper in which it had been written out for him. 'The English officers all admired the way the Germans kept their countenance notwithstanding the absurdity of the exhibition.'

Princess Victoria, however, was not taken by Louise, and Queen Victoria wrote to her in reply to some remarks: 'You are rather unfair, dear, and a little quick in your judgement about the Duchess of Manchester; since we have known her well – we (Papa is of the same opinion) have found her very amiable, anxious to improve herself – fond of reading, very kind to the poor (she even teaches in the schools in Ireland) and very domestic, and not foolish. As for her beauty, I admire her profile very much; the front face much less – and I fear it will not last. The waist and throat are too short for me to admire her figure.'

That a young German girl of twenty-six should have reached the highest position open to a lady in English society was not received without envy in some quarters. The 2nd Duke of Wellington thought that his stately wife, who had been a Lady of the Bedchamber for years, ought to have had the Robes and was so annoyed that he made her resign her existing office. But then the Duke was not a party man (his wife in fact received the honour from Lord Palmerston three years later). Other critics, with that refusal of the English to take seriously any aristocracy but their own, spread stories that Louise was a bookseller's or a schoolmaster's daughter. In fact, given how short of loyal dukes he was, Lord Derby's choice was a reasonable one, and it might even be called a clever coup to find a Hanoverian duchess for the Court of Victoria and Albert.

One of the ladies who hated Louise was the wife of the Prussian ambassador, Countess Bernstorff, and she describes a house-party given by Lord Derby at Knowsley in October 1858. The Prime Minister spent his time joking with Louise, teasing her about her accent, and paying a lively court which she found a little embarrassing under the furious eye of Madame Bernstorff. The house was full of high-spirited young men who surrounded Louise, while her husband was left completely in the background.

Lord Derby's ministry, alas, after struggling on without a parliamentary majority, was forced out in the summer of 1859, and Louise went too. Lord Clarendon told her six weeks later what he had heard from Lady Ely of the Royal Family's feeling: 'It's not only the Q & Pss Alice, she said, but everybody is so *very* fond of the Duchess of M: & the laments at her loss are as great now as they where 6 weeks ago.' One thing her tenure as Mistress of the Robes had done for Louise, however: it had placed her at the very top of English society, and she was out to consolidate her position by keeping a political *salon* in rivalry with the leading hostesses of her day.

The social scene in London of the 1850s was one of almost complete Whig and Peelite monopoly. Among the great houses of the time first place perhaps belongs to the spectacular Stafford House (now Lancaster House), which had been built by the 1st Duke of Sutherland a generation previously; it was known for its support of liberal causes, especially under the sway of Harriet Duchess, who was Mistress of the Robes in all the Whig administrations until the death of her husband the 2nd Duke in 1861. Montagu House was a French-style château in Whitehall newly rebuilt by the Peelite Duke of Buccleuch, whose wife was also an important social figure. The greatest political clout was wielded by Lady Palmerston, who had been Countess Cowper and already a leading Whig hostess before she married Palmerston in 1839; the Palmerstons entertained from Cambridge House, which still stands as the old 'In and Out' in Piccadilly, and their regime shows the power that could be exercised in the Victorian scene by a woman married to an active politician. Lady Palmerston's influence was decisive in her husband's emergence as Prime Minister – rather than Lord John Russell – when the Tory government fell in 1859. Lord John had discredited himself over the negotiations for the ending of the Crimean War in 1855; but Palmerston had blundered more recently over the Conspiracy to Murder Bill. Between these two men the difference was made in the drawing-rooms: while Lady Palmerston's receptions kept the political world in her grip, Lady John Russell was as socially hopeless as her husband. Cambridge House was a political force in its own right, and it brought Palmerston back to the premiership. It was a lesson that Louise Manchester could not fail to notice.

All these ladies were too well established for Louise to contemplate an assault on their positions, but there was one rising force with whom she at once joined battle. Frances Countess Waldegrave was the widow of the 7th Earl Waldegrave, whose fortune and title she kept through a succession of later marriages; at the moment her husband was an elderly Peelite MP, George Harcourt. She had established her claim as the most active hostess in the small Peelite circle, and as her party merged progressively with the Liberals she was casting her influence wider. Her house was in Carlton Gardens, and she also kept up Horace Walpole's Gothick extravaganza of Strawberry Hill, which was conveniently close for house-parties popular with the liveliest talkers of the political world.

Louise Manchester at once identified Lady Waldegrave as the opposition. Ostensibly, her own aim was to set up a Tory drawing-room – *the* Tory drawing-room, since there was hardly another hostess in the party worth the name; but there was the problem. The Tories were, frankly, a dead weight outside the hunting-field and were regarded by Whig society as a collection of boneheads. Louise would have to poach across the party boundary to make her salon the sparkling meeting-place she wanted. This she did without a qualm; Lords Granville and Clarendon, her most assiduous correspondents, were the leading politicians on the Whig side, but they were happy to come over and be entertained by the Tory Duchess. 'You who are cleverer, more natural, and more sunshiny than anyone in your talk,' wrote Granville to her in 1859, '. . . you have in the course of the year compliments enough to turn that very well furnished lovely little head of yours.' Compliments to her, it was understood, were to be balanced by remorseless ridicule towards Lady Waldegrave; they referred to her as Maria, in derisive allusion to a fine Reynolds of her predecessor Maria Countess Waldegrave in which she took great pride.

One of the rising young men whom Louise lured over was the bachelor Lord Cowper. Clever and extremely good-looking, he had inherited one of the great Whig fortunes; his main house, Panshanger in Hertfordshire, had already been a glittering Whig centre when the present Lady Palmerston was its châtelaine. Lord Cowper was expected to go far in politics. He was a little hampered by the lethargy which was a tribal characteristic of the Whigs (Lady Salisbury said that the Whig pulse beat ten seconds slower to the minute than the Tory one). It was widely accepted that there was little point in speaking to the Cowpers at breakfast, since they would not have woken up. At lunch-time the situation was little improved, and only at dinner was there any chance of tempting them to social intercourse. Nevertheless Louise aroused Lord Cowper sufficiently to make him a keen visitor at Kimbolton for the hunting season from the late 1850s. He became one of that group of admiring young men before whom the Duke of Manchester retreated into eclipse in his own house. Some of them were perhaps her lovers, and certainly with Lord Cowper Louise began an affair that lasted for several years.

Louise had already secured the Manchester succession in ample fashion. Her first child was a boy, the new Lord Mandeville, born in 1853; twin girls, Mary and Louisa, followed just after Christmas 1854; a second boy, Charles, was born in 1860; and the fifth child, Alice, appeared in 1862. In November 1864 Louise gave birth to a stillborn child a week after being peppered in a shooting accident, and that was her last pregnancy. As they grew older Louise organized her children in private theatricals at Kimbolton, and Sir David Hunter Blair recalled being at school with the eleven-year-old Mandeville at Malvern, where the Duchess 'used occasionally to drop down on us like a celestial visitant – a perfect vision of grace and loveliness – and entertain us to an al fresco luncheon or tea party'.

Louise's amusements with other men did not imply any quarrel with her husband. For his part he was happy enough to be husband of the beautiful Duchess whom people stood on chairs to see as she drove through Stanhope Gate to the Park. 'My darling pet,' begins a letter from him in 1862, when her affair with Lord Cowper was well under way, and he rounds it off with a love poem. She kept his adoring affection all his life, it seems, and addressed her own letters to 'My darling Mandy'. It was one of the better sides of Louise's nature that she was never tempted to unkindness towards those who did not win her respect. If she made enemies, it was not in her family circle. She kept warm friendships with her sister-in-law, with her children as they grew older and with her father and the rest of her own family. But Louise could not admire her husband, who is presented to us in a character sketch by the Marquis of Huntly: 'His Grace William Drogo, seventh Duke of Manchester, was a curious mixture of good nature and oddity; he was continually airing some extraordinary theory or complaining of some hitherto unknown ailment. One day he asked me to examine his eye, as he felt sure there was "a small volcano" in it. I assured him that I saw no eruption, but he went on to the next person he came across and made the same enquiry. He posed as an ardent soldier, was wont to attend the military manoeuvres, both in England and on the Continent, and held forth on tactics. He raised the Huntingdonshire Light Horse, and was a well-intentioned bore.'

In the course of his military tours, in which he forged an alliance with Louise's brother Carl, the Duke contrived to be awarded the Prussian Iron Cross. He was a prominent Freemason, and in 1864 he published the collection *Court and Society from Elizabeth to Anne* in two volumes, from historic documents at Kimbolton. One of his fads deserves particular mention: in 1858 he was invited to join a group who claimed to have revived the Knights Hospitaller of St John in England. Three years later he was elected Prior, and he soon got the Prince of Wales to accept membership. In 1888 Queen Victoria gave this body official status as the 'Venerable Order of St John' and the Duke gave way to the Prince of Wales as Prior; the Order is now the controlling body of St John Ambulance. There can be no doubt that without the royal approval the Duke obtained, the self-constituted Priory would never have acquired the resources to organize the vast ambulance work it still maintains today. Thus it may be that the 7th Duke of Manchester with his crotchets was responsible for doing more lasting good to mankind than any other actor in this story.

As for Louise, a glimpse of her unconventional ways is given by Lady Eleanor Stanley, describing a paper-chase at Kimbolton in 1859: 'The Duchess of Manchester, in getting too hastily over a stile, caught a hoop of her cage in it, and went head over heels, alighting on her feet with her cage and whole petticoats remaining above her head. They say there was never such a thing seen – and the other ladies hardly knew whether to be thankful or not that a part of her underclothing consisted of a pair of scarlet tartan knickerbockers (the things Charles shoots in) – which were revealed to all the world in general and the Duc de Malakoff in particular.' Lady Eleanor says that the other ladies hardly knew whether to be thankful because at this date a lady's normal wear under her petticoats was only a pair of leggings laced up to the waistband, an arrangement that could be unduly revealing in combination with a crinoline.* But some of the more active ladies were beginning to adopt

---

*Hence the anecdote provided by Lord Cowley of the visit to Paris by King Victor Emmanuel of Sardinia. After observing with interest a young lady slip and fall flat on a ballroom floor, he remarked to a friend: 'I have discovered that Parisian ladies do not wear knickers. It is an azure heaven opened to my eyes.' When Palmerston made this dispatch known to the Cabinet, the laughter, as the Foreign Secretary notified our ambassador in Paris, 'might have been heard at Westminster Bridge'.

Louise's expedient of donning a hidden pair of breeches for rambles in the country.

Another of Louise's habits is illustrated by an anecdote she liked to repeat all her life. It was her humour to walk about the streets of London quite alone, in defiance of convention; apart from the fun of it, she enjoyed the exercise. Victorian rules demanded that no respectable lady should go about unless accompanied at least by her maid; for a duchess nothing less than a footman would do. A nice lady, likewise, would not be found taking a cab. The effect of these rules was to make it virtually impossible for a woman to keep secret assignations; and it followed that any woman who flouted the rules could be treated as fair game. One day Louise was on a solitary excursion when she stopped to look into a bonnet-maker's window. A stranger excited by this dazzling vision sidled up to her, made himself pleasant and sought the privilege of buying her a bonnet. They went inside and Louise, amid much elegant dalliance, took care to choose the most expensive hat in the shop. The man then offered to bring it to her house. Probably he belonged to the degraded class who carried their own shopping home, but in any case it was a good way of taking his conquest further. Louise, however, said the shop should deliver it, and gave the assistant her address: 'The Duchess of Manchester, 1 Great Stanhope Street.' Hasty exit of Lothario. This story must be seen as an early example of Louise's taste for snubbing people, since her contemporaries would have said that she had asked for it; they would also have agreed with Queen Victoria, who when she heard of them viewed such expeditions as not just 'fast' but for a duchess positively vulgar.

Louise's relations with the Court seemed rosy for some years. Princess Alice showed her special affection ('I am glad to have to write to you dear Louise,' runs one of her letters with rare informality); the Queen wrote to her cordially in October 1861, and the royal family, although devastated by the recent death of Prince Albert, were delighted when she spent a day at Windsor the following spring. Then came the marriage of the Prince of Wales to the beautiful Princess Alexandra of Denmark, due to be held at Windsor in March 1863 with a glittering attendance. It was a thunderbolt when Louise Manchester was not invited to the wedding – and without a word of explanation. Lord Clarendon, her busy correspondent, was baffled by the slight, and reported the equal astonishment of the other guests. A stiff message came from Lord Granville that the Queen 'regrets your not having been at the marriage'.

What had happened was that Queen Victoria got wind of the compact by which Lord Derby had made Louise Mistress of the Robes, and she was not amused at her Household appointments being awarded in that fashion. From now on she was to observe Louise's 'fast' ways with cold disapproval, and the royal Court was one scene where Louise could abandon her ambitions, even when Derby returned for his last term of office in 1866.

All in all, 1863 showed signs of being a bad year for Louise, not lightened when she looked across at her main rival. Old Mr Harcourt had died, and Lady Waldegrave had just married her fourth husband, the Whig minister Chichester Fortescue, a much more stylish and able man who was a step away from the Cabinet; Frances Waldegrave's influence was growing steadily as a result. By contrast, Louise's lover was not getting his political career started. Perhaps this was what made her look afresh at another young man who had been in Lady Waldegrave's circle for the past four years. He had just been made Under-Secretary for War and was making his mark in the House of Commons; his friends were beginning to talk of him as the future leader of his party. He was the 29-year-old Marquis of Hartington and was the heir to the Dukedom of Devonshire, one of the grandest titles in the kingdom.

2
Whig Inheritance

Among the great Whig families, one of the two chief places was accorded by common agreement to the Dukes of Devonshire. Their family history was wholly typical of the tradition they represented. They had been prominent in the birth of the Whig cause in Charles II's reign, when the party names came into being, and were at the heart of the Glorious Revolution of 1688, which had settled the British Constitution on lines that were to be virtually unchanged for a century and a half.

The Cavendishes traced their descent to the fourteenth-century Chief Justice Sir John Cavendish, who had met his death in the faultlessly aristocratic pastime of suppressing a Peasants' Revolt. Their rise to greatness, however, began with Sir William Cavendish, who acquired Chatsworth in Derbyshire after serving as one of Henry VIII's commissioners for the suppression of the monasteries. The real foundation of his fortune was his marriage to Bess of Hardwick, the richest and perhaps the most remarkable woman of her time. She accumulated the estates of four husbands, of whom only Sir William Cavendish gave her sons and reaped the benefit for his descendants, She built the breathtaking Elizabethan prodigy-house of Hardwick Hall, and when she died, aged eighty, in 1608 she had seen her son advanced to the barony of Cavendish, with the earldom of Devonshire to follow in 1618.*

The Cavendishes showed a foretaste of their Whig tendencies by a lack of enthusiasm for the royal cause in the Civil War, which the 3rd Earl of Devonshire contrived to spend abroad. Whiggery under that name was born in 1678, when the Country Party (as opposed to the Court) sought the 'Exclusion' of

---

*The choice of the title Devonshire, when the family had no estates in that county, has long been commented on. But there was already an Earl of Derby (incidentally he had no estates in Derbyshire, where the Cavendishes were now the leading family); choices of name were on a fairly hit-and-miss basis, as has been seen with the Manchesters, and Lord Cavendish seems to have chosen the most similar-sounding county for his title.

the Catholic Duke of York from succession to the throne. While the party's founder was Lord Shaftesbury, one of his most zealous followers was Lord Russell, who was to be executed for supposed treason in the Rye House Plot. Russell's bosom friend was the 4th Earl of Devonshire, who posthumously sealed the friendship by marrying his son to Lord Russell's daughter, thus consecrating the partnership of the two families. In 1688 Lord Devonshire was one of the seven lords who wrote to William of Orange inviting his intervention against the despotism of James II. The Russells and the Cavendishes received their dukedoms on successive days of 1694 and remained the foremost of the great Revolution families that controlled England's government for the next seventy years. When the young George III tried to break free from this oligarchy, he viewed the 4th Duke of Devonshire, who had been Prime Minister under George II, as his principal enemy. 'The Duke of Devonshire', in Macaulay's words, 'was especially singled out as a victim by whose fate the magnates of England were to take warning', and the King's own hand struck his name from the list of Privy Councillors.

On the failure of George III's monarchical plans, the pure Whigs returned to office in 1782, inaugurating one of the most glittering periods of their history. Charles James Fox was the guiding spirit of this society, and Devonshire House was its playground. The solidarity of the Devonshire House set became all the more vital when the French Revolution frightened the English governing class into Toryism, and only the Foxite Whigs dared propound the logic of the freedom which the aristocracy of 1688 had asserted against the Crown.

The 5th Duke of Devonshire (1748–1811) was an incongruous prince of this Whig world, a foil to the brilliance of the men and women around him – although Fox deferred to his judgement and his scholarship. His life and character provide a curious parallel to those of his great-grandson the 8th Duke. Brought up in solitude at home, he emerged silent and ungraceful; when he received his Garter from George III, an observer viewed him 'with his phlegmatic, cold, awkward air, like a clown [i.e. yokel]'. He lived a life of late nights, and only gambling seemed able to rouse him from his apathy. At Devonshire House he maintained a curious *ménage à trois* with Lady Georgiana Spencer and Lady Elizabeth Foster, whom he successively married. Georgiana was the fascinating Duchess of Devonshire who bought a butcher's vote with a kiss, while an old Irishman said that he could light his pipe at her eyes. But after eight years of marriage to this impetuous, lovable, vulnerable woman the

Duke turned his affection to the cool, calculating and equally beautiful Lady Elizabeth; and at last, on his first wife's death twenty-four years later, he married her.

Our subject demands attention to a younger brother of the 5th Duke of Devonshire, Lord George Cavendish (1754–1834). The two brothers were much alike in character, and there is a well-known story of their once sharing a bedroom at an inn; the room had an extra bed in it, whose curtains were drawn. One of the brothers peered inside and saw a corpse in the bed but said nothing; later the other looked, too, and remained equally silent. The following morning as they left, one of them remarked: 'Did you see what was in that bed?' 'Yes,' said the other, and that was all the allusion they made to the matter.

In 1782 Lord George Cavendish married Lady Elizabeth Compton, the only daughter of the 7th Earl of Northampton. Although the bulk of the Compton estates had descended with the title to another branch, her father had bequeathed Lady Elizabeth a fine property at Eastbourne, which had come into the family from his uncle Spencer Compton, a distinguished Speaker of the House of Commons and then First Lord of the Treasury as Earl of Wilmington. Lord George Cavendish was only a younger son, but his brother's marriage had been childless for eight years and he looked like being the next Duke of Devonshire, that prospect being only broken by the birth of the Duke's heir in 1790. In 1803, however, the inheritance from an uncle of the Holker estate in Lancashire made Lord George a landowner in his own right; and seven years later he was left the vast fortune of another relation, the scientist Henry Cavendish. In this savant the intelligence and taciturnity of the Cavendishes reached a peak; he was the first man to calculate the weight of the Earth, and he lived the life of a recluse, dining on a leg of mutton every day. The result was that by accumulated interest he left a fortune of £1,175,000, and his heir became one of the richest men in England.

By this time Georgiana Duchess of Devonshire had died, and the 5th Duke promptly married his mistress. Although the two ladies had been the best of friends while they shared the Duke's bed, the son, Lord Hartington, was less tolerant and was hurt by his father's second marriage; this is said to have been a reason why, after he succeeded as 6th Duke in 1811, he himself avoided marriage, and the dukedom was to pass eventually to the descendants of his uncle.

Lord George Cavendish used his new wealth to buy from his nephew Burlington House, the creation of the connoisseur 3rd Earl of Burlington, whose daughter married the 4th Duke of Devonshire. It stood just a little way up Piccadilly from Devonshire House, and two eighteenth-century palaces side by side were a little more than the young Duke could use; but Burlington House would serve very well for the rich cadet branch of the Cavendishes of which Lord George now appeared as the founder. He was blessed with four sons, of whom the eldest, William, had taken an Irish wife, Louisa O'Callaghan. The O'Callaghans were relations and hangers-on of the Dukes of Devonshire, and on their recent ennoblement (they were big landowners in their own right) had taken their title from the chief Devonshire seat in Ireland, Lismore. William Cavendish, who appears in a glamorous portrait at Chatsworth, had entered Parliament and reached the rank of Colonel in the army by the time he was twenty-eight and had himself fathered three sons, but in 1815 his curricle overturned as he returned from shooting in Holker park, and he was killed by being thrown on his head. Louisa mourned her young beau for the forty-eight remaining years of her life, the prototype of the inconsolable Victorian widow.

Her eldest son, also William, born in 1808, turned out a studious boy. He was sent, as was traditional in the Cavendish family, to Trinity College, Cambridge, and he emerged in 1829 as Second Wrangler – that being the name by which Cambridge designates its inoffensive first-class men in mathematics. Besides being the heir to his grandparents' estates in Lancashire and Sussex, he was now looking likely to inherit the dukedom of Devonshire.

The 6th Duke, young, good-looking, cultivated, generous, amiable, and incomparably grand in his life, had eluded all the ladies who would have killed for so eligible a match. Now approaching forty, he settled down with a mistress and had caught the epidemic despair at his ever marrying. He resolved on a plan to settle the succession and carried it through with masterful swiftness: his sister Georgina had married the 6th Earl of Carlisle, and her daughter Lady Blanche Howard, the Duke's favourite niece, was seventeen in 1829; she would marry young William Cavendish and her descendants would be Dukes of Devonshire. Lady Blanche and William had never met, but that was soon remedied. On 27 April the Duke held William's coming-of-age party at Devonshire House; on the 30th he presented Blanche at Court. The following day he gave her coming-out ball. The two were betrothed, and three months later they were married. At the same time William was elected Member of Parliament for the University of Cambridge.

Sidney Smith commented on the young mathematician and his graceful bride: 'Euclid leads Blanche to the altar – a strange choice for him, as she has not an angle about her.' But any idea that it was a marriage of incompatibles would have been wrong; William and Blanche Cavendish were like a pair of love-birds from the beginning. At this time, too, political sunrise was bursting on the Whigs after their forty years in opposition. In 1831 Lord George Cavendish was offered an earldom by Lord Grey's government, and he revived the title of Burlington, becoming the first Earl of the second creation.

The new Lord Burlington died in May 1834 and his grandson William inherited the title; but only eleven days later his eldest son died, aged two and a half. The status of heir devolved on the next son, who had been born on 23 July 1833 and is one of the two subjects of this biography; he had been christened Spencer Compton after his great-grandmother, Spencer being the traditional given name in the Compton family, but he can never have learnt to answer to it. He now became Baron Cavendish by courtesy title and was called Cavendish or Cav by his family. Three more children followed: Louisa, born in 1835; Frederick, in 1836; and Edward, in 1838.

The Burlingtons made their main home at Holker on the edge of the Lake District, where there was an estate of 12,000 acres. The hall is set in a beautiful rolling park with spacious views over Morecambe Bay; even after Lord Burlington rebuilt it in Elizabethan style in 1838–42 it remained quite a modest house for so large an estate. The other residence was Compton Place at Eastbourne, where 11,000 acres were inherited from old Lady Burlington in 1835. Although the town had scarcely yet begun its development, the Burlingtons helped to boost the Victorian taste for seaside holidays by coming here to spend the summers with their children.

Everywhere the Cavendishes looked, domestic happiness and family success seemed to surround them. The 6th Duke's elder sister, as we have seen, was Countess of Carlisle and thus mistress of a great Whig house; the second, Harriet, had married Lord Granville Leveson Gower, brother of the Marquess of Stafford. The Leveson Gowers shared in the Whig accession to favour after 1830, the Marquess being created Duke of Sutherland just before his death in 1833, and his brother becoming Earl Granville in the same year. A second family alliance with the Leveson Gowers was made by Blanche's elder sister Lady Harriet Howard, who married Lord Stafford's son and who became on her husband's succession in 1833 the second Duchess of Sutherland.

The Duke of Devonshire put away his mistress and became the very ideal of an early Victorian duke: his hospitality was princely; his estates were vast and managed in the grandest fashion. His gardener was Joseph Paxton, who built the Crystal Palace and received a knighthood; his auditor was Sir James Abercromby, who became Speaker of the House of Commons and then Lord Dunfermline. In 1838 the whole village of Edensor, next to Chatsworth, was uprooted and rebuilt further away in handsome style, as the Duke remodelled his great house and park in harmony with the best taste of his day; the house itself, already unrivalled in grandeur, was enlarged with a long sculpture gallery and stately tower and belvedere thrown out to the north and commanding a grand view of the valley.

This scene of contentment was broken by tragedy in 1840 when Blanche Countess of Burlington died. The Duke wrote of her, 'She had the art of giving life and charm to everything that approached her', and called 1840 'the year of his sorrow'; a monumental urn with the simple word 'Blanche' upon it still closes a vista in the gardens at Chatsworth. But for Lord Burlington it was a grief which he never got over; to crown the calamity, Blanche had died on his birthday, and he could never bear to hear the day mentioned again; instead, in his long widowerhood, he would remember anniversaries such as the day on which he had first seen his wife. Never avid for society, he withdrew even more to his beloved Holker and his family circle.

Lord Burlington made the decision not to send his sons to school. He himself had been to Eton in what was probably its worst period, under the headmastership of the boorish Keate, who was celebrated mainly for his flogging exploits. He therefore decided to tutor Cavendish and the two younger boys himself. This was a serious misfortune; by the later 1840s both Eton and Harrow were well on the road of reform, and either of them would have been a good training ground for the young heir, where he would have had the company of clever boys with the great world of politics and society before them. Instead he grew up in the isolation of north Lancashire, learning no manners either from his father or from his retainers. Sir Frederick Ponsonby observed him near the end of his life at Lismore: 'He never by chance said "Thank you" to any servant who helped him.' That was the way he had been brought up, among servants who showed all deference to the heir but were themselves short on ceremony.

Another well-known story depicts him in old age listening in the House of Lords to a peer who was speaking bombastically about something that made it the proudest day of his life; he turned to his neighbour and said, 'The proudest day of my life was when my pig won first prize at Skipton Fair.' It was pointed out a long time ago that this story can only refer to Cavendish's boyhood at Holker, since subsequently he maintained an aloofness from pigs that would have satisfied a rabbi. This, therefore, is how we are to see the young Cavendish, immersed in rural interests amid a laconic, level-headed peasantry impatient of frills. He never threw off a clumsy Hodgelike manner, looking at those who approached him, as Sir Almeric Fitzroy described it, 'in that peculiar way of his, as if half inviting, half forbidding communication'. We should bear in mind, too, as he stands in gilded drawing-rooms or walks the corridors of power, that he is, in his own estimation, just a lad from Lancashire, treating others as plain men and women, contemptuous of 'humbug' (a favourite word of his) and enjoying a large but silent amusement at the pretentious and the over-deferential.

One avenue out of this earthy existence was the glittering world of 'Uncle Duke'. Cavendish got to know the splendours of Chatsworth, and regular visits were paid to Lismore Castle, the centre of the Devonshire estates in southern Ireland. In 1849 the Duke took a fancy to this romantically situated house above a gorge of the Blackwater River and began transforming it into a large castle. The Burlingtons joined him for the first three Christmases he spent at Lismore, and the love of Ireland that gripped the Duke in old age became part of Cavendish's life from his boyhood.

His first real encounter with the wider world came when he was sent to Cambridge at the age of eighteen. In October 1851 he entered his father's college of Trinity. Cavendish was entered as a Nobleman, a rank which gave him, with the equally privileged Fellow Commoners, the right of dining with the Master and Fellows at the high table. It was not a distinction he relished, as he said in his first letter to his sister: 'It is highly disgusting being a nobleman as I have to sit at dinner or *hall* quite away from the other undergraduates, on the left of the Master.' But he never escaped from the set of Noblemen, Fellow Commoners and a few of the more aristocratic Commoners into which he fell in his first weeks. He joined the Athenaeum, a club virtually confined to this circle, and told his father, 'the other commoners bother us considerably & are a beastly set of snobs'. This attitude, combined with the shyness born of his home education, prevented him from mixing with a wider society and in particular that of academic ability and ambition. He made no really close undergraduate friends, although his isolation was relieved by the presence at Trinity of two first cousins, Leo Ellis (later 5th Viscount Clifden) and Lord Frederick Leveson Gower, who was to die at Sebastopol.

Cavendish's letters home from Cambridge could be those of any young aristocrat of the time. He furnishes his rooms 'at a vast expense', attends balls in London, insists on buying his champagne there 'as the stuff here is nastiness', keeps horses, hunts a good deal and does a little shooting with fellow undergraduates who have neighbouring estates. The Athenaeum were far from upholding the learned connotations of their name and spent their time holding private dinners in their rooms, followed by supper parties at about nine (the ordinary humble undergraduate made do with evening tea following dinner at four), then playing cards until well after midnight, with some not-too-serious gambling. Many of them went racing at Newmarket, also a lifetime taste of Cavendish's. The fact is that his generation of Trinity men was short of men who displayed intellectual distinction in later life. Perhaps the best known of them was the refined and dandyish Christopher Sykes, who was to spend his life entertaining (in both senses of the word) the Prince of Wales.

Already at Cambridge Cavendish showed the views expected of the heir to a great Whig name. Attending his first debate at the Union, where there was a motion against the aristocracy, he told his sister: 'The radical side, I am sorry to say was very unpopular.' Although he found the experience 'rather good fun' and although, at his father's wish, he remained a member of the Union, he was never tempted to break his silence there.

One of the privileges of a Nobleman was that of acquiring his Master of Arts degree after only seven terms' residence instead of ten; and Cavendish accordingly took his finals in January 1854. After a little cramming, and staying up at Cambridge for Christmas 1853, he was placed in the second class. To put this achievement in perspective, it should be pointed out that Cambridge at that time awarded nine classes and that most men took at least a year longer before proceeding to finals. Here, as throughout his life, Cavendish showed the performance of a first-class brain never bothered about being underrated. He had exerted himself little and had never honed his mind by contact with the cleverest of his contemporaries. He lamented in old age: 'All through life I have had to work with men who thought three times as quick as I did.'

As he approached his majority, Cavendish was much in favour with his great-uncle the Duke of Devonshire. But that nobleman's horizon was overcast early in 1854 by the looming war with Russia. The Duke had been a strong Russophile since 1826, when he had conducted with great pomp Britain's special embassy to the coronation of Czar Nicholas I. He proposed to take Cavendish with him on a mission of reconciliation he wanted to make to Russia; but his plans were overtaken by the outbreak of war in March 1854.

Given his great-uncle's views, it was not to be expected that Cavendish should go out to fight, and one avenue of employment was thus closed. He was sent to round off his education with a few months' travel on the Continent, and he left for Paris in April. Here the Duke of Cambridge was on his way out to command the Guards Division in the Crimea, and Cavendish writes to his father: 'I was invited to a ball at the Elysée given by their Majesties for the Duke of C. I was introduced to Ld & Ly Cowley & by him to the Emperor; also by the Georges [the Duke of Cambridge and his wife] to a host of swells, & am going to dine to-morrow with a female of that species the Marquise de Caraman.'

Cavendish went on to the Rhineland, Berlin and Dresden before returning to Holker to celebrate his coming of age on 24 July. The Duke, with his gift for the grand manner, settled on Cavendish £2,000 a year. It was just as well, since Lord Burlington would probably have had less generous views, even after he succeeded to the ducal estates. The allowance was a lavish one in the days when a young man with £500 a year could rent chambers in Mayfair, keep a manservant, dress in Savile Row, belong to a club and have a little over for hunting and shooting at his friends' country houses.

In the young heir thus launched into the world the blood and the characteristics of his family were peculiarly concentrated. Not only was he the grandson of two Cavendishes but his paternal grandmother had also been a quarter Cavendish, making him descended three times over from the 3rd Duke of Devonshire. His life was to prove him the embodiment of the family's punning motto *Cavendo tutus*, 'safe through caution'. The phlegmatic, taciturn strain in his ancestry was strong in him, and so was plainness of manner, accentuated by his rustic upbringing at Holker. When he transposed this to the drawing-rooms of Mayfair, as his biographer was to put it, 'he successfully established early in life the principle that little was to be expected of him in the details of polite etiquette'. Not many years passed before this lesson was widely learnt, and one hostess remarked that she always invited one man spare when she asked Lord Cavendish to her house; he turned up late if he remembered to turn up at all. But it did him little harm with the mothers who were hurling their daughters at him as the prize coconut-shy in the London marriage fair. He was not bad-looking, at least before he retreated behind a shaggy Victorian beard, and his tall gawkiness was softened by small, elegant hands and feet. His letters at this period are full of humour and charm, and those who knew him well valued him warmly, recognizing a rock-like honesty and straightforwardness underlying his contempt of frills. His gaucherie was not that of a man afraid of society; he had told his sister after attending his first ball from Cambridge: 'I thought it very good fun and intend to take to it vigourously when I come to London.' Country sports pleased him equally; he was a first-rate shot, before the duties of office made him rusty, and was reputed one of the best horsemen in the country. He was a keen hunting man to whom Lord Spencer wrote in March 1856 offering him the Mastership of the Pytchley – a striking expression of confidence in a man of twenty-two. He turned the offer down but remained a well-known figure in the Leicestershire fields for a decade, until personal ties made Kimbolton his favoured haunt.

We come back to him, though, in the first months of his majority. In August 1854 he took up an invitation from his aunt the Duchess of Sutherland to deer-stalking in Scotland, where her son Lord Stafford was his congenial companion. Lord Mandeville was renting a nearby shooting-box from the Duke that autumn, and he looked in at Dunrobin with his wife and her sister Julie, who took away the memory of a very shy and silent young man. Lady Mandeville, however, made no appearance in Cavendish's letters home. His attention was engrossed by the eighteen-year-old Lady Louisa Hamilton (nicknamed Tiny). A verse alphabet composed by her, of the sort with which the Victorians amused their house-parties, found its way into Cavendish's letters to Holker. In this,

> S was a Stafford who is so fond of laughing,
> T was the Tiny he's so constantly chaffing.

(C, uninventively, 'was a Cavvy who breakfasts on porridge'.)
Just before Christmas Lady Louisa was his fellow guest again when he stayed with the Cowpers at Panshanger, in a party which included the young Guards officer Lord Grey de Wilton. Lady Cowper wrote to her son on 22 December: 'Today Ld Abercorn and Tiny come . . . They say she wont posi-

tively marry Cavendish, and likes Grey the best, which old Lascelles* wont believe; and thinks Cavendish quite irresistible.'

Tiny Hamilton was the second of four daughters of the Marquess of Abercorn, a family who were the mirror of aristocratic accomplishment. Disraeli was so taken by them that he raised Lord Abercorn to a dukedom as soon as he became Prime Minister and represented him as the distinguished Duke in *Lothair*. His description in that novel of the Hamilton daughters at home was romantic but scarcely exaggerated: 'Beautiful forms in counsel leant over frames glowing with embroidery, while two fair sisters more remote occasionally burst into melody, as they tried the passages of a new air, which had been communicated to them in the manuscript of some devoted friend . . . They were all alike with their delicate aquiline noses, bright complexions, short upper lips, and eyes of sunny light.' G.W.E. Russell wrote more factually: 'Few sets of sisters have been so universally liked and admired', and to Lady Louisa especially he ascribed 'that bright humour, that love of fun and pleasantry and innocent mirth, which she inherited, through her mother, from Georgina, Duchess of Bedford'. (Russell, of course, inherited it, too – hence this tortuously genealogical compliment.) The romanticism of the time liked to think of a young lady as attached to one particular young man, and over the next five years Lady Tiny's name and Cavendish's were commonly linked in the gossip of their circle.

The year 1855 saw Cavendish's first real expeditions in London society, launched from his 'garret' (as he called it) in his father's house in Belgrave Square.† In February he was elected to Brooks's, that headquarters of the Whig world, with its beautiful eighteenth-century house in St James's Street. When he cared to, he could look in at a neighbouring Whig sanctum of equal prestige, Devonshire House. The Duke had returned to London life with a vengeance some years earlier, after his time of discreet retirement with his mistress, and his magnificent reign was at its height: Devonshire House was one of the grandest private houses in London. Standing with its entrance court on the north side of Piccadilly, it occupied the whole space between the present Berkeley and Stratton Streets. A deep garden behind it, dotted with classical statuary, ran back to the adjoining garden of Lansdowne House, so that the

---

*Perhaps Cavendish's uncle William Lascelles, who had married Lady Burlington's sister.
†The 1st Earl had chosen to leave Burlington House to his third son, and it had just been sold to the government for use by the Royal Academy.

windows of Devonshire House commanded a view of a quarter of a mile to the north side of Berkeley Square.

Within the plain brick exterior the Duke carried out a remodelling of the house to adapt it to Victorian notions of grand living. On the garden front he had thrown out a large bow to contain the new marble staircase he built, rising in a semicircle to the main floor. It was known as the crystal staircase from its swirling handrail of glass, and it made a stage for the grand entrance parade required of Victorian social functions. From two of the old rooms on the garden front the Duke put together a great ballroom, at sixty-six feet long one of the three most spacious in London; and from the old entrance hall he made the Saloon, which rose the full height of the first and second floors, its arched ceiling richly painted in the style of a *salotto* in the great Italian palaces. The remaining seven state rooms were preserved in their eighteenth-century form and were packed with an incomparable collection of works of art. A description by Lady Eastlake of a reception in May 1850 conveys this newly opened splendour: 'The apartments were a perfect fairyland, marble, gilding, mirrors, pictures and flowers; couches ranged round beds of geraniums and roses, every rare and sweet oddity lying about in saucers, bouquets without end and white camellias in gorgeous pyramids . . . The Duke looks just fit for the lord of such a mansion; he is tall and princely-looking, with a face like a Velasquez Spanish monarch.'

A sterner scene, that of militia training, took the young Cavendish away from such pleasures. Already as a Cambridge undergraduate he had become captain of a company in the Lancashire Yeomanry (the Duke of Lancaster's Own), and in the spring of 1855 he took the same rank in a newly formed body called the Chatsworth Rifles, part of the Derbyshire militia. These duties, which he took very seriously, took up much of Cavendish's time and obliged him to spend the summer at Chesterfield, a town he much disliked. Nevertheless, in a contingent officered mainly by Cavendishes there was a limit to hardships, and after a nepotistic appeal to Chatsworth regarding the sad privations in the mess he was able to tell his sister in July 1855: 'We now revel daily in grapes & peaches, & to-night we are to have a haunch of venison.'

That September Cavendish was with his great-uncle in the visit which formed the climax of the Duke's restoration of Lismore. As one of the great landowners of Ireland, the Duke wanted to pay honour to his nephew the 7th Earl of Carlisle – Cavendish's 'Uncle Morpeth' – who had just been appointed

Lord Lieutenant of Ireland. The visit of September 1855 is related by Cavendish in a series of letters home, with a gently satirical view of the Duke's efforts. On the 19th he writes to his sister: 'The Duke has had some of the natives to dinner twice, which was rather a bore.' On the 22nd: 'Yesterday the Ld Lieutenant arrived in considerable state . . . There is to be a big dinner this evening but no speeches wh. is a mercy, for it is frightful to see his Grace on the point of oratory.' After a ball and other celebrations to everyone's great satisfaction, the visit ended five days later. 'It seems to have been one of the Duke's great wishes,' wrote Cavendish to his father, 'to receive Uncle Morpeth here in this way.'

In August 1856 Cavendish was given the opportunity to go to Russia in the embassy headed by his cousin Lord Granville, known as 'Pussy' for the soft amiability which had carried him to the leadership of the House of Lords. The Czar had died during the war, and his successor Alexander II was due to be crowned in September. In the civilized manner of the time his recent enemies were sending embassies to celebrate the occasion with undiminished honour. Lord Granville, asked to head the English delegation, described his response in a letter to Lord Canning: 'I consulted Marie [his wife], who pronounced some sage aphorisms, but danced a hornpipe, and lamented that it would be necessary to buy twenty gowns and have her diamonds reset.' As Lord Granville was not a rich man, he turned to his uncle the Duke of Devonshire, who insisted on his accepting. He himself had spent £26,000 on his embassy of 1826, and he was prepared to back this one with equal lavishness. Loaded with sumptuous Devonshire plate and other trimmings, Lord Granville's cortège set out in August 1856.

The large party of young aristocrats in his train included Cavendish, his cousin Lord Stafford, heir to the Duke of Sutherland, and Lord Dalkeith, heir to the Duke of Buccleuch. They were kept amused by Lord Granville's quips, original and repeated, such as the French ambassador Morny's remark at a ball that there were thirty women present and thirty teeth, pretty equally divided. On arriving in Russia Cavendish described to his father the reception of the English visitors, which involved their being 'in a state of perpetual presentation to some member of the Imperial Family'. To the same correspondent, tactfully casting his remarks in the plural, Lord Granville wrote: 'Too many of our young men are shy, which the Russians take for pride, but they look very gentlemanlike, although some of them are too partial to a combination of coloured flannel shirts, false collars, and cheap jewellery. I think the expedition will do many of them much good. It has given several of them a wish to learn French, which they have hitherto neglected.'

At a parade on 31 August the Emperor opened the proceedings by riding with his staff at full gallop along a line of troops; the English party followed. As this display closed the big grey horse Cavendish had been given, over-excited by the mode of entry, reared up and struck with its forefeet close to the Emperor. 'But his rider', wrote Granville to Lord Burlington, 'pulled him up, sat him beautifully, and has thrown additional lustre on the name of Cavendish by his courage and horsemanship.' A fortnight later Granville adds: 'Cavendish appeared on the big grey horse which he has made perfectly quiet with troops.'

After the return home Cavendish faced the question of his political future. For a Cavendish there was no alternative to entering the House of Commons; his father, two uncles, grandfather, great-uncle and great-grandfather had done so more or less at the earliest opportunity, and his two brothers were to do the same. Some of them hardly opened their mouths there, and Lord Cavendish might want to copy their reticence; but he would do so in the same place. The Duke of Devonshire offered his interest for a seat in Ireland or a seat in Derbyshire, but Lord Burlington decided to put his son up on his own home ground, North Lancashire.

The occasion for this came sooner than was expected. In March 1857 Lord Palmerston was defeated in Parliament and appealed to the country over his bullying treatment of China, where he declared that an 'insolent barbarian' had insulted the British flag. Cavendish supported the jingo policy, but his views hardly mattered since he was assured an uncontested election by the ploy of putting up £5,000 as a war fund to frighten off opponents. He continued to be elected unopposed for North Lancashire until 1868, a not unusual experience in the political conventions of the time. On his entry into the House of Commons Cavendish found there two other members of his family. One was his uncle George (Lord Burlington's younger brother), who sat for the Chatsworth domain of North Derbyshire from 1834 until his death in 1880. A great-uncle, Charles Cavendish (fourth son of the 1st Earl of Burlington), had just given up the county seat of Buckinghamshire after twenty-five years and was created Lord Chesham; the seat was passed on to his son William Cavendish until he succeeded as 2nd Baron in 1863. These gentlemen were examples of the Cavendishes who spent a lifetime in Parliament without show-ing the slightest interest in office.

The General Election of 1857 saw almost the high-water mark of Whig fortunes in the nineteenth century. The Whigs, after two generations of oppo-sition, had in 1830 seized the leadership of the popular reform movement and kept themselves in office for twenty-eight of the next thirty-six years. The Great Reform Act, which wiped out the irredeemably rotten boroughs but kept many small constituencies amenable to landowners' influence, estab-lished the political pattern of a strong middle-class interest controlled in the House of Commons by aristocratic leadership. The arch-Whig of the time was Lord John Russell, younger brother of the 7th Duke of Bedford, with his sense of family and his harking back to the Revolution of 1688. The Cabinet he had formed in 1846 was the epitome of Whig dominance; people said that it con-sisted largely of his cousins, and it focused attention on the vast ramifications of the Whig aristocracy. Russell's pedantic manner, however, was not a success, and he had to give way to Palmerston, who formed the next all-Whig adminis-tration in 1855.

A Tory writer, A.J. Beresford Hope, gave in a novel called *The Brandreths* a satirical view of the Whigs in the middle years of the century: 'It was a party which for all practical purposes existed in, through, and for its leaders, while these leaders made up a huge partnership of cousins. They had all of them a common great-great-grandmother, and there was none of them who had not, in the person of some ancestor, been beheaded, and all of them, in the persons of some other ancestors, made William III king. They were all very proud of their peerages, which they enjoyed with a zest unknown to any other class of Her Majesty's subjects, and they all intermarried within the sacred circle of the great-great-grandmothership. Of the rights of property, particularly if it happened to be landed, they had all the most positive convictions, and all owned the finest houses, the best cooks, the highest bred horses which money could command. All these attributes were accommodated to a keenly devel-oped self-consciousness of intellectual superiority.'

The roots of this clannishness were in the two generations of political exclusion and in the memory of that brilliant and attractive circle – of Charles James Fox, of his nephew Lord Holland, of Lord Grey – who had kept alight the candle of English liberty when the whole country was in Tory darkness. Family affection was a peculiar virtue of the Whigs, and they extended it to all their rambling cousinhood. It was a mutual admiration that made it hard for Lord John Russell to believe that a Cabinet could be better formed than within the 'sacred circle' and which caused the Duke of Argyll to say that 'some of the Whigs talked of themselves as if they were a particular breed of spaniels'.

This was the background against which Lord Cavendish began his career in 1857. Just two years before, a Radical member, Henry Layard, had attacked the government, saying that it attached more importance to having a Cavendish in the Cabinet than to the proper conduct of the war. 'A Cavendish in the Cabinet is a very important thing, but the public think more of 20,000 lives than they do of a Cavendish.' This gibe was all the more striking because, of the four Cavendishes then in Parliament, none was anywhere near the Cabinet; but it was precisely that deficiency which it was now hoped to correct. Some of the Whigs, like Lord Granville, were well aware of the new heir's talents and were looking to him as future Cabinet material. That was far from being his young cousin's ambition.

In June 1857 Cavendish made his maiden speech, defending Granville against a complaint on his management of the Duchy of Lancaster. It was everything that was expected of a young man's maiden speech, brief, modest, correct and with just that reminder of high political connections which made the flood of congratulations all the more cordial. Many years later, when Cavendish had acquired the reputation of a practised but lethargic speaker and Disraeli that of an oracle of epigrammatic wisdom, a story was invented that Cavendish had yawned in the middle of the speech and Disraeli had commented: 'He'll do. To any man who can betray such extreme languor under such circumstances the highest post in the gift of the Commons should be open.' The anecdote badly misrepresents Cavendish's character at this time. Quite apart from the occasion, and the brevity of the speech, he was still far too shy and unsure of himself to do anything of the sort, and he showed little eagerness over the next five years to increase his experience.

Later that year the Duke of Devonshire perversely went to spend the winter at Hardwick. It reminded him of Blanche, who had laid out the garden there, but in the hall's windy vastness he caught cold and died on 17 January 1858. Lord Burlington thus succeeded to the dukedom and to a patrimony which, added to his own, gave him a property of 200,000 acres. Besides Holker and Compton Place, these comprised the Chatsworth and Hardwick estates in Derbyshire, amounting to 85,000 acres – one-seventh of the whole county;

20,000 acres with excellent grouse moors at Bolton Abbey in Yorkshire; a few hundred acres forming the estate of Chiswick House; and 60,000 acres at Lismore in southern Ireland.

By Bateman's survey of twenty years later the Duke of Devonshire was the seventh-largest landowner in the three kingdoms, the first six being all masters of vast clan territories in Scotland, with rentals far below English levels. Of these, only two had larger incomes, the Whig Duke of Sutherland with his gigantic 1,200,000 acres, and the Peelite Duke of Buccleuch with 460,000 acres. Of English estates, only the Tory Duke of Northumberland's was larger than Devonshire's, with 186,000 acres; but he had nothing outside England, whereas the Duke of Devonshire was also one of the twenty greatest Irish proprietors. In addition the Devonshire estate included valuable urban interests: the spa town of Buxton had been developed by past dukes, and Lord Burlington himself had begun in the 1850s the great expansion of Barrow and Eastbourne, the former as an iron town and port based on newly discovered haematite ores, and the second as a genteel seaside resort. Barrow was to grow in twenty years from a mere hamlet to a town of 40,000 inhabitants by 1874, producing at its peak nearly half the Duke's income.

This inheritance, however, as the 7th Duke took the helm in 1858, filled him only with gloom. He calculated his income at £115,000 a year, but half was swallowed up in interest payments on a debt of nearly £1 million, part of it occasioned by his own recent urban investments but most stemming from the late Duke's extravagance. He took counsel of the 7th Duke of Bedford (Lord John Russell's brother), of whom it was said that his life's ambition, made possible by his large town holdings in Bloomsbury and Covent Garden, was to bring his income up to £200,000. Bedford advised against selling land, and Devonshire found that for a huge estate a debt of a million pounds was not as daunting as it seemed; apart from the sale of two small outlying estates in Ireland, he kept his inheritance together and concentrated on increasing its value, which he did for a time with great success. One measure of economy was to relieve Sir Joseph Paxton of his duties as master of the ducal works.

Of these details Cavendish – who is now to be recognized under his new title Marquis of Hartington – seems to have been allowed rather scanty knowledge. We find him three weeks after the 6th Duke's death passing on to his father Paxton's opinion: 'He says if you sell Ireland, you can pay off the whole debt and have £100,000 a year.' But that may well have been the last piece of advice on his affairs that the new Duke received from either Paxton or his own son. The latter enjoyed telling the story of his great-uncle, of whom, when he was himself the heir in waiting, the family agent had complained to his father, 'Lord Hartington appears disposed to spend a great deal of money.' The 5th Duke had replied: 'So much the better. He will have a great deal to spend.'

His father's elevation meant a move from Hartington's 'garret' in Belgrave Square to a room in Devonshire House. For much of the year he had the place to himself, since the 7th Duke maintained his hatred of London and was even reluctant to spend much time at Chatsworth, keeping Holker as his usual home. Hartington grew used to life in a very small patch of London ('A delightful place, when you succeed in getting here,' he once murmured to a host who had chosen to install himself in an admirable residence in South Kensington). Brooks's was four minutes' walk away; his other favourite club, the Turf, was even closer. To stretch his legs, as he liked to do, he could stroll down to the House of Commons, or he would drive there with a phaeton and pair which he handled with the careless skill expected of a fashionable young man. Another bow to fashion he made about this time was the growing of a beard, a decoration favoured by Volunteer officers and which was soon to engulf most of Victorian manhood.

In 1859 Lord Derby called a General Election, in the hope of giving himself a parliamentary majority. He failed, and when Parliament met the 25-year-old Lord Hartington was chosen to move the amendment which would force the Tories to resign. On 7 June he thus made his first important Commons speech, a fifty-minute criticism of the government's record. It showed the features that were to be familiar for many years: a wooden stance, a drawling tone and repetitive intonation which lost the ends of sentences in the facial undergrowth, an apparent ignorance of the very possibility of rhetoric. The speech was nevertheless a sound piece of work, displaying Hartington's characteristic grip of the essential. It was the sort of opportunity given to young men to win their spurs with a view to taking office, and without showing brilliance Hartington had risen to the occasion.

Unfortunately, however, Lord Palmerston proved unable to find a place for him in his new government. The Tories, while falling short of a majority, had dented the Whig numbers, and Palmerston had to return to a Peelite coalition, with careful attention to Radical support. Even two years later, when a reshuffle raised hopes again, he had to give preference to Henry Layard – the mocker of

Cavendish claims in 1855. It was a pointed demonstration that by the mid–Victorian years 'a Cavendish in the Cabinet' was not to be had for the asking. Hartington was kept kicking his heels, with only his sport and his Volunteer regiments to occupy him.

He himself bemoaned that fate less than his friends did. One of the latest of these was Lady Waldegrave, who had been impressed by his 1859 performance and started inviting him to her brilliant political gatherings at Strawberry Hill. Lady Waldegrave was the daughter of a well-known singer, John Braham (originally Abraham), and was an example of the way a person of no birth could, with exceptional talents, rise almost to the top of Victorian society. When she first scaled the aristocratic heights by marrying Lord Waldegrave she had tried to model herself on Hartington's aunt Harriet, Duchess of Sutherland. Finding the *grande dame* manner too taxing, she reverted to her own clever, risqué, vivacious self, so different from the proper deportment of ideal Victorian womanhood. She backed up her social skills with a somewhat coarse, dark-eyed beauty. All through his life feminine charm was something that could pierce Hartington's reserve, but the conventional and the vapid bored him. One writer alleges that Lady Waldegrave (who was twelve years his senior) became his mistress, but that is just a bit of sensationalism. Lady Waldegrave's behaviour did not go beyond a loose flirtatiousness, if Lord Clarendon is to be believed; and if she had a lover at this time it was probably Chichester Fortescue, whom she was lining up as her next husband. Hartington nevertheless formed a devotion to Lady Waldegrave that lasted to the end of her life.

A glimpse of Hartington's amorous career is given by a diary entry he made in Paris just before the 6th Duke's death: 'I have been to two Bal Masqués at the Opera, wh. rather amused me as curious sights, but not knowing any women & again the bad French, prevented me getting on there very well: I have however made the acquaintance of a little woman I go to see sometimes who is pretty & amusing but not a swell.' A year later his diary records cryptically a conversation he had with Leo Ellis's sister Diana about a romantic subject, which may be an allusion to Lady Louisa Hamilton. In that quarter, however, he made no progress over five years. In 1858 the supposed favourite Grey de Wilton married someone else, and Lady Louisa saw her younger sister wedded before her, an unconventional thing for the times. Hartington's House of Commons success in 1859 might have given him new prestige with her, but he failed to capitalize on it. Two months later Lady Abercorn took the matter into her own

hands; the party of her choice was Lord Dalkeith, the young heir to the dukedom of Buccleuch who had gone with Cavendish to St Petersburg. At the end
of the season the Abercorns left London for Brocket Hall, and Dalkeith was
invited to stay later in August. In Lord Clarendon's description to Louise
Manchester, 'She got him down to Brocket for 6 days and nailed the thing.' By
the end of the month the engagement was announced. The young Lord Cowper told his mother that he was surprised at the marriage; Clarendon's remarks
to Kimbolton were more explicit: 'If Hartington really cared for Tiny it will
have served him right to lose her by his shilly shallying.'

Louisa Hamilton became Duchess of Buccleuch on her husband's succession in 1884, and she was Mistress of the Robes to Queen Victoria in all the
Conservative administrations from 1885 to the end of the reign, going on to
hold the same position under Queen Alexandra. G.W.E. Russell wrote that she
'had the charm of perpetual youth', but she was more widely reputed as one of
the few great hostesses to maintain the old canons of social acceptance. She
abhorred the showiness of the Prince of Wales's Smart Set, one of whose
cosmopolitan female members once remarked: 'Who is this Duchess of Buccleuch? I never heard of her. Is she smarrt?' The Duchess was content to be as
unknown to this circle as they were to her, and she was the only hostess to resist
Edward VII's penchant for revising the guest lists of houses he was invited
to in favour of his moneyed friends. On the one occasion he attempted it she
wrote back regretting that she did not know the person in question and
begging to resign the Robes, before the King hastily assured her that it did not
really matter.

If Hartington had married Louisa Hamilton he would have remained
faithful to her all his life; she would have proved a priceless although conventional hostess for him and, as will be seen, would have smoothed his way to a
more successful political career. The consequences that would follow from his
failure to cast anchor in a safe marriage cannot have been foreseen at the time
he let Lady Louisa slip away; but at about the same time he began his three-
year affair with the bewitching young horsewoman Catherine Walters, better
known as Skittles.

3
Skittles

CATHERINE WALTERS WAS born in Liverpool in 1839, the daughter of a customs officer who would have enjoyed the status of a minor clerk. When she was twelve, her parents crossed the Mersey estuary to settle in the Wirral, where they are said to have kept an inn. They sent their daughter to a convent school which was opened in Chester in 1853. Although it was extremely cheap with fees of £20 a year, the choice of this school shows the family's middle-class pretensions, and it is wrong to depict Skittles as a slum girl, as some writers have done. Nevertheless, Skittles took brief benefit from this education, for she ran away after assaulting one of the nuns. There was certainly family trouble, of the sort that often underlies such outbursts, but whether Skittles also ran away from home is not clear.

From the street-ballads that were made up about Skittles in the 1860s comes the story that she earned her living in a low skittle-alley in Liverpool. This is a popular attempt to extract some biography from her nickname, which in fact is no more than the last of a series of variants on her name – Cathy, Katie, Kitty, Skitsy – all of which she used. There is no evidence that she ever worked in Liverpool, even in a less innocent trade. Absurd as such a dashing ascent may appear, it seems that she found her fortune in the hunting-field. While still well in her teens, she was hunting with the Cheshire Hounds, a body which was in a very bad way until in 1858 it was taken over by Lord Grosvenor, later 1st Duke of Westminster. It may have been a propitious setting for an upwardly mobile innkeeper's daughter to catch the eye of rich protectors.

Skittles was soon known as a superb horsewoman. In words that capture her dash and daring, Wilfred Scawen Blunt was to write of her:

> Brave as a falcon and as merciless
> Untamed, unmated, high above the press.

And to these skills she added her wonderfully slim girlish figure, her dark-blonde hair and blue eyes and her look of childlike innocence. One admirer said she had 'one of the sweetest faces I ever saw . . . a face like a Magdalen with such an innocent mouth, and tender, timid eye'. But she could belie this look with highly colourful language. Once a Master of Foxhounds congratulated her on her rosy cheeks after a hard day's riding. 'That's nothing,' she answered. 'You should see the cheeks of my arse!' Nowadays every public-school girl talks like that, but in the age of the crinoline young aristocrats found it refreshing and hilarious. Skittles also made the most of the new fashion which was driving out the doll-like look of the early Victorian period in favour of close-fitting sleeves and bodice called the 'cuirass bodice'. Worn as it normally was over a corset it did indeed give a cuirass-like appearance; but Skittles, with her breathtaking figure, squeezed the maximum of effect from the style by having her dresses tailored skin-tight over her naked body. To the male eye frustrated by the over-dressed bundles of the day it was like finding champagne in a desert.

Skittles's first known patron was the Hon. George Fitzwilliam, a brother of the 6th Earl Fitzwilliam; he had recently inherited his father's estate of Milton, near Peterborough, and was the Master of the Fitzwilliam Hounds. By the 1858–9 season, he had released Skittles from her Cheshire rides and introduced her to the smart Shire hunts, where she caught the attention of many well-born young men. At some point – it may not have been until 1860 or 1861 – Fitzwilliam pensioned off Skittles with an income of £300 a year, but he continues to feature in the letters which record Hartington's affair.

Skittles met Hartington in 1859. We may discount the story that she collided her horse with his in Hyde Park to be sent sprawling on the grass for him to rescue. She was too well connected to need such an outsider's trick – certainly Fitzwilliam and Hartington knew each other well. She probably met him on one of his hunting visits in the Shires; but it was in London that the first stages of their affair developed. There is no reason to suppose that Hartington was experienced in this sort of thing, and the problems of finding a hotel or lodging-house to meet in are mentioned in his letters. She may even have begun as she did with another shy young man four years later, and treated Hartington to an exhibition of the sort which her costume made it easy to improvise. Wilfrid Scawen Blunt tells in poetry how she met him in Lyons in October 1863 and took him to a house which she said was her dressmaker's. For a while she discussed a confection with the dressmaker and her assistants, until:

In a moment more
She had thrown off her hat, her veil untied,
And motioning all the women to the door,
While I sat speechless by who would have gone,
Undid her jacket and anon her dress,
With the jet buttons of it one by one,
And stood but clothed the more in loveliness,
A sight sublime, a dream, a miracle,
A little goddess from some luminous field
Brought down unconscious on our earth to dwell,
And in an age of innocence revealed,
Naked but unashamed. Nay, wherefore shame?
And I ah, who shall blame me, who shall blame?

Poetry was not one of Hartington's talents but, as Lillie Langtry was to find eighteen years later, he was a man for the grand gesture where a pretty woman was concerned. Disdaining the custom of hiding a girl-friend in a discreet suburb such as St. John's Wood, he set Skittles up in the heart of the West End, a stone's throw from Devonshire House. The house, 34 Park Street, can still be seen; it is not as large as the typical family house in Mayfair but was commodious enough to be occupied later in the century by a Rothschild, who remodelled the front, forming the present shallow bow. Before that it would have provided a spacious drawing-room on the first floor with three tall windows on to the street, and two more floors above.

Skittles kept practically every letter she received from Hartington during their affair. He destroyed hers, or at any rate they have not survived. Her wild and wilful outpourings resonate in his replies, though, and it is perhaps just as well that they do not exist verbatim to tarnish her brightness. Nearly all of the letters date from the years 1860–3, and although many are impossible to date they make up a detailed chart of the affair. Hartington writes in an affectionate, playful tone, like a grown-up writing to a child and sometimes descending to lovers' baby-talk; but his letters show a warm personal interest of a sort which few outside his close family glimpsed. He signs discreetly, 'Your affectionate H', but the letters show that he had asked Skittles to call him by his family name of Cav. When Skittles began her affair with Wilfrid Blunt in 1863 we find her writing to him, not too appropriately, with exactly the same endearments and in exactly the same emotional tone as Hartington had used to her. There are not many front-rank statesmen who could boast of having taught the tricks of her trade to the leading courtesan of their time.

The letters begin with a series of notes which show how Hartington fitted in the affair round his attendance at the Commons, whose debates began in the afternoon and often went on until after midnight. 'I am afraid that I shall be at the House all night; but if I get away before 1 o'clock, I will come & let myself in. You must not expect me later than that.' Or: 'I have only just got back from the House (past 2 o'clock) . . . I hope the poor little darling is fast asleep now & wont expect me. I shall come & see you about half past two to-morrow.' Sometimes the talk is about meeting her in the Park, or at Cremorne, a fashionable pleasure garden which Hartington often patronized. The following note is probably from June 1860: 'I have been all day at Epsom. I am going to dine at Brooks' & go to the Opera; & will come & see you after if you like. If you do not want me to come to-night send me a line to Whites.'

Meeting at the opera is several times mentioned but perhaps not to sit together: 'I shall only be able to go there for a minute, as I shall have to go the House afterwards,' reads one of the notes. It must have been a similar occasion mentioned in Chichester Fortescue's diary for 23 February 1860, which is the earliest independent reference to Skittles in London: 'Late to St James's Theatre. Lady W[aldegrave] was curious to see the celebrated "Skittles" who was there.'

After the Season Skittles would leave for the Continent, to coincide with Hartington's absence from London. In 1860 she visited Rome. These Continental stays introduce us to other young men who clustered round her. Hartington's cousin Leo Ellis is repeatedly mentioned, as well as Jimmy Ellis, a relation whom the official genealogy does not help one to identify (*Burke's Peerage* shows no James Ellis in the family of the Viscounts Clifden); Jimmy seems to have lived in Paris and was used by Hartington as an intermediary to keep Skittles supplied with money. George Fitzwilliam often appears, and Skittles at times was not above pricking jealousy between the past and the present lover: 'I am sure you talked to George much more than to me. Why did you?' An unexpected acquaintance is the elderly Lord Lucan, fresh from losing the Light Brigade. Skittles heard much aristocratic gossip from these and was sometimes able to give Hartington news about his own relations: 'I am quite shocked at what you tell me about Granville; such an elderly gentleman; he ought to be ashamed of himself.'

In the autumn Skittles was back in England for the hunting, but here she brought on herself an unpleasant incident. One of the less charming sides of Skittles's character was her jealousy of rivals, and indeed of all other women in general. At this time her *bête noire* was the wife of Lord Stamford, who was Master of the Quorn. Lady Stamford was a gamekeeper's daughter and had started her career as a show-rider in Astley's Amphitheatre – a calling that was regarded as tantamount to that of a whore. For this reason, although she was a naturally shy, well-bred and inoffensive person, no lady in the Shires (although very few ladies at this date hunted at all) would consent to join the Quorn while she rode with it. But that ostracism was nothing to the outrageous insults which Skittles flung at the Master's wife, and eventually Lord Stamford told her that if she showed her face with the Quorn again he would call the hunt off. Skittles defied him, and the result was told in an item in the *Illustrated London News* for 17 November 1860, which Hartington refers to in a letter of the following day. The article is written by an insider for insiders, but a little amplification will make the story clear.

> The Quorn met at Lowesby on Friday; but Treadwell [the Huntsman], in accordance with the strict orders from the noble master threatened to take the hounds home unless a certain unwelcome person withdrew from the field. When the departure (after a good deal of persuasion) had been duly accomplished, a fox was found in John o'Gaunt, and crossed the path of the homeward bound [Skittles]. This was too much for any one's philosophy [and Skittles galloped after the fox]; but Treadwell got to his hounds in his old style and stopped them when they were going, racing pace, over some of the finest country in Leicestershire. After this contretemps a final departure was taken and a capital twenty-five minutes from Baggrave Spinneys ensued. [The *News* does not mention that as Skittles rode away for the second time she turned in her saddle and bawled: 'Tell Lady Stamford *she's* not the queen of our profession – I am,'] Public opinion fully supports the Earl in the very decided step he has felt bound to take in this matter.

Hartington's letters, however, are full of sympathy at the 'bullying' Skittles was suffering, and the incident only boosted Skittles's popularity in the neighbouring hunts, where any number of young men (including George Fitzwilliam) gave their support. There are numerous letters from this hunting season, concerned with Hartington's purchase of a horse for her: 'Dearest little Skits, I send you a cheque for £250 wh is all I can manage just now. George told me that he would let you have Luxury for 200 guineas, so I think it will do. You see I am not a bit cross with you, but think you are a very nice little thing. Only you are a very expensive little thing to mount, & I am as usual very poor, & I dont think I shall be able to give myself Magnet after this.' He did buy this horse, though, which he rode for a couple of seasons. A story of their hunting days which Skittles liked to remember in old age was her jumping of the Whissendine brook in the Cottesmore's country. The brook was normally twenty feet wide, but it was flooded that day and its banks had been trodden in by many riders. Everybody begged Skittles not to try, and Hartington was ill with anxiety for her; but she cleared a measured thirty-two feet.

As society moved back to London in 1861 Skittles set out to conquer a new field; she took her place among the smartly turned-out women riders who flaunted themselves in Hyde Park. These 'pretty horsebreakers', as they were called, were the English equivalent of the *poules de luxe* whose Paris heyday began with the Second Empire and who represented the top of their brazen profession. An article of 1858 by the journalist George Augustus Sala celebrates their vogue:

> The Danaës! The Amazons! The lady cavaliers! The horse-women! Can any scene in the world equal Rotten Row at four in the afternoon and in the full tide of the season? Watch the sylphides as they fly or float past in their ravishing riding-habits and intoxicatingly delightful hats . . . And as the joyous cavalcade streams past . . . from time to time the naughty wind will flutter the skirt of a habit, and display a tiny, coquettish, brilliant little boot, with a military heel, and tightly strapped over it the Amazonian riding trouser!

The aristocratic habit of admiring horseflesh and admiring and discussing feminine beauty made it possible for these professionals to compete on lips for which, in any other context, the very notice of such persons would have been shocking. They became a fashionable subject of conversation, and the elderly man-about-town Captain Gronow, as he recalled in his memoirs the demure young ladies of his prime, marvelled that well-bred ladies now 'discuss the merits of Skittles and her horses'.

Probably even Hartington's and George Fitzwilliam's largesse would not have equipped Skittles to appear in this guise. Like the other riders, she was fitted out by a Mayfair livery stable with her horses and habits – an arrangement which enabled the stables to advertise their horseflesh while the girls advertised their bodies. But Skittles rapidly imposed herself as the most glamorous and the most dashing rider, as Gronow's singling-out of her implies. She was also supposed to be referred to in the satirical poem 'The Season' published by the future Poet Laureate Alfred Austin in 1861: 'Or more defiant, spurning frown and foe, / Rules with loose rein Anonyma the Row.'

Her fame gained an unlooked-for boost from a picture which Landseer exhibited at the Royal Academy in May of the same year. It was titled 'Taming the Shrew' and depicts a lady rider and the horse she has just been breaking in; the horse, a magnificent animal, rests in the straw, while his exhausted mistress reclines in a distinctly post-coital pose against his glossy flank. Even the unpuritanical Lord Clarendon, writing to Louise Manchester about it before the gossip started, remarked that 'a lolling damsel always looks saucy', and the picture quickly became a scandal. There were comments on the impossibility of the lady, gowned and jewelled as she was, having been taming a horse, and the official title was replaced by that of 'The Pretty Horsebreaker,' which was the contemporary code for a tart. And if she was a 'horsebreaker' she must be Skittles, despite the fact that the facial resemblance was non-existent. Thus the consensus grew that Skittles had added to her other audacities by taking several feet of advertising space on the sacred walls of the Royal Academy.

Her affair with Hartington grew steadily more intense. She showered him with little presents. 'You will make me quite a swell some day for all the nice things I have got come from you, my own little pet.' These tokens, though, had a way of bringing out the clumsiness in Hartington's manners: 'You need not send me whatever you call the thing you have been working for me, but give it me when I come.' More gallantly he often mentions the locket she had given him with her portrait, which he tells her he was always taking out and kissing. Hartington encouraged Skittles's efforts to improve herself, commenting on the spelling and grammar of her letters. In the summer of 1861 she was learning music and Greek; she even took a governess, although – typically – this effort did not last; but her cleverness cannot be doubted. By the time Blunt met her in France in 1863 she was speaking fluent idiomatic French and was able to play the title role in a public production of *Manon Lescaut*.

In August 1861 Hartington and Skittles parted again; she going to Paris. Towards the end of the month Lord Clarendon wrote to Louise Manchester: 'Skittles was at Paris with Ld: Listowel Mr Petre and Mrs. Howard and they are all gone to Baden together! The Skittles Joint Stock Company, what a pleasant investment – I wonder what the shares are at!' The Earl of Listowel was a young Whig peer whose rivalry was fleeting since he was on his way out to a tour of India. Mr Petre is possibly Henry Petre of Dunkenhalgh Hall, a well-known *bon vivant*. Hartington mentions him in his letters – without helping to identify him – writing to thank him that August for having protected Skittles from some threatening characters: 'You will get him shot or ran through the body if you dont mind.' Hartington was well aware of these and other supernumeraries in their affair: 'I hear that Jimmy is very much in love with you as well as all the others . . . but every body tells me that you have been behaving very well, but they dont know what a little darling you are, do they Skitsy?' A different code, however, was expected of him, and protestations such as one from a house-party at Hardwick – 'There are a lot of people here but I dont look at any of them because Skits said I mustnt' – are typical of a stream of reassurances to her jealousy.

Skittles was back in England in September, but Hartington could not well go to London at such an improbable time of the year. 'I dont want my people here to know anything about you Skitsy, if I can help it,' he tells her; 'but I am afraid they soon will, for people do nothing but talk.' He had a visit to Dunrobin for the stalking, and in October he stayed with the Duke of Newcastle at Clumber, where the nineteen-year-old Prince of Wales was a guest. 'The Prince of Wales is a very nice little fellow I think; but I have not got much to tell you about him, except that he smokes from morning till night.' In November, when she would normally have been disporting herself on the hunting-field, Skittles went back to Paris. There is no indication of what brought this about, but Hartington was by now becoming alarmed at the intensity of their relationship and at Skittles's possessiveness and jealousy, as she dropped other lovers and became more and more dependent on him. He wrote to her on 20 November: 'Sometimes I think that it would be better for you if you could forget me and leave off loving me . . . some day you ought to find some one who will take care of you for the rest of your life & make you happy – which I am afraid I shall never be able to do.' Skittles reacted with frantic distress, and all the more so when in early December the newspapers announced that Hartington was about to marry his cousin Susan Pitt.* Hart-

---

*Daughter of Lord Granville's sister, Lady Rivers.

ington told her: 'it is no more true than that I am going to fly. I scarcely know her to speak to.' But Skittles's desperate pleas to him continued. All through her life, there is no sign that she exercised any power over men beyond that of her bubbling, childish charm, and she knew of no lure for Hartington but to accuse him of desertion. On 29 December he wrote to her the most explicit letter in their correspondence:

My own dearest darling,

I got your letter of Thursday yesterday, but as I had to go out shooting very early & the post goes out in the afternoon I was not able to answer it. You dont know darling how miserable I have been ever since thinking of my little child crying and making herself unhappy. Poor little thing I have read the letter over & over again and I can see all the places where the tears dropped, & it made me cry too I can tell you Skitsy. It is not true my own darling. I dont want not to have any more to do with you, and I am sure nobody ever heard anything of the sort from me. Do you think my little darling I would part from you in that way and not even say good-bye to you? My little child I will promise you that whenever the time comes, for us not to be as we have been, I will tell you myself & you need not mind what any body else says. But I will tell you all the truth, Skitsy; I know darling, & you know too, that I dont love you in the same way as you do me; I dont think it is my nature ever to be so; but I do love you really & truly & sincerely; and what I should like best in the world to see would be to see you married some day to some one whom if you could not love very much you could like, & who would take care of you all your life & make you happy . . . Then darling there is always the chance of something happening to make my father interfere . . . Whatever happens my own darling child, there can never be any reason for your *never never* as you say seeing me again. If I was to cease to be your lover, nothing on earth would prevent me going on seeing you, if you would let me, & being I hope your best friend . . . You tell me my little Skitsy that you will do everything I wish; and I am going to tell you what I want. I want you not to ask me to go to theatres &c with you. If people dont see me with you in public, they will soon leave off talking about it. And one more thing Skitsy, I want you to try not to be jealous of my going out anywhere, or talking to any-body. I never give you any real cause darling, and you must please give me a little more liberty. Now darling can you do these little things? They are not as bad as asking you to say goodbye to me, are they darling.

It is proof of the terror Skittles had been in of losing Hartington that she annotated this cautious statement 'A pretty letter to be kept'. By February she was back in England hunting with Hartington, and the correspondence is smooth again.

Skittles had been complaining about 34 Park Street, which she found inconvenient, and a letter of Hartington's, probably before 1862, tells her that he will not be jealous if 'Lord L' gives her another house, at the same time good-humouredly acknowledging her criticisms: 'You know I dont know anything about houses; do I darling?' Listowel, the young Lord Londesborough, or even Lord Lucan would be, to judge from the correspondence, possible identifications for this patron. But by the beginning of 1862 such alternatives had fallen away. Skittles had 34 Park Street lavishly done up from top to bottom, although authorities are divided as to whether it was done in the style of a high Victorian whore-house, with cerise-coloured wall-hangings and gilt cherubs all over the place, or whether it was all quite tasteful and elegant. Skittles later spun a wonderful tale out of her affair with Hartington, saying that he had offered her marriage, that he had taken her to see his father and that the Duke had kissed her but demurred to marriage on the grounds of her health (which was indeed wretched). From the evidence of 250 letters this can be absolutely ruled out; but it gives us a glimpse of the fantasy the 22-year-old girl was weaving: to be the next Duchess of Devonshire. Was it this dream that made her cling to Hartington, or was she really in love with him? It is easy to be cynical about the motives of a girl in her position, but we should throw in the judgement of Henry Labouchere, who later knew Skittles well: 'She had the most capacious heart I know, and must be the only whore in history to retain her heart intact.' For the moment at least her relationship with Hartington floated on this illusion.

Early in June Hartington took Skittles to the Derby, where she was paraded all day on his arm. This may seem curious in view of his request that she should not ask him to take her to theatres, but in those days the Derby was an event which very few ladies attended; as far as society was concerned it was a male occasion, and therefore one to which gentlemen could take their mistresses without scandal. What Hartington failed to take into account, however, was that it immediately made his affair with Skittles public property. From this moment therefore is born the popular version of the affair – one which superseded the true history until quite recently – a version which confined its duration more or less to June and July 1862 but added various other sensational trimmings which will be presently described.

Skittles soon had another national outing with a letter planted in *The Times* on 3 July. It sprang from the increasing ostentation which her position with Hartington was encouraging in her; not content with her appearances on horseback she had joined the ultra-smart set in Hyde Park by driving out in a spanking carriage with a pair of perfectly matched black Orloff ponies of the kind for which the Park served as such a competitive display. Referring to her as 'Anonyma' – the name to which Austin had given his authority – the writer playfully describes her stopping the traffic and setting the fashion in both clothes and horses, as people now paid between four hundred and six hundred guineas for a pair of ponies as handsome as hers. The letter was signed 'H', but someone on *The Daily Telegraph* found out that its author was a young *Times* journalist, Matthew Higgins, who had thus relieved the usual stodgy fare of the correspondence columns. There was a fierce circulation war between the two newspapers, and in such a conflict moral indignation was a useful weapon in the mid-Victorian climate. *The Daily Telegraph* launched a thundering attack on *The Times* for giving advertisement to a whore. Those who were watching the Skittles affair naturally took note.

This publicity may have influenced Hartington, but he had by now come to the conclusion that Skittles must be weaned from her dependence on him and that putting the moment off would only make it worse. He decided to embark that August on a tour of America, where the Civil War had been raging for over a year. His brother Edward had been sent out there with his regiment the previous December as a precaution against trouble on the Canadian frontier, and a fraternal reunion together with a study of the war gave a pretext for a long absence. He may have taken alarm at the amount of money Skittles was swallowing up ('You are to be economical now,' he was to warn her in November); in the correspondence alone we find payments of at least £750 or £800 mentioned in the two and a half years up to this time. He shirked telling Skittles until the last moment, and even on 28 July he was writing to his father that he wanted the journey kept secret – no doubt for fear the papers would announce it. It was on the very next day that he saw Skittles and told her two things: he was leaving on a six-month trip, and he wanted her to give him up; he would continue to see her and support her, but the affair could not continue as it was.

Skittles was taken so much by surprise that her violent reaction of eight months ago in Paris was muted. 'I think I was worse than you instead of giving you a good example,' wrote Hartington on 3 August recalling their parting; but the storms came in her desperate letters over the next two months, and in a stream of replies he tried vainly to assuage her grief.

Skittles also left London for Paris – presumably her usual August retreat which was already planned – and the simultaneous disappearance of both led to a first rumour that they had eloped. With better information a more elaborate story was concocted: that the Cavendish family had taken fright at the newspaper notoriety given to Skittles, that it had descended on Hartington in its mighty array to make him give her up, that he was being whisked off to America to get him out of scandal's way, and that he had been forced to desert Skittles without a parting word. All this is pure gossip's make-believe. The Duke at least was still blissfully unconscious of the affair. Hartington saw out the parliamentary session, went to Holker for a Volunteer review, proceeded to Bolton as he always did for a few days' shooting at the beginning of the grouse season, crossed to Ireland and embarked on the Cunarder *Persia* on 17 August. With him travelled Colonel Charles Leslie of Glaslough, an Irish landowner and MP who was a family friend. A six-day voyage brought them to New York.

Hartington was handsomely received by the rich banker August Belmont, who was Chairman of the Democratic Party; he had recently been in England and knew Lord Frederick Cavendish. Belmont's house was one of the finest in New York and his wife was perhaps *the* society lady of the time, with a taste for hunting social lions. One of Belmont's keenest aims at this time was to woo European support for the Union cause, but the drive did not lead him to affect any esteem for the Republican administration. New York was probably the most pro-Southern place in the Union states, both at the highest level, at which the Mayor, supported by some of the leading citizens, had advocated at the beginning of the war that the city should secede and continue its trade with the South, and at the popular level, at which there were riots on the introduction of conscription in 1863. It was thus with a slanted preparation that Hartington went on to an interview with the President in Washington towards the end of September. True to his habit of making facetious remarks on such occasions, Lincoln opened the meeting by saying, 'Hartington! Well, that rhymes to Partington.' (Mrs Partington was the heroine of a popular comic book of the time.) His visitor naturally concluded: 'I never saw such a specimen of a Yankee in my life. I should think he was a very well meaning sort of man, but as almost every body says, about as fit for his position now as a fire shovel.' But Lincoln had one trait in common with Hartington, of being underestimated by people until they found out what he could do: it took assassination to turn Lincoln into a hero, an apotheosis which Hartington was spared or denied. When Hartington had withdrawn, Lincoln remarked to his companion Mr John Rose that he expected to hear more of his friend in the coming years, although he seems to have been thinking as much of Hartington's special opportunities for rising in the British political system as of any talents he had prophetically discerned.

Mr Rose (later Sir John), together with Lord Edward Cavendish, had been picked up in Canada in the month's travelling that Hartington did between New York and Washington. In this time Hartington received two letters of impassioned despair from Skittles. She told him that she wanted to enter a convent, to which the level-headed reply was returned: 'It would never suit you I am sure to remain in one long.' But in mid-October came a bombshell: Skittles had come out to America in the *Persia* and was asking to join him. Hartington must have been appalled, but he responded calmly: 'I am very sorry that you should have come out here . . . Of course darling I shall see you now that you have come.' He insisted, though, that she should await his return to New York and not try to follow him. From this point a growing firmness creeps in ('you know I am going to keep you in great order now') with the gentleness of his letters to her. Skittles's presence would not have embarrassed Hartington with Colonel Leslie, who was no slouch when it came to amorous susceptibility,* but he was determined not to let her impulsiveness throw out his companions' travel plans.

After leaving London Skittles had gone to the spa town of Ems, and there made a bizarre liaison with an Irish squire, Aubrey de Vere Beauclerk, a rather sickly individual whose sexual exploits consisted mainly in endless anecdotes of how women took off their clothes for him. Deserting his wife, Beauclerk escorted Skittles to America. If Skittles hoped by this manoeuvre to make Hartington jealous, she could not have picked a weaker rival. Hartington

---

*One of the many ladies he ardently pursued was a beautiful Swedish prima donna. Once as he watched her from his box at the opera he expressed a wish that he could make passionate love to her on the stage. 'That would never do,' replied a friend. 'The audience would call for a encore.'

added in his letter: 'I have been looking over the list of passengers in the Persia & cannot find your name, but I find Mr & Mrs Beauclerk . . . Has that unfortunate man come out with you, and are you travelling in his name?' The presence of such an undesirable escort only added to the distastefulness of the situation. In fact Hartington continued travelling about America with his companions and kept Skittles waiting for him in New York until after mid-November. Before arriving he wrote firmly but sweetly insisting that Skittles should go back as soon as he had seen her: 'You see darling, I am in a great hurry to get you home.'

The gossips circulated two stories about their meeting: one was that Skittles came upon Hartington unawares in a hotel and he exploded with anger; the other was that she confronted him for his desertion, calling him spineless and a prig. What the letters of the next six months show are Skittles's desperate efforts to win Hartington back. This whole episode is the best proof that she was really in love with him; a calculating woman would have seen that she had lost him and tried to tweak what advantage she could out of the situation. Instead Skittles took a course which would make her a laughing-stock to her rivals when they learnt how she had pursued her vanishing protector all across the Atlantic. Her distress wrung some change of mind from Hartington, for in a later letter he referred to their meeting in New York: 'I gave way though I knew I was wrong because I could not bear to see you suffering.' But it was no skilful game Skittles was playing; when on 24 November Hartington saw her off on the train to Boston, he lost his temper – only to send a contrite letter after her: 'I have been so sorry ever since, for being cross with you a minute yesterday.'

There follows a four-month gap in which there are only three letters – only three, at any rate, which reached Skittles from Hartington's complicated travels. In mid-December, after a second visit to Canada, where he left Lord Edward with his regiment, he went on to Baltimore, intending to cross the lines to the Confederate side. The party failed to get passports and had to cross unofficially, reaching Richmond before Christmas. A month later Hartington wrote to Skittles: 'I have lost all my luggage, & I cant get any things here; at least very few things; & I have had to get along on one suit of clothes for a fortnight & shall for some time longer . . . We have had some hunting as they call it, but it is not much like Leicestershire.'

His stay in the Confederacy confirmed Hartington's political leaning to the

South. He had studied the Northern lines at some length, and from the less than Moltkean standards of the English militia regiments had been astonished at the amateurishness and ill-discipline of the Union army. The Confederates impressed him much more. What he failed to witness were battles, lamenting that he arrived ten days late for both Antietam and Fredericksburg. ('Both were excellent battles for a spectator,' he told his father.) His regret is characteristic of a wish to be at the centre of action. All through his life he was to show an itch to be on the spot where events were unfolding, instead of watching them from behind a desk in London.

The American Civil War exemplifies the truth that history is written by the victors, its consequence in this case being that anything short of ardent Unionism is seen by modern historians as sympathy for the slave-holding Confederacy. Thus we have the frequent assertion that English opinion in general, and aristocratic opinion in particular, was pro-Southern. That was certainly not the case in Hartington's circle; the Stafford House set was strongly abolitionist and had lionized Harriet Beecher Stowe on her visit to England; one of its members, the Duke of Argyll, was probably the only Cabinet minister who would have resigned if Palmerston had decided to intervene in the war; Hartington's brother Lord Frederick was so pro-Northern that his bride called him 'old Yankee Freddy'. Nor was the feeling confined to Whigs: the Duke of Manchester's brother Lord Robert Montagu, who was a Tory MP, was a strong pro-Unionist. It would be hard to find any comparable strength of feeling on the other side. What many people saw, though, was the paradox that a nation which derived its existence from asserting a right of secession was denying that right to eleven of its members, calling them 'Rebels' and forcing them back into a supposedly free partnership of equals. Hartington's attitude had started from his instinctive resistance to idealistic gush; when he reached America he saw that for many people in the North the war was not an anti-slavery crusade but very much an effort to avert a grave blow against their national greatness. He regarded Lincoln's Emancipation Proclamation as a political manoeuvre and was derisive of people in England – including his own constituents – who were taken in by it. His response was always a reasoned one, but by 17 February 1863 he was telling his father: 'I am very decidedly Southern in the main.'

Prevented from recrossing the lines, Hartington eventually got out of Charleston by sea and sailed to New York in February 1863. Here, before he left, he starred in the most notorious incident of his American visit. On 17 February, August Belmont gave a ball for General McClellan, whom Hartington had met and admired at Antietam five months before. At that time he was the leading Union general, but he had since been dismissed by Lincoln, and Belmont had his eye on him as the next Democratic presidential candidate. The general and many of his officers were thus being fêted in New York at a *bal masqué* – an occasion where the women wore masks and dominoes but the men were undisguised. A young Confederate sympathizer, Mrs Yznaga del Valle, whose husband was a Southern planter, came up to Hartington (it is not clear whether he knew her), stuck a miniature Confederate flag in his lapel and dared him to introduce her to General McClellan. Perhaps Hartington really thought that a jape like that would be taken lightly in New York, or perhaps it shows what he could be led into by a pretty woman. The two began to make their way through a throng of Union officers. One of these, a diminutive young Lieutenant who had been wounded in Florida, jostled Hartington twice, adding, 'Offence was intended.' When this had no result, he took Hartington out of the ballroom and furiously ordered him to take the badge off. Hartington complied, apologized, protested ignorance and said that he had not meant to offend. In the mean time a ferment was growing among the officers back at the ball, and someone had gone to fetch Mr Belmont. He arrived on the spot and took Hartington out of the house by a side door to the stables, where he made his escape. Unfortunately we have not got Hartington's account of this fiasco, since his last letters to both his father and Skittles were written on the day of the ball itself.

The incident had a long resonance in America and was recalled years afterwards by James Russell Lowell in an article 'On a Certain Condescension in Foreigners'. Although he asserted that at the ball 'nobody minded it', that was evidently not the attitude of the writer, who cited it as an example of English arrogance; he went on to claim that at Hartington's interview with the President – which Lowell places later – Mr Lincoln deliberately addressed the visitor as Partington in revenge for the insult.

Unconscious of the long-term trauma he had wreaked on the American psyche, Hartington embarked for England a week after the ball. Skittles had given up 34 Park Street after their separation, for it seems that she had been going to move anyway. The contents had been auctioned in November 1862 amid great public interest, fuelling gossip about the crisis that had 'forced'

Hartington to America. Hartington's next letters to Skittles were therefore addressed to Paris, and those of 11 and 15 March announce a new turn in the affair: 'My father heard about your going out to America to see me & since that he has been told all about the whole thing, which he had no notion of before ... My father of course is in a terrible state about it ... I told him you had given me up & he knows that I am very unhappy.' We can only note how far this is from being reflected in the Duke's diary (10 March 1863): 'Cavendish arrived this morning & I had the great happiness of finding him here on my return from Windsor this afternoon looking extremely well & in excellent spirits, apparently much pleased with his expedition.' The rest of the diary is equally free from any hint of the scandal. One is tempted to suspect a subterfuge on Hartington's part to rub in Skittles's error in pursuing him, and if so it would show how much pressure he was feeling obliged to put on her. Skittles for her part was squeezing emotional blackmail for all it was worth, asking Hartington to look for a convent for her to enter (a subject he knew decidedly less about than she did), while at the same time she went on showering him with little presents: 'such a lot of gloves & pct handkerchiefs, that I shall never want any more; & a little "*from Skitsy*" written on the boxes. Thank you for them all darling.'

On returning to England, Hartington was faced with an offer from Lord Palmerston of government office in the Admiralty, and, as the law then stood, this required his presenting himself for a re-election, which took place on 24 March.* The following weekend he nipped across to Paris to see Skittles, but would not agree to go back as they had been. In early June she sent an intermediary, Madame Guillotte, to London to make the same plea, but Hartington still refused. Madame Guillotte, being like all Frenchwomen a specialist in affairs of the heart, concluded that Hartington was wholly cold towards Skittles and told her so. This provoked a renewed crisis. Hartington's next two letters have been tightly crumpled up, as one can still see; but Skittles later rescued them from the waste-basket and carefully smoothed them out again. A sharp talking-to from Leo Ellis to Madame Guillotte and Hartington's unceasing protestations gradually calmed Skittles down.

All through this spring and summer the letters zig-zag over whether

*It is worth contradicting the story, repeated by so well informed a source as G.W.E. Russell, that Hartington's ministerial career was a diversion engineered by his family to draw him away from Skittles. Lord Palmerston had been trying to find an office for him for four years; and the eventual offer came eight months after Hartington had decided of his own accord to break with her.

Skittles is to come back to London and whether Hartington really wants her to come or not. On 26 May he writes:

> Two sad little letters from you this morning darling. I do so wish you could get over this a little & try & be a little happier again. Poor little darling, I can fancy it sitting in the Park where I took you & crying, & picking her little flowers & sending them to me. My poor little Skitsy, you dont know how fond I am of you though I am so unkind to you, & how unhappy it makes me when I think I have given you so much pain . . . Of course you may come over darling, & of course you shall see me as often as I can possibly manage it. and if I can you shall have some dinner with me some-where; but it wont be good-bye dear, & I shall see you very very often again I hope my little darling.

Hartington started looking for another house for her, but at the end of June Skittles told him that she looked forward with horror to returning. Probably by now she had seen through her grief enough to realize how she had destroyed herself, by her dash to America, with those who were watching her progress with a mocking and rival eye. She had by now gone for a month to Wildbad, in the Grand Duchy of Baden, where Hartington felt able to send her items of fashionable intelligence: 'There was a wonderfully swell ball . . . on Friday last given by the Guards to the Prince & Princess [of Wales]; & you never saw anything so smart; but I didnt think there was anybody near so pretty as poor little Skitsy used to be.' It is worth noting that one of the ladies at this ball, held on 26 June, was Louise Duchess of Manchester.

Skittles finally made a fleeting visit to London at the end of July, when she knew that Hartington was at Goodwood (as was Louise Manchester) and would then be going to the country. He came up to see her at her hotel, and a note asks to see her again, but it looks as though that did not happen, and she seems to have left without saying goodbye or at least without leaving sweet memories. In a letter of perhaps a few weeks later Hartington writes to her in a tone of unwonted stiffness: 'I still intend to do everything that is in my power to be kind to you, and to help you, and to repair as well as I can any harm I have done you, which God knows was not intentional on my part . . . I think you do not know the unhappiness & anxiety you give me.'

Probably at their parting in July 1862 Hartington had given Skittles a cheque for £400 and told her: 'I will give you £500 a year for the present at least. When I come to settle anything upon you, I may not be able to do quite so much for you.' He gave her some more cheques in New York and £100 in June 1863. To the period of constraint after July 1863 seems to belong a letter in which he writes: 'I cannot think that there was anything unreasonable in what I proposed you to do . . . I can do nothing but make you the same offer as I did when you were here . . . Re money I told you it will be paid every quarter to the same bankers as G. Fitzwilliam; & as it ought to have begun sooner I send you a cheque for £200 wh. I hope may be useful to you.' The final allowance he made her was £400 a year.

That October Skittles began her affair with the young English diplomat Wilfred Scawen Blunt, whom she met at Lyons; and soon afterwards she became the mistress of Achille Fould, Napoleon III's Finance Minister. Besides giving her security, this liaison conferred a prestige that allowed her to look her rivals in the face again, and she took to coming back to England for the hunting season, where she basked in continued male admiration. She also took a house in Chesterfield Street, in Mayfair, where she held court for the next few years. She met the young Prince of Wales, who was at this time beginning his pleasure-loving leadership of London society. She used to tell the story of when she, Hartington and the Prince went to see a stud farm in the country and the Prince remarked on the shabby umbrella she was carrying that day, saying, 'It wants recovering.' 'Yes,' she replied, 'I have had it covered twice, but there has been no produce.' That was the sort of joke the Prince enjoyed. Another new admirer was Lord Hubert de Burgh, later 4th Marquess of Clanricarde. As a younger son, Lord Hubert was kept on a tight allowance and was famously mean; on one occasion when he lent Skittles money it was only on the security of her jewels, and then, so she told Blunt, he refused to return them to her 'except on a certain condition and that it should be in her riding hat'. Hartington and the Prince tried to get her to drop Lord Hubert, saying that he was too disreputable and not a gentleman, but he kept coming round to Chesterfield Street, and one night the Prince, who was there with Arthur Ellis and Lord Charles Beresford, emptied a chamber-pot on his head from an upper window. In 1867 Skittles was still sufficiently interested in Hartington to stay at an inn on the Chatsworth estate and go round the house while the family were away.

These amiable meetings concealed needling relations, of which the last letters give a glimpse. At one point she suddenly asked Hartington for £2,500 to move into a house (perhaps Chesterfield Street). He replied: 'I would do a good deal for you, I think you know darling, but it is certainly not convenient to me to give you this now, and I dont like to stop what I allow you, for I want you always to have that regularly. Tell me what it is you want it for, and whether any less will do, and I will see what I can manage . . . it is a good deal of money you ask me for. Bless you darling.' They had a meeting, after which Hartington wrote her one of his stiffest letters: he would pay her the £2,500 provided he could be sure it would be spent on nothing else but the house. He promised to continue her allowance, but if 'you intend only to live in London, to annoy me, and give me trouble, things might happen which might make me wish to take it away from you . . . I cannot tell you how unhappy it has made me this last year to think that you have been going all wrong.' But Skittles had not dropped her winning little ways, and a postscript adds: 'The studs are very pretty darling.' It may be one of the last letters that assures her: 'I shall *always* like to know all about you, and I should like to think you are happy at last after all your troubles.'

Skittles was watching the first stages of Hartington's affair with the Duchess of Manchester, of which she wrote to Blunt: 'I never put myself in her way & ever showed her anything but the greatest politeness when she cut me out.' In October 1867 her own protector Achille Fould died, and her brief glittering career among the *grandes horizontales* of Paris came to an end. She set about building a following among a wider circle in London, none of whom stood out as her special patron. In 1872 she moved into a new house in South Street, where a blue plaque recalls her 48-year residence. She still rode in Hyde Park, amazing everyone with her superb figure under her skin-tight riding-costume. Visitors to her drawing-room were expected to be turned out with spick-and-span formality. Besides the Prince of Wales and his friends, eminent figures who paid court to her included Lord Hopetoun, who had been Master of the Pytchley. The popular sporting peer the 9th Earl of Coventry is said to have paid her an allowance to the end of her life (Hartington of course would have neither blinked at nor begrudged such assistance). The Radical MP and journalist Henry Labouchere was a respectful acolyte at her tea-table; and in the 1880s Skittles earned the ardent devotion of the young Prince Wilhelm of Germany (soon to be Kaiser), to the mortified jealousy of his uncle the Prince of Wales.

As for Hartington, his affair with Skittles remained one of those open secrets which Victorian deference knew so well how to keep. In 1864 no fewer than three fictionalized biographies of Skittles were published, without so much as a veiled reference to the connection. Yet the affair had been public knowledge since that Derby Day in 1862, together with the romantic embell-ishments which gossip liked to hang on the great aristocratic names. Puritanism might rule the respectable middle class, but the underlying opinion preserved a more sporting tradition; it was shown in 1863 when the 79-year-old Lord Palmerston was caught in an affair, provoking Disraeli to mutter: 'Don't let this get out or he'll sweep the country.' Similarly Hartington's dalliance did him no harm and was alluded to discreetly by a writer in 1886 as a venial escapade of his youth which was fondly remembered and endeared him to the public now that he had climbed to the top of the political system.

4

The Prince of Wales and Friends

Before Hartington returned from America Lord Palmerston wrote to the Duke of Devonshire offering his son a Civil Lordship of the Admiralty and stating the reason: 'I feel very strongly that it is of great importance to the country, and is highly conducive to the working of our Constitution, that young men in high aristocratical positions should take part in the administration of public affairs, and should not leave the working of our political machine to classes whose pursuits and interests are of a different kind.' Since forming his government in 1859 Palmerston had had some trouble with one of those whose pursuits and interests were of a different kind: this was W.E. Gladstone, who was his Chancellor of the Exchequer. The son of a Liverpool merchant, he had begun his career as a High Tory, then was converted to Sir Robert Peel's free-trade commercial policy and resigned with him in 1846. After serving in the Aberdeen coalition, he was left in the political wilderness during the first administration of Lord Palmerston, whom he regarded as immoral and unprincipled, and, as he also shrank from rejoining the Tories (he was equally censorious of Disraeli), his future looked barren. When Palmerston formed his second administration, however, Gladstone's high sense of duty led him to take office, a move that allowed him to succeed Palmerston on his death in 1865 as Leader of the House of Commons. Russell's retirement then made him Leader of the whole party, with a subsequent career as four-times Liberal Prime Minister.

His exhausting political trajectory took up only part of Gladstone's energies; another realm of interest was formed by his strong religious convictions and the austere work into which they led him. Already from his undergraduate days he had laid on himself a duty of rescuing fallen women, in whose search he spent many nights walking the streets. To chasten any passions that might be excited once he had taken them home, he would subject himself to secret sessions of self-flagellation, conscientiously entered in his diary. In this humanitarian cause Gladstone braved social disapproval: when Lillie Langtry appeared on the London scene he was alone among respectable people in visiting her (his efforts tended to be drawn the more decorative members of their profession), and he founded a friendship which lasted for a number of years while she kept her main interest as the Prince of Wales's mistress.

It was in line with this concern that Gladstone turned his attention to Skittles. They are said to have met in Hyde Park, where she asked Gladstone to one of the Sunday afternoon tea-parties patronized by so many distinguished and broad-minded gentlemen. Gladstone was a strict sabbatarian, but the man who had not scrupled to submit to 'strange and humbling acts' in his sessions with capricious converts was not to be put off by such a thought. Soon he was sipping tea in Skittles's drawing-room, whose intimacy emboldened him to courtly compliments; he kissed her hand, admired the slimness of that famous waist and went on to test its size by manual measurement. The visits were repeated; he brought her flowers and sent her cases of Russian tea, desiring her to write to him and to mark her envelopes 'Private' with a little cross that he would recognize as a code. So the work of rescue progressed. There was no sign that his efforts were raising Skittles any higher than Hartington's and Lord Coventry's annuities had placed her, but Gladstone went on trying; it was proof of that dauntless determination that kept him coming back to the premiership, wearied with the political battle, until the age of eighty-four.

We see here a case of the ways in which Hartington's and Gladstone's lives touched and diverged. There is no evidence that Hartington ever had to do with street-walkers, and no doubt his attitude would have been on the lines of his nephew's, when he heard Stanley Baldwin's charge that the press barons were seeking 'power without responsibility, the prerogative of the harlot throughout the ages'. The 9th Duke of Devonshire, as he then was, exclaimed: 'There! He's gone and lost us the tarts' vote now.' As we follow Gladstone's and Hartington's political lives we shall trace the same counterpoint of likeness and divergence; we find it almost from the beginning of Hartington's ministerial service, which was to make him within four years, in the wishes of a section of his party, a competitor of Gladstone's for the leadership.

Hartington first took office as a Civil Lord of the Admiralty on 23 March 1863, but at the end of April he moved to the War Office as Under-Secretary. To the Radicals, the appointments seemed a case of aristocratic favouritism. Hartington had spoken a mere five times in his six years in the House, and only his No Confidence speech of 1859 had gone beyond the briefest intervention. 'The cheekiest thing I ever heard of, but it is like old Pam' was a typical reaction. But Hartington's post was not a sinecure, since the Secretary for War, Lord De Grey, was a peer, and this made Hartington responsible for presenting his department's policy in the Commons. Within a few weeks he had surprised the House by his grasp of his subject and the competence and clarity with which he explained it, and he was being seen as the quiet success story of the session. He caused even more astonishment in 1864, when the Army Estimates were submitted in May. By an oversight, all of the Cabinet were absent; Palmerston, who would normally have been there to support an Under-Secretary, was at home with gout; yet for six hours Hartington warded off attacks from all quarters, rising to his feet twenty times to explain points of the Estimates clearly, concisely and without frills. Over the next two years he continued to show the same mastery of his department's business, but he remained shy of general debate. His speech on the 1866 Reform Bill was his first for three years not on Army affairs, and it was a halting performance, not helped by heckling from Tories who, in Lady Frederick Cavendish's opinion, had dined too well earlier in the evening.

An observer of these developments, as we have seen, was Louise Manchester, and she must have been looking at Hartington with new respect when she asked him to tea with her in the summer of 1863. She had known him for some years, of course, and had thought it worth while since 1859 to annoy Lady Waldegrave by competing with her for his attendance. Some writers say that he had already become her lover, but this view is linked with the error which confines the affair with Skittles to a couple of months in 1862. We may assume that Louise had received full details of the break-up with Skittles from Colonel Leslie, who was her strong admirer, and she saw her opportunity. In January 1864 Hartington paid his first visit to Kimbolton for the fox-hunting, and the friendship developed. He displaced the little circle of courtiers whom Louise had held in her teasing, commanding thrall; Lord Cowper, who had been an annual visitor to Kimbolton, practically drops out after 1864. We need not see this as particularly ruthless, since Louise, like most women, doubtless found one lover at a time enough for a quiet life; but certainly Hartington now gave her a better spy-hole than Cowper into the world of high politics. As for her new lover, he made a good exchange by passing from Skittles to Louise Manchester. These were the years of which an old gentleman told Hartington's biographer: 'No one knows how gloriously beautiful a woman can be who did not see the Duchess of Manchester when she was thirty.' To beauty she added qualities to which Skittles had been, very naturally, a stranger; Hartington found in her an intellectual equal, a woman of the great world, of discretion and judgement; she not only spared him the headaches of Skittles's childlike storms but provided support and guidance in his political and in his social life. There are no letters to record their affair as there are with Skittles, but a few surviving notes which Hartington wrote when Louise had become the formidable Double Duchess hint at the devotion there must have been in the first years. He addresses her as 'darling little angel' and as 'my own own darling', and when they are parted tells her how he longs to see her 'little face again'. It is the same voice that we heard thirty years before in the letters to Skittles. We see in it proof that the masterful society lady stirred in Hartington the same tenderness as had the childish little body from Liverpool; and Louise, used to awe and distance, melted at the treatment, replying with an affection which she had never given to her deferential court.

Of all Louise's rivals in Victorian society, none perhaps except Lady Palmerston had an intelligence so focused on power. She was not without more obvious feminine tastes, such as a soft spot for flowers (Lord Clarendon jokingly looked forward to 'Louise Cultivatrice' appearing at a ball adorned in the rare blooms she was developing at Kimbolton); but even her frivolities leant more to the male worlds of hunting, racing and gambling. The serious business of life for her was power, both social and political; but she did not make the feminist's mistake of becoming mannish to pursue it. Together with wit, intelligence and a commanding effrontery, she used her beauty as part of a well-integrated armoury; nor did she, like Lady Waldegrave, allow the pleasures of flirtatiousness to sidetrack her and get her laughed at. Her contemporaries, and especially those who remembered the grand tyrantesses of Regency Almack's, would not have found anything unfeminine in her spirit. All the conventions of the day – the sweeping costumes, the queenly deportment, the deferential manners – conspired to place women on a pedestal, and Louise occupied it like a throne.

It was this single-mindedness that turned the Prince of Wales's marriage from a rebuff into an opportunity. She was quick to spot that social leadership had passed from the widowed Queen to the young Prince, and she nimbly shifted her allegiance. After twenty years of repression under his father's serious regime, the Prince was out to enjoy life; and there was no one better placed to help him than the glamorous Duchess. They had met well before the marriage; the Prince had made a hunting visit to Kimbolton in December 1861 on the very day after the Prince Consort went to Cambridge to confront him with his wicked dalliance with Nellie Clifden, the girl whom some young hearties had manoeuvred into his bed that summer at the Curragh. One surmises that the Manchesters did not find their guest chirpy on that occasion; but things were changing. The Prince now set up his own establishment at Marlborough House in London and bought Sandringham in Norfolk, at both of which Hartington and Louise Manchester were soon habitués. Newmarket was another frequent venue, Louise being one of the few ladies of the period who favoured that horsy scene. There was never any suggestion that Louise became the Prince's mistress (according to Anita Leslie he was faithful to his wife for the first five years of his marriage), but a woman of her beauty and talent to amuse was his ideal social mentor. One thing that linked them was their social energy. They could both spend the night dancing or gambling until the small hours of the morning and be up again early and ready for frolics the following day.

Hartington could accommodate himself to the late-night part of this routine, but early rising was a virtue he never cultivated; he was none the less taken up as one of the Prince's most intimate friends. If a fanatic for social exclusiveness had wished to reduce London Society to its innermost trinity, he would have had to choose the Prince of Wales, Hartington and Louise Manchester, and this state of affairs remained unchanged until the deaths of the three principals over forty years later.

The circle of the Prince's close friends included Hartington's first cousin the 3rd Duke of Sutherland (hitherto Lord Stafford). He was a man who affected a rough directness of speech, while his clothes looked as if they had been stuck on with a pitchfork. His special eccentricity at this time, into which he enlisted the Prince, was to rush about London when a big fire was declared and fancy that they were assisting the fire brigade. Hartington and Sutherland were similar rough diamonds nestling in the sumptuous settings of Stafford House and Devonshire House. Louise Manchester did her best to tidy Hartington up, making him brush his hair and sit up in public, but it was too late to do much about his rustic manners. When a dinner party was kept waiting at Marlborough House, it was usually Hartington who was to blame. The suave G.W.E. Russell was irritated by Hartington's habit of replying to a question by

drawling 'a monosyllable which sounded like "Whor?" and meant "What?"'
Those who got to know him, though, found Hartington an easy companion. As
Lady Randolph Churchill was to discover, 'His rather stern countenance
belied a mirth-loving soul, and he thoroughly appreciated a joke.' Margot
Asquith also found in him 'the noisy sense of humour of a Falstaff. He gave a
great wheezy guffaw at all the right things.' He was a raconteur in a gruff and
irreverent vein; his jutting lower lip would waggle for some moments as he
assembled his thoughts, then out would come the story. At the Turf Club it was
said that if every member were forced to resign and stand again, Hartington
would be the only man certain of re-election.*

The satirical eye of Disraeli has left us in *Lothair* a character-sketch of the
young Whig of this time. His Lord St Aldegonde is mainly modelled on
Sutherland, but has touches of Hartington in him:

> St Aldegonde was the heir-apparent of the wealthiest, if not the most ancient
> dukedom in the United Kingdom. He held extreme opinions, especially on poli-
> tical affairs, being a Republican of the reddest dye. He was opposed to all
> privilege, and indeed to all orders of men except dukes, who were a necessity. He
> was also in favour of the equal division of all property, except land. Liberty
> depended on land, and the greater the landowners the greater the liberty of the
> country. He would hold forth on this topic even with energy, and was amazed at
> any one differing from him: 'as if a fellow could have too much land', he would
> urge with a voice and a glance which defied contradiction.

Hartington no doubt contributed to this picture by enouncing, according to
G.W.E. Russell, 'advanced opinions with the amiable intention of shocking his
friends'. That may be, although in the Turf Club, where a Liberal politician was
almost as strange a sight as a pink horse, shocking his friends was easily
achieved. It could be done by a no-nonsense comment such as his reply when
someone expressed horror at a political demonstration introducing a 'mob' into
Hyde Park; Hartington growled: 'But there always is a mob in the Park; only

---

*A recent political biography, Patrick Jackson's *The Last of the Whigs* (1994), perpetuates the
image of the aloof, public Hartington. After accepting the story of his yawning during his maiden
speech, and attributing to him, perhaps on the strength of this, 'a languidly affected manner', the
author treats Hartington's affair with Skittles as a suspiciously undocumented interlude of perhaps a couple of months and goes on to describe him as 'socially isolated' and with few close
personal friends. These judgements merely reflect the author's lack of interest in Hartington's
private life.

some of the mobs are better dressed than others.' Hartington, his younger
brother Lord Frederick Cavendish and their cousin Sutherland were examples
of the Radical younger Whigs who were coming forward at this time. The very
name Whig was not one that Hartington would have acknowledged politically;
he defined himself as a Palmerstonian. To later historians Palmerston may be a
crypto-Tory who managed to hold up reform for the ten years of his leadership;
but to the classic Whigs of the day like Lord John Russell he was the exponent
of a populist type of politics which they found distasteful. That was not Hartington's view. He was never an admirer of Russell, although Russell, with his
'sacred circle' predilections, looked kindly on the Cavendish heir. What Hartington saw was that Palmerston's jingoism was a popular policy which the
Whigs needed to endorse if they wanted to keep the support of the electorate.

Further, to the extent that Hartington was not a Palmerstonian he was a
Gladstonian, as was seen in the affair of the paper duties in 1860–1. In his first
Budget Gladstone attempted to abolish these duties and thus make newspapers cheaper and more available to a democratic electorate. Conservative
opinion found this abhorrent, all the more so since it meant raising income tax
to tenpence from its already high level (for the time) of ninepence. Palmerston
himself was secretly delighted when the House of Lords threw out his Chancellor's proposal, manufacturing for the occasion the doctrine that, although it
was improper for them to reject a new tax, they could oppose the abolition of
an old one. Gladstone returned to the attack in 1861, and Hartington, in one of
his rare speeches, supported him in forthright terms, calling the House of
Lords 'a body which never had, and ought not to have, the control of the taxation of the country'. Gladstone wrote to Hartington's father appreciating 'the
warm and generous tone of the support which he gave'. The sequel was Gladstone's first visit to Chatsworth that November and a rapprochement to the
Cavendish family which was soon to be more than political. Already the
Devonshire connection formed Gladstone's most sympathetic point of contact with the Whig aristocracy. The Dowager Duchess of Sutherland was his
warm supporter, and her son-in-law the Duke of Argyll his most consistent
ally in the Cabinet. Lord Granville was perhaps the only aristocrat who managed to find a path of easy friendship through Gladstone's pedantic manner.

In April 1864 Hartington's brother Lord Frederick announced his engagement to the Hon. Lucy Lyttelton, who was Gladstone's niece by marriage.
Frederick was not yet in Parliament, but was already known for Radical political

views which soon made him take Gladstone as a leader. His keen anti-slavery partisanship in the American Civil War has been mentioned, but in this it took Gladstone some years to catch up with him, since at first he expressed pro-Southern views. When Gladstone made an unexpected speech in 1864 supporting a virtually unlimited extension of the franchise, Lord Frederick was zealously in favour. His election to Parliament in 1865 allowed him to support the Reform Bill of the following year, which failed through the defection of some Liberals of less generous views. As Gladstone, by now the standard-bearer of advanced Liberalism, suffered a rough ride with his adoptive party over the next two years, Lord Frederick remained his most ardent supporter. Ardour was not his elder brother's style, but in loyalty he yielded to none, and the family connection gave him a special closeness to the party leader.

It was a source of special strength that the link came through the character of Lucy Lyttelton, now Lady Frederick Cavendish. Her beautiful portrait painted at this time dominates the library at Holker, a house which her husband loved perhaps even more passionately than this two brothers did. Lady Frederick was a woman of great sense of humour and love of fun and at the same time of deep religious feeling and nobility of character. These qualities had drawn her to Frederick's generous idealism and were to take her from her hereditary Toryism to throw herself into the politics of her husband ('wicked Radical Fred' as she called him at first) and her leftward-rushing uncle. Ease with the excruciatingly shy Duke was something she perhaps never attained, but she advanced quickly in affection for Frederick's sister and brothers. Of a luncheon at Devonshire House a month after her engagement she notes: 'I am hardly shy at all with Ly. Louisa now; my chief awe centres round Lord Hartington, who is very kind to me however.' Step by step her diary traces her pleasure as she managed to get Cavendish, as she was taught to call him, into intimate little tête-à-têtes as the years went on.

In August 1865 Lord Edward, the youngest brother, married Emma Lascelles, the remarkably ugly grand-daughter of the 2nd Earl of Harewood. But the most moving event for the Cavendishes was the marriage less than two months later of Lady Louisa to Captain Frank Egerton, a naval officer and aide-de-camp to the Queen.* For twenty-five years Louisa had been doted

---

*He was really a member of the great clan of Leveson Gowers. His father, a younger son of the 1st Duke of Sutherland, took the name Egerton on inheriting the estate of the Dukes of Bridgewater, with its vast income from the Bridgewater Canal, and was created 1st Earl of Ellesmere.

over as the only girl in the all-male household of Holker. From the age of fourteen she had run the place for her father with a competence which she later extended to the other ducal palaces. Her loss at the age of thirty to a mere second cousin stirred all the Cavendishes up like an egg-whisk. Louisa was married from Holker, and Lady Frederick thus described the wedding day:

> I did not expect to be upset by the service which is a calming thing, I think; but when dear Lou came up the choir with the poor Duke, to the sound of a beautiful wedding-hymn, and one looked at her dear, tall, bending figure standing by her father, to whom she has been all in the world! – Cavendish's face, too, struck me and moved me exceedingly – full of deep feeling which I have never seen called forth in him before. My poor Fred's love for her I knew all about, and pretty well Eddy's too; so that I did not wonder at their regularly crying . . . She kept herself composed with some difficulty, and broke down more than once in private, especially when Cavendish went to her room before, and was much overcome himself. Most of us went to the tenants' dinner which I would not have missed for anything. The Duke could not trust himself to go, so Cavendish returned thanks for him, his voice trembling, and his face quite white. What he said was *perfect*, in its simplicity and depth of feeling: it gives me a new affection for him, showing me how tender his heart is.

The loss was really quite small, since the Egertons made their home at Holker; luckily the Captain was used to a ship-board economy of space, for his study consisted of a writing desk in a recess of the drawing-room. As for the Duke, his career proceeded on its distinguished but quiet way. He had been elected Chancellor of Cambridge University on the Prince Consort's death and munificently founded the Cavendish Laboratory there. He improved his vast estates and was a founder of the Royal Agricultural Society. Conscientiously he attended the House of Lords, especially on Irish questions; but he could not be got to expose himself to a more public role. Lord Esher, who knew him in his seventies, wrote: 'His bowed figure tacked into a room like a vessel finding an intricate channel.' He shunned the grandeur of Chatsworth as much as possible, although it would be an exaggeration to think of the place as deserted through his long reign. Here, as at Holker, house was kept for him by Lady Louisa, who is described by Sir Almeric Fitzroy as preserving 'the best traditions of English womanhood of the patrician type'. In the library there was a portfolio of racy Italian Renaissance sketches, which she sealed up with the inscription 'Not fit to be seen'. But this only incited the red-blooded Victorian noblemen who visited the house, and the band was cut through many times, only to be resealed by Lady Louisa's vigilance. Sir George Leveson Gower, who imparts this confidence, gives us also a glimpse of life at Chatsworth when he describes Lord Frederick Hamilton, 'that prince of drolls', giving a performance as a dying pianist, playing diminuendo until he eventually slipped off the stool and finished pianissimo from a position lying on the floor.

It was natural that Hartington should wish to bring Louise Manchester to Chatsworth, and he had her invited with her husband in December 1866. Louise was on her best behaviour, striking Lady Frederick as 'too beautiful and winning, with the most perfect manners – high-bred, gentle, and intelligent'. Such impressions were not exceptional; the undergraduate Lord Ronald Gower,* staying at Kimbolton in April 1865 along with Hartington, spoke of 'The Duchess in great beauty, in a white gown bespattered with diamonds. I think that loud ringing laugh of hers the prettiest music possible.' Louise's glamour for the young also shows in Lord Clarendon's letters, where he tells her how his teenage daughters 'rave' of her and, after a visit of one of them to Kimbolton, finds that 'Constance as usual has returned from you excited by *Louise worship*'. In June 1865 Lady Frederick Cavendish recorded: 'Dined at Lady de Grey's, to meet the D. of Cambridge, and encountered great swells, viz. the Duke and Duchess of Manchester, she looking brilliantly beautiful and attractive as usual; he certainly a foil!'

The jolly Duke of Cambridge, who was Commander-in-Chief of the British Army, was much in the Manchesters' circle. His boyhood in Hanover, when his father had been Governor, was sufficient reason for his interest in Louise, quite apart from rash rumours that they were brother and sister. She was a useful bridge between him and the Under-Secretary for War, so that when Hartington was promoted to head that ministry the Duke wrote to him: 'No successor could have been selected to fill the post more acceptable or more agreeable to me'. The Duke retained a lifelong preference for Hartington, in whom he recognized a straightforward man and a sportsman, so different from the other politicians who blighted his enjoyment of his command.

Hartington's elevation followed on the death of Lord Palmerston in Octo-

---

*Brother of the Duke of Sutherland, to whom he formed a marked contrast in character; he was a suave and cultivated connoisseur, said to have been the model for Lord Henry Wotton in *The Picture of Dorian Gray*.

ber 1865, when Lord John Russell, now endowed with an earldom, succeeded him as Prime Minister. In a reshuffle in February 1866 Lord De Grey moved to the India Office, and Russell took the opportunity to make Hartington Secretary for War; at thirty-two he was the youngest Cabinet minister for many years, but his competence as Under-Secretary was held to have justified the choice. To celebrate his success the Duke gave a big 'drum', as receptions were then called, at Devonshire House on 19 June, but it was an ill-omened occasion. The government had just been defeated over Russell's Reform Bill, and the Cabinet came to Devonshire House early for a brief meeting on how to respond; their decision was to resign, so that the celebration that followed was, in Lady Frederick's words, 'rather like inviting people to see Cinderella after 12 had struck!' Hartington's first Cabinet experience thus came to an end after only four months.

In foreign affairs a matter that had tangentially concerned him at the War Office was that of Germany. In 1863 the question arose of whether the Duchies of Schleswig-Holstein were to be governed by the King of Denmark or by the Duke of Augustenburg, who embodied the hopes of the German nationalists. The confederation of minor German states opposed a solution which would have led to the incorporation of Schleswig into Denmark. Palmerston described this meddling as 'the Duke of Devonshire's servants' hall assuming to decide who shall be the owner of a Derbyshire country gentleman's estate', and he took a high line, following a pro-Danish policy which had been made popular in England by Princess Alexandra's marriage. But when the German states went to war with Denmark in 1864 it became obvious that the British Army was far too weak for intervention. Palmerston had to eat his words, and the German victory was the first act in the drama of unification. The second was played two years later as Prussia turned on its former German allies. The Six Weeks' War broke out just as the Liberal government fell in England, and Hartington, with his usual urge to see action, went straight off to Germany to observe the conflict; but again he was disappointed. The war, as its name implies, was over too quickly for him to see any fighting; he saw only the battlefield of Königgratz, and he also watched the victorious Prussian army march into Berlin, where he conversed with Bismarck, now the arbiter of Europe.

The war had consequences for Louise's family, for Hanover was one of the German states that had resisted Prussia and was swallowed up by it, the dynasty being deposed and the capital becoming a provincial town. The Altens were curiously undisturbed by this revolution; Louise's brother was in the Prussian, not the Hanoverian service, and her aged father spent the rest of his life in Berlin, where Louise used to visit him every year until his death in 1879. When Prussia crowned its triumph with the formation of the German Empire in 1871, Louise made the ungrudging transition to an all-German patriot.

Domestic politics concerned Hartington more closely. On Lord Palmerston's death Gladstone succeeded him as Liberal leader in the House of Commons, but the exchange was not a happy one. In his journey from High Toryism to Radicalism, Gladstone never rid himself of the notion that policy was a thing to be handed down by ministers and accepted by an obedient following. A more tactful leadership might have avoided the Liberal defeat over the Reform Bill, and on the close of the session Gladstone fled abroad, 'leaving the wound of the Liberal Party to the healing powers of nature'. When Parliament reassembled early in 1867, the party was so much at sixes and sevens that the customary dinner was not held on the eve of the session, and Gladstone wrote: 'In the singular mental condition of our party, it may be well that I should lie low for a little while.' This was the background to the revolt noted by Lady Frederick Cavendish on 30 January 1867: 'There are dismal indications of a plot among the Whigs against Uncle William's leadership of the Opposition, and some have dragged up Cavendish's name to take his place. He has heard nothing of it directly, and would have nothing to do with such a dirty job.' Among those involved in this *Fronde* was the Whig MP Hastings Russell, soon to be 9th Duke of Bedford. Doubtless he felt the same as his great-uncle the 7th Duke, who, when told that Gladstone and Disraeli were likely to be the next Prime Ministers, replied that they were both equally unqualified for the post. That was the view of many of the governing class, to whom the passing of control from its traditional holders seemed a violation of the order of nature.

The worst sign of Gladstone's failure was his inability to get even the Liberals who had rebelled against the 1866 measure to combine with him against Disraeli's far more radical Reform Bill in 1867. The 'Tea-Room Mutiny', in which many Whigs including Hastings Russell and his brother showed their hatred of his leadership, gave the Tories an unexpected taste of victory. Gladstone remarked to Lord Russell on 'The condition of things in which a nominal leader is regularly deserted by his men at the moment when he orders a charge', and concluded that it would be best to avoid all acts of leadership that could be dispensed with. Further Whig intrigues sought to prevent Gladstone's succession as overall leader on Lord Russell's retirement early the next year. It was this loss of authority which kept the minority Tory government in power until December 1868. In such circumstances one cannot underestimate the effect if Hartington had chosen to put himself at the head of the Whig section; he could hardly have attained the leadership himself, with his brief ministerial experience, but he might have put an end to Gladstone's expectations of the premiership.* Such an act was ruled out by one reason especially: neither now nor later did Hartington regard himself as belonging to the right wing of his party, which would have looked to him as its natural head; he rejected any notion of the Whigs clinging to power, unless it were by adapting to the demands of a popular electorate. This view made him a progressive and therefore a Gladstonian, and his conviction combined with family links to assure his loyalty.

These rumblings in the Liberal Party, coming on top of Hartington's rise to Cabinet rank, could not but make Louise Manchester feel how right she had been to select him as her lover. Her visit to Chatsworth in December 1866 marked a new step in intimacy, and it is from this winter and the next that we trace Hartington's really assiduous attendance at Kimbolton, where he took to keeping his hunters. Even now Louise can hardly have envisaged the kind of parallel marriage that was developing, or the part she was to play behind the scenes of his political career. It was Hartington's loyalty that was making the running – the same sense that had kept him obedient to Skittles's close possessiveness; and Louise's response was to return his loyalty. Their affair became known to those who had the entrée to such circles, but discretion was preserved. In public they addressed each other as 'Duchess' and 'Lord Hartington' and preserved a slight formality at odds with their obviously close friendship. The convention was not designed to deceive but to instruct; an observer who saw the relationship presented as colder than it ought to be was given to understand that it was warmer. Daisy Maynard as an unmarried girl in the 1870s tried to eavesdrop on their conversation in the hope of catching them in some romantic lapse, but she never managed to. Only one breach has come down to us, when the two were staying with the young Duke of Portland at Welbeck in 1881 and the Duke's mother overheard Louise murmur, 'Harty,

---

*The agreeable Sir George Grey, veteran of six Cabinets, would have been an obvious Commons leader from the established Whig ranks, while Lord Granville would have had the best claim to the premiership.

darling, stand me a stamp', as she sealed a letter.* Such discretion took skill, especially to preserve the quiescence of the cuckolded husband. Both Hartington and Louise had the manners and the good feeling to avoid rubbing the Duke's nose in their affair, and he preferred to shut his eyes. He had early resigned himself to the cloud of admirers around Louise, content, no doubt, to be the man with legal possession; and Hartington went on treating Kimbolton as a second home and discussing politics with the Duke from time to time without causing any souring of relations.

An affair with a lady presented in Victorian times much greater difficulties than with a kept woman. Hartington could no longer make those late-night visits after the House rose such as he had made to 34 Park Street. There was no question of using the empty vastness of Devonshire House to cover their affair; the Duchess of Manchester could not have called there alone without destroying her character. Custom admitted only one loophole by which a gentleman might see a lady alone. By a curious convention a lady's tea-time was a public occasion at which men could drop in uninvited, knowing that her husband had made himself scarce until dinner-time. But a visitor must take with him his hat, stick and gloves into the drawing-room; with these symbols of transience laid on the floor by his chair, he might sit for an hour or more taking in his hostess's tea and small-talk. Tea, like breakfast, was a meal at which servants did *not* attend, once the essential elements had been brought in. It was then open to the hostess, if her preferred gentleman had got there first, to give orders that she was not at home to any other callers, and the meeting could become even warmer. All the same, such encounters made a hasty scramble of the undressing and dressing which was usually a leisurely process with the help of a servant, although the lady's plight was eased by the invention of the tea-gown, a flowing confection that could be worn without a corset. There was no doubt a certain piquancy in receiving one's dinner guests on the same gilded furniture that had supported a thrilling half-hour earlier in the afternoon; but the situation was not exactly designed for comfort, and many women must have felt with Mrs Patrick Campbell when she spoke of 'the deep peace of the double bed after the hurly-burly of the chaise-longue'.

---

*The subject of names prompts comment on the alias 'Lottie' which a contemporary, wishing to seem to know more than he did, fastened on Louise, followed by some incautious later writers. Nobody called her anything but Louise. 'Louisa' is another common error – no doubt because it represented the German pronunciation of her name.

It was these restrictions that made the country-house visit such a favoured setting for adultery. The social arrangements of the time required Lord and Lady Blank to be accommodated in a suite of bedroom and dressing-room. The husband had the option at night of joining his wife in the bedroom or retiring (or pretending to retire) to the single bed provided in his dressing-room; sharing a bedroom was not taken for granted by married couples as it is in our own confined days. As he passed the leisurely time of day about the house it was open to an enterprising gentleman to make other arrangements with one of the ladies of the party, although presumably it took some nerve to execute this if she, too, had been invited with her husband. When Hartington and Louise Manchester were invited together to country houses, as they often were, the Duchess was sometimes asked alone and sometimes with her husband. Hartington's rank and political standing no doubt ensured that he was allocated a proper bedroom rather than one of those monastic cells reserved for bachelors in Victorian houses. At Kimbolton there would have been little problem, for it probably followed the practice of many houses of providing completely separate bedrooms for the master and mistress.

Unlike the Skittles affair, Hartington's liaison with the Duchess of Manchester does not seem to have been known to the general public; but it was an open secret in their own circle. People with a less impregnable position in society would not have been able to get away with it, but Victorian censoriousness had to take account of rank up to a certain point; where lesser folk would have been damned, a duchess and a duke's son could get away with being viewed as fast on the one side and casually racy on the other. There was one quarter, however, which did not need to defer to such concerns: the royal doors were now more firmly closed against Louise than ever. But by the conventions of the day, to which the Queen subscribed, such condemnation only fell upon women. As Hartington's public career put him unavoidably in the Queen's presence, he proved able to enjoy her tolerance and even her favour.

5
The First Gladstone Ministry

I<small>N</small> N<small>OVEMBER</small> 1868 a General Election was called under the provisions of the Second Reform Act, and a Liberal majority brought Gladstone to office, but the occasion was ill-fated for the Cavendish family. Gladstone had raised the cry of granting justice to Ireland by disestablishing its Anglican Church, and the Duke of Devonshire conscientiously supported his policy. But the measure allowed the Tories, beating the Protestant drum, to put up an opposition in Lancashire for the first time, and the Duke, in spite of spending £16,000 on the election, saw both Hartington and Lord Edward lose their seats. Gladstone offered Hartington the post of Lord Lieutenant of Ireland, which did not require a seat in Parliament, but it took only a little thought to see that the offer was impracticable. The Lord Lieutenant was the Queen's representative and was required to entertain lavishly, the post being usually given to great noblemen whose wives were accomplished hostesses; it was not a duty which a bachelor with no fortune of his own could discharge well. In point of fact Hartington's uncle Lord Carlisle, who had served as Lord Lieutenant twice, had been unmarried, but he was a sociable and popular man and, more importantly, the master of a great aristocratic estate. The Lord Lieutenants were expected to bring over their households, carriages and plate, and this expense vastly exceeded the reach of the incumbent's official salary. Even if the lack of a wife were ignored, Hartington could only have accepted if the Duke of Devonshire dug into his pocket and parted with a section of his household and equipage. Hartington refused Gladstone's offer.

In fact this ill-thought-out proposal had not depended on Hartington's defeat. With sweeping reforms planned in the army, Gladstone did not want Hartington back at the War Office, which he earmarked for the more ruthless Cardwell. It was convenient to have him out of the way in a ceremonial post, and his knowledge of Ireland made the Viceroyalty superficially attractive. When that was ruled out Gladstone grudgingly proposed the Home Office, but he really wanted to give that to the lawyer H.A. Bruce. He produced the argument that Hartington could not expect a Cabinet position unless he got himself back into Parliament, but the irony was that Bruce had also lost his seat; for that matter Gladstone himself had been defeated in Lancashire, although he had taken insurance by simultaneously standing for Greenwich, where he was returned. Hartington could have chosen to pull rank on Bruce, who had not held Cabinet office before, but as he later admitted to Granville, 'He considered that he had been pitchforked into the War Office, and that it was quite natural that he should have a lower office.' He therefore agreed to be Postmaster-General and was returned for a Welsh constituency, whose sitting MP was rewarded with a baronetcy for giving way. Bruce became Home Secretary, and his puritanical Licensing Act proved a contributory cause of the Liberal defeat of 1874, when Gladstone judged, 'We have been borne down in a torrent of gin and beer.'

Government posts in those days were sharply divided between the Secretaries of State, with salaries of £5,000 a year, and minor ministers who were paid £2,000 or less. There was a marked hierarchy between them, giving rise to the offence caused by Gladstone when Joseph Chamberlain asked for the Colonial Office in 1886, to be met by the lofty reply, 'Oh, a Secretary of State!' The Post Office was one of the lowest positions in the Cabinet and as often as not failed to carry Cabinet rank at all. Few men would have consented to take it after being a Secretary of State; a Whig would have stood on his dignity, and any other politician would have reckoned that accepting demotion was not the way to further his career. If, as is generally supposed, Louise Manchester was busy trying to push Hartington on in politics, she slipped up badly in 1868 by allowing him to take a position which kept him in the background for the next six years.

The mishap of 1868 illustrates the importance of a wife to a Victorian politician. If Hartington had married Lady Louisa Hamilton back in 1859 he would have been able to accept the Lord-Lieutenancy and play a resplendent part in Dublin. It was a post which could be made much of by an able man, and his standing in the government when he resigned would have been a strong one. But if Louise Manchester had been his wife it is probable that Gladstone would not even have dared to offer him the post: his position as the husband of such a political hostess would have assured him one of the highest offices – supposing, that is, that it had not succeeded in ousting Gladstone from the leadership at some time in the previous two years. Louise would not have allowed Hartington to get away with the self-effacing role which he followed on his own account. The partnership would have greatly strengthened the Whig section and its influence in the party, and an unpopular import from the Peelite ranks would have found a less easy path to power.

Louise herself had not been forgotten in this Cabinet-making. When Gladstone first proposed to send Hartington to Ireland, the Queen 'referred to the Duchess of Manchester as "another lady who must not do the honours"'. This was a bizarre suggestion which would have occurred to no one else, but Queen Victoria's disapproval of Louise Manchester had been mounting steadily, and she was especially annoyed to see her influence with the Prince and Princess of Wales. The innocent Princess, who would never listen to scandal, was a particularly unfortunate victim of Louise's charms, and the Queen would tell her emphatically: 'Believe me, dearest child, the Duchess of Manchester *is not a fit companion for you.*' She and the Prince should show their disapproval of frivolous society 'by *not* asking people like the Duchess of Manchester to dinner or down to Sandringham and above all *not* going to their houses'. Alexandra gracefully ignored these warnings, and Louise remained her dearest friend.

The Queen's fears about her son's bad company were confirmed when the Mordaunt scandal broke a year or so later. The young Lady Mordaunt had been one of the Prince's merry companions, but in February 1870 she was sued for divorce by her husband, to whom she admitted adultery, implicating the Prince of Wales. The fact was that Lady Mordaunt was going mad, but the Prince was obliged to go into the witness box and deny the charges. Although his innocence was accepted, some frivolous letters to Lady Mordaunt which were read out in court, and the disgrace of the heir to the throne having to enter a court of law for such a purpose, brought down on him the indignation of middle-class opinion. A week later he tried to resume normal life by going to the theatre with Louise Manchester and they were greeted with a deafening roar of booing. In mid-March the Waleses were due to stay at Kimbolton, provoking Queen Victoria to comment: 'This visit to Kimbolton (which is an old engagement) is a great misfortune.' And to Princess Alexandra she wrote begging her to drop the Duchess of Manchester, who although 'she may not, and, I believe, *does not* do anything positively wrong . . . has done more harm to Society from her *tone*, her love of admiration and "fast" style, than almost anyone'. A curious comment, in view of the Queen's awareness of her affair with Hartington; or did she cling to the hope that Louise was merely leading him by the nose? In any case, the Kimbolton visit went ahead, as did many others afterwards.

A special reason for the Prince of Wales's closeness to Louise Manchester came from the Queen's determination to exclude her son from any contact with state affairs. His thirst to be in the know was gratified by Louise, who took care to be one of the best-informed people in London, and it was largely through their friendship that the Prince was able to break the pall of ignorance. Louise was not constrained by the same misgivings as Lord Granville, who also took pity on the Prince and as Foreign Secretary agreed to keep him informed about the progress of the Franco-Prussian War. He dropped the practice when he received messages from four separate friends that one of his confidential notes had been handed round a dinner party.

Her affair with Hartington was not Louise's only window into the government camp. We find her at Mrs Gladstone's at home in the Downing Street garden in July 1870 when the rumour came of the outbreak of the Franco-Prussian war, and the Prime Minister arrived to confirm the news. She rightly forecast that all Germany would support Prussia. Three months later Gladstone dined with her at Holland House and noted: 'I was much pleased with the Duchess of Manchester. Plenty of mind in her.' The impression was not mutual, however. Louise could no doubt have done much for Hartington's career by cultivating Gladstone, but that was one sacrifice she found too much to make for him.

By these years Louise Manchester had delimited spheres of influence with Lady Waldegrave, now supreme as the Whig hostess, and the two were genuinely the best of friends. This fact earned her the deference of Lady Waldegrave's acolyte, the well-known journalist Abraham Hayward, who was normally the most poisonously witty commentator on society. Lady Waldegrave's husband Chichester Fortescue had been appointed Irish Secretary (he was said to have dined his way into the Cabinet through his wife's much-coveted entertainments). Fortescue was an ineffective speaker, with some of the worst meanderings of the parliamentary manner ('And when I say that I mean this . . .' he would drawl) but he was an able minister and one of Hartington's chief friends in the Cabinet. Abraham Hayward, exchanging gall for honey, gives us a picture of Louise Manchester as Lady Waldegrave's guest at the Chief Secretary's Lodge in Dublin, where an old gentleman exclaimed: 'I have come fifty miles to attend this ball, and I would have come a hundred to look at that beautiful Duchess.'

One of the duties of Cabinet rank which Hartington did not take to was his attendance on the Queen. Her Private Secretary, Sir Henry Ponsonby, gives an impression of one of his early visits: 'Hartington has talent and tact but terrible idleness. If he has work to do, no one does it better but he takes things very easy indeed* . . . He talked a great deal at dinner. Perhaps too much. Whereon he was rather set down as a bore. He doesn't know where and when to stop.' A similar visit (if not the same one) was noted by Lady Frederick Cavendish on 17 April 1869: 'I dined again with the Queen [at Windsor]. Who should be there but Cavendish! It was great fun meeting him for the 1st time on his good behaviour. He enlivened the dinner a good deal.' Hartington, however, was annoyed at the exhibition, and showed it by being deliberately 'disloyal' in his talk when he met Lady Frederick three days later. One can detect not just the irritation of a plain man forced to polish his manners but the Whig pride over having to treat the Sovereign as more than a social equal before one's friends. He showed the same attitude when he told Lady Spencer in 1872 what a bore it was to have to go to Baden with the Queen as her Minister in Attendance.

The Prince of Wales's company posed no such problems. In 1869 the Prince founded the Marlborough Club in Pall Mall opposite his own residence of Marlborough House. He was provoked to do this by the fogeyism of White's in refusing to allow smoking except in the smoking-room, and he kept a veto on membership of the new club, which was to consist entirely of his friends. Hartington was of course one of the first recruits (it was the seventh club whose membership he had accumulated almost without noticing), although he preferred playing whist upstairs in great gravity and silence with a few like-minded spirits to joining the noisy frolics favoured by the Prince downstairs. Smoking at least was a taste they shared and another was the informal attire which the Prince had brought into fashion. Already in the 1860s they were wearing short jackets in place of the frock coats which had been the rule hitherto, and Hartington showed very twentieth-century

---

*This comment seems to date the occasion to Hartington's time at the Post Office, which he regarded as 'almost a sinecure'.

preferences in costume: he wore shoes instead of the usual ankle-length boots, together with brightly coloured socks, checked trousers and flat, low collars to his shirt, sometimes striped; and in an age when even street urchins were more likely to be seen barefooted than without a cap on their heads he often astonished people by appearing out of doors without a hat on. In those days no respectable person removed his coat in public, and, as the phrase 'shirt-sleeves' indicates, retention of the waistcoat was a basic minimum; but in March 1880 a friend came upon Hartington sitting in the Library in Devonshire House with his coat and waistcoat off and his braces down as he worked on his election address as party leader. Yet, although casual about dress – he certainly did not share the Prince of Wales's obsession with it – he was not slovenly. He had once told Skittles that he supposed a dozen gloves would do for a present. A painting of the House of Commons depicting the various members in character shows him lounging on the front bench in a smart white waistcoat, with a brightly coloured handkerchief stuck in his breast pocket and a pale top hat tilted over his eyes, markedly the showiest creature among his respectable colleagues. In the 1860s a London tailor even christened a *tout-ensemble* with the new short jacket the 'Hartington', as a type of casual but stylish costume that might be favoured by the more unstuffy man about town.

All this made Hartington fit in well to the Prince's easy-going circle. A courtier, when someone remarked on the Prince's informality, once replied: 'Yes, His Royal Highness is always ready to forget his rank, as long as everyone else remembers it.' There was no danger of Hartington's behaving like the elated guest who called out, 'Come on, Wales, pull yourself together!' in response to a bad billiard shot and promptly found his carriage called for.

Not that everyone was equally happy with Hartington's manners. Lady Frederick Cavendish's brother Alfred Lyttelton spoke of 'that sullen Marquis' whose sociability would have been improved by a couple of years at Eton (a judgement with which Hartington ruefully concurred). Lyttelton noted on a country-house visit: 'He has no manners at all, but it must be said that his rudeness is splendidly impartial – he was rather affable to me, I only mean relatively. That is to say he would answer five times out of six if I spoke to him whereas he frequently deigned no reply even to ladies.' We must understand this in the context of the strict rules of Victorian manners, which required that all small talk be scrupulously taken up, however vapid; but Hartington, if he could not think of anything to say, simply said nothing. He was often at a disadvantage with ladies, those guardians of social amenities, who were trained never to let a conversation drop, just as they must never trespass on contentious subjects, or disagree with a remark or express criticism of anyone. To avoid the last, it was *de rigueur*, when a person's name came up, to praise some good quality of his, and in cases so frightful as to tax the ingenuity, the convention grew of attaching to the individual one or two recognized accomplishments, which would be scrupulously brought out on the mention of his name.

Hartington's conversation followed different rules. While he was no wit, his jokes tend to depend on shocking this convention of niceness. Thus to his secretary Reginald Brett who was about to get married: 'When does your melancholy event come off?' To Lady Randolph Churchill enthusing about a recent visit to Chatsworth and its beautiful treasures: 'Did you break anything?' In old age to Lady Maud Warrender when she was discussing the proper way of responding to the American greeting 'Pleased to meet you', he suggested: 'So you damned well ought to be.' The attribution to Hartington of the dictum 'The greatest crime is to be found out' would have a distinct appropriateness if true, and may perhaps be classed in the same genre. On the other hand, his remark 'I think my motto should be "Never do today what you can put off till tomorrow" and then very often it need not be done', is an expansion of a *Punch* joke of 1849 but is no more than sober sense; anyone over twenty-five knows from experience that far more harm is done in life by precipitancy than procrastination.

One of Hartington's close friends was the young Tory MP Harry Chaplin, a genial member of the Marlborough House set and one whose huge figure and monocled face were well known at Newmarket. Chaplin was a large landowner and a big man in every sense. As one of the leading men in racing in the 1860s he had been the owner of Hermit, who won the 1867 Derby in one of the most sensational races of the century. A few years before, he had been engaged to Lady Florence Paget, but she eloped with the Marquess of Hastings, a foolish young man who then made a point of betting heavily against Chaplin at every opportunity. His bet against Hermit ruined him, and he was left owing Chaplin £120,000. With splendid magnanimity, Chaplin then wrote to Hastings giving him unlimited time to pay the debt and even apologizing for broaching such a delicate matter. Despite this glittering success, Chaplin now cut back severely on his stables. Hartington had long been a spectator on the Turf (we find him in the mid-1860s laying bets in cross-party sportsmanship with Lord Derby), and towards the end of the decade he began his tentative career as an owner in partnership with Chaplin. In 1870 he first raced his own horses under the pseudonym of C.J. Stuart, and three years later he began racing under his own name, reviving the 'all-straw' colours of the 1st Duke of Devonshire, said to be the oldest racing colours in the world. The Prince of Wales was taking to racing with equal gusto; his purchase of Sandringham put him within easy distance of Newmarket, where Hartington too set up his house and stable at Beaufort House. Louise Manchester, with her passion for betting, was no less familiar a figure at this and other venues and was known for the Derby Day balls she held in Great Stanhope Street for the racing set, a custom which she eventually extended to the grandeur of Devonshire House.

Hartington received a blow to his social life at the end of 1870 when Gladstone moved Chichester Fortescue to the Board of Trade and asked Hartington to become Chief Secretary for Ireland. The thought of having to leave Louise Manchester for long spells in Dublin was hideous to him, and he showed whence his reluctance came in his reply: 'to me as a bachelor the necessity of constant residence in Ireland would be still more irksome [than to Fortescue]'. But Gladstone was adamant and told Granville: 'I fear I must be very rude to him,' by which he presumably meant mentioning the Duchess of Manchester. The only alternative was to resign, and both Granville and Louise urged him to accept the bitter pill. In an overnight stay at Hawarden Hartington allowed his repugnance to be overcome, and he went straight from there to Kimbolton for New Year's Eve and his last enjoyment of Louise's company. The exile proved less complete than he feared, since the Irish Secretary had to be frequently in London for parliamentary duties. In Ireland he had a congenial Lord Lieutenant to work with: Lord Spencer, known as the 'Red Earl' for his huge bristling red beard and moustache, was Hartington's second cousin and a close friend of the Cavendish family. G.W.E. Russell wrote of him: 'He was one of the greatest gentlemen I ever saw, with that absolutely perfect manner, both dignified and gentle, which no one nowadays can even imitate.' The charm of his wife as Vicereine earned her the title 'Spencer's Faery Queene'. Spencer had been keen to get Hartington as a colleague, urging him: 'The Irish MPs are a queer lot and want management, but a real Gentleman can rule them very well.' His faith in Hartington's little-known talents in that line proved well founded, for as Granville told Gladstone three years later, 'Rather odd to say, Hartington has been very civil to everybody in Ireland, and there is no doubt that with their temperament the Irish prefer the son of a great landed Irish proprietor of high rank.'

Spencer and Hartington were a partnership well qualified to rule Ireland with a firm hand. The state of the country was quiet at that time, but disturbances in County Westmeath obliged Hartington to go to the House of Commons for a measure of coercion in 1872. He had sat down after making what he thought an innocuous proposal, when Disraeli produced one of the surprises he liked to spring on an unsuspecting House. In Lord George Hamilton's words, 'he delivered a twenty minutes' speech of the most scathing invective and ridicule I ever heard . . . "You have legalised confiscation . . . you have condoned high treason . . . you cannot govern a single county . . ."' Hartington was completely taken aback. He may have felt even more outplayed by a curious exhibition of Disraeli's presence of mind. It was his custom to wave a handkerchief airily about to accompany his words, and in the middle of a sentence he suddenly put the handkerchief up to his mouth, turned to his neighbour Lord John Manners and apparently asked him a question. 'What, what are you saying?' said Lord John, but Disraeli replied, 'It is all right', and resumed his speech. Two days later a Liberal member who had been sitting opposite told Lord George Hamilton what had happened: in the best part of his speech Disraeli's false teeth had flown out; he caught them with extraordinary quickness in his handkerchief, turned round to cover his replacing them and resumed the sentence at the exact word where he had left off.

The end of 1872 was marked by the Waleses' first visit to Chatsworth. On his regular stay at Sandringham that November Hartington was questioned by his anxious father: 'Glad you are staying at Sandringham, for you will be able to get answers to several things I want to know. How long do they stay? How many servants do they bring? How many maids for the Princess? Do you think they could bring any horses? Am so afraid that our own may not stand the cheering.' The result, described by Lady Frederick, did justice to Cavendish efficiency. The royal party arrived on 17 December, driving by carriage from Derby and coming upon Chatsworth's west front picked out in the dark by fireworks which were set off as they approached by the picturesque bridge. They found the great hall full of sulphur as a consequence, but clarity was restored at dinner, which was 'very fine, with feathery cocos palm springing *out* of the table in the midst and overshadowing us. Whist and music in the evening.'

The following day 'the P and Pss breakfast tête-à-tête in the Red Velvet room; and did not appear till 12 or so'. The Prince went shooting with the other males, being joined by the ladies for luncheon in the 'Russian cottage'. In the evening there was a big county ball, 'a great success for all the company, who were over the moon'. It started with illumination of the Emperor Fountain and water steps; the Prince opened the ball with Lady Frederick and Hartington with the Princess; supper was held in the great sculpture gallery, superbly decorated with red carpet, flowers, palms and ferns, and the orangery lit with coloured lamps. On the 19th there was a dinner of forty-four, followed by 'a truly enchanting dance of only the houseful and the few dinner-guests. Delicious was the dining-room for this much of a ball, and everybody looked their best and thoroughly enjoyed life. Supper was at various little tables in the big drawing-room, capitally managed. Ly. Macclesfield, Mr Cockerell, and I made fun at our table, all the more comical from the dignified condescension of my neighbour, Ld. Cowper, Ly George's silent laughter,* and the poor dear Duke of Rutland's puzzled Manner-ish high-shouldered aspect through it all.'

On the 20th the party visited the Duke of Rutland's Haddon Hall, and that evening the Princess inaugurated what would one day be a tradition at Chatsworth: 'At bed-time, high jinks with all the ladies in the corridors.' On the 22nd, 'The curtain dropt on our fine great drama! . . . We were all a little comatose, and Lou [on whom all the arrangements had presumably fallen] vanished to bed at 9 o'clock.'

The previous year a domestic blow had struck the Duke of Devonshire. In the night of 8 March 1871 Lord Frederick woke up in his bedroom at Holker to find his dressing-room on fire. He called help, but the fire spread, and he sent word to the Duke's bedroom by means of a footman who burst in shouting, 'The house is on fire!' 'Very well, go and help put it out. It's your business, not mine,' replied the Duke with true Cavendish phlegm. But it quickly became his concern, for the whole of the new wing which he had built thirty years before was burnt to the ground. He rebuilt the house much as it had been, with fine spacious light-filled rooms and panelling immaculately crafted by the workmen of the estate. The work cost a fairly modest £38,000, and the Duke

---

*The wife of the Duke's brother, Lord George Cavendish.

had little difficulty in paying it, for he had become at this time the richest landowner in England. His income in 1874 reached £310,000, nearly half of it from the booming steel works of Barrow, but because of the Duke's quiet way of life no one suspected this colossal wealth.

Hartington's policy as Irish Secretary will be treated in a later chapter, but we must take note here of a measure that was imposed on him in 1873, the Bill to set up an Irish University. Ireland's only ancient university was Trinity College, Dublin, an institution comparable in status, although not in size, to Oxford or Cambridge; but it was obnoxious on religious grounds to the non-Anglican majority of the population. A few non-denominational colleges had been set up in the middle years of the century, but they were very much poor relations. Gladstone's University Bill of 1873 was typical of the measures taken in Ireland in the nineteenth century. Although meant as a generous attempt to give the majority a proper university, it was based on the premise that Ireland must be governed by enlightened British principles, with provision against the teaching of religion and such subjects in which the natives might peddle their retrograde views. The Catholic Church in Ireland pronounced firmly against accepting this secularist gift-horse. Hartington, with his usual practicality, argued in Cabinet against giving the Irish something they would reject, but there was no stopping Gladstone when he had resolved on a gesture of sweeping generosity. He turned to Chichester Fortescue, who had himself done the groundwork for the scheme while Irish Secretary. Gladstone did not acknowledge this contribution, feeling that his own amendments, designed to make the Bill as unwelcome as possible to papist feeling, made it an original work of vision. He asked Fortescue to speak first in Parliament in favour of the Bill, before the Irish Secretary whose responsibility it was. Fortescue, less than flattered, refused to speak before Hartington, telling Gladstone that he had no right to ask such a thing. The Prime Minister, in Fortescue's account, made no reply but looked majestically down his nose.

The Bill was introduced in February 1873, and one of the first speakers was the Radical Fawcett, who was Professor of Political Economy at Cambridge, a doctrinaire Benthamite and secularist and therefore a warm supporter of the Bill. Such was Hartington's distaste for this kind of fanaticism that when he rose to speak he began uncharacteristically with a personal attack on Fawcett, saying that his ideal of a professor in the new university would be a type of man as dissimilar as possible from the Professor of Political Economy at Cambridge. This did not help party unity, and as the Irish members were opposed the Bill was defeated. The government decided to resign, and the delighted Hartington went hotfoot to Kimbolton. The Prince of Wales fished for news, writing to him there on 12 March: 'Would you consider it very indiscreet if I asked you to let me know what steps the government are going to take since the meeting of the Cabinet?' But Hartington's pleasure was shattered a few days later. Disraeli was not confident of getting a majority if he dissolved Parliament at that time, whereas he calculated that if the exhausted Liberals had to struggle on they would only lose further support. He refused the offer to form a government; Gladstone had to return to office and Hartington to Ireland.

Later in the year Hartington's relations with Gladstone took a new blow. Lord Spencer had made it known that he wanted to retire as Lord Lieutenant before the end of the year, and Hartington had made unofficial noises that he would not care to continue under a different viceroy. In August 1873 he received a curt letter from Gladstone proposing that as he intended to resign he should return without delay to the Post Office. It was a slap in the face in every way: Hartington had not said officially that he intended to resign; Lord Spencer was still in office; the proposal that he should again accept demotion to Postmaster General looked like a studied insult; and the unceremoniousness of Gladstone's letter did nothing to put a different complexion on it.* Hartington had tried to rid himself of the Irish Office at the time of the March resignation, and he wrote back to Gladstone placing the office at his disposal, but he refused to be Postmaster General again. He commented to Spencer: 'The alacrity with which my supposed wishes are now considered is a contrast to the pressure put on me to stay in April.' Gladstone called in Granville to pour his diplomatic balm over the situation and was told that Hartington was sore over the brusque letter. With his talent for refashioning reality, Gladstone wrote back as if it were the departure from Ireland rather than the demotion to the Post Office that was the cause of offence and told Granville: 'I cannot admit Hartington's right to be sore . . . Hartington has many good and fine qualities besides his birth; but I am tempted to say he sells them rather dear.'

This remark was the opposite of the truth: what disconcerted Gladstone about Hartington was precisely his lack of interest in selling his qualities.

---

*In fact the offer was in a way a compliment: the affairs of the Post Office had fallen into a sad mess since Hartington's departure, and Gladstone wanted to put them back into a safe pair of hands.

Gladstone enjoyed the hold that his power of patronage gave him, even over Whig grandees, and was ill at ease with one to whom political office was a chore rather than a prize. Having assumed that he could be fobbed off with minor posts. Gladstone was taken aback to find him simply proposing to resign and, what was more, meaning it. With Granville's soothing intervention, the offer was withdrawn and Hartington was asked to stay on in Ireland. He took only modest satisfaction in his office's record, and when the government resigned next year, he advised Lord Spencer against accepting the marquisate he was offered, telling him: 'The Irish Administration of the present Government, though I believe its merits will be recognised some day, has hardly been so immediately and brilliantly successful as to prevent some cavilling about the thing.'

In January 1874 Gladstone called an election, and the Tories were swept to power – their first majority since the split over the repeal of the Corn Laws. Hartington welcomed the opportunity to devote himself to Louise Manchester, and 1874 was an agreeable year for him. Family life kept Louise busy as her children grew up. Her husband had developed an interest in the Colonies and went to America in 1873; he was to make long journeys to Australia in 1884–5 and 1887–8. Louise had brought up her daughters knowing that they were all expected to marry eldest sons. They learnt the outward preservation of proprieties which Louise used with such ruthless skill; when one of the girls made a saucy joke she was ordered to her room for three days on bread and water. For Mary, the first of the two twins, nothing less would do for Louise than a ducal alliance, and she imperiously arranged her marriage in 1873 to the 28-year-old Duke of Hamilton. She knew him well as a leading race-horse owner, but the Duke was also a supreme example of aristocratic arrogance and self-indulgence. He had been expelled from Eton within a few months of arriving and had been sent down from Oxford after a mindless riot in which the busts in the Christ Church library were burnt. He then took up with a beautiful Italian known as Gioia, and his mother was anxious to rehabilitate him in respectable society. The two duchesses laid their plans together, and Lady Mary Montagu was their pawn. She cannot be called a particularly reluctant one, and the Duke's race-going passion was certainly one she shared. Hartington probably had no misgivings when he wrote to Louise: 'Please give her my love, & very best wishes, & that I hope she will be very happy. Tell her also that I hope she will condescend to speak to me still when she is a Duchess.'

It would be fair to add that the Duke of Portland thought Hamilton a charming man, while his trainer Marsh was devoted to him; Hartington, too, was happy to train his horses with him in the 1880s. By those years the Duke, a heavy, burly man, had settled down quietly to enjoy hunting and racing in company with his wife, and they disappointed the glittering social ambitions which Louise had formed but for which neither of them had any taste. If Mary was discontented, one can only judge it from her conduct after the Duke's death in 1895, when she made a modest second marriage to a commoner.

The fate of the heir, Lord Mandeville, was of even greater moment. Lady Frederick Cavendish, after meeting him in July 1874 when he was just twenty-one, called him 'an ugly youth, but rather taking'. He took the question of his marriage into his own hands when he went to the United States and met the dusky Southern beauty Consuelo Yznaga del Valle. By an extraordinary chance she was the daughter of the mysterious lady who had got Hartington into trouble at the masked ball in New York in 1863; her father, a big Cuban and Louisianan planter, had survived the Civil War a rich man, and they cut a figure in the *seconde société* of New York. After meeting Consuelo at Saratoga, Mandeville had gone to stay with the Yznagas at their country place, and the eighteen-year-old Consuelo nursed him through a bout of typhoid fever. They married in New York at the end of May 1876, the carriages of the 1,200 guests creating a traffic jam in Broadway; but the family of the heir to the Manchester title were not there to see him paired off. The Duke had initially been distraught at his son's marrying a 'little American savage', although on acquaintance his opposition was softened by Consuelo's charm. Hartington was staying at Kimbolton on 3 June when Louise arrived from London with the Yznagas' account of the wedding. Very different was the sensation caused in America, for Consuelo Yznaga was the first American of the time to marry the heir to an English dukedom, the sort of alliance which the rising plutocracy had not yet begun to dream of. One of those impressed was the ambitious Alva Vanderbilt, who made Consuelo godmother to her own daughter, born this same year and also named Consuelo in the hopes of a similar destiny. The omen proved fruitful, for in 1895 Consuelo Vanderbilt became the wife of the 9th Duke of Marlborough, catapulting the Vanderbilts through the hitherto closed doors of old New York society.

When the Mandevilles' son was born in 1877, William K. Vanderbilt stood godfather, and things looked rosy as Lord Mandeville in the same year was elected to Parliament. Twin girls were born two years later. Consuelo Mandeville, in the Duke of Portland's words, 'took Society by storm by her beauty, wit and vivacity'. She was one of the very few Americans in England at that time and provided the model for Conchita Closson in Edith Wharton's *The Buccaneers*. Among the storming party of coronet-seekers that Consuelo led was her sister Natica, who was later to marry Sir John Lister Kaye, a member of the Prince of Wales's circle; the petite Yznagas came to be called 'the little Sisters of the Rich'. In 1877 Mrs Adair wrote to Lady Waldegrave: 'We have just been staying up at Tandragee with Lord and Lady Mandeville – poor little thing, she is so delicate – so utterly helpless – and *most* charming. What a contrast to the Duchess. She cannot endure a country life and is quite miserable.' Sir Henry Ponsonby also found her 'blue with cold' at Balmoral in 1884 and not appreciative of the royal residence. Consuelo was certainly a creature of the sun and more unbuttoned than the Yankees who trod the English path after her. People such as the Duke of Portland enjoyed the anecdotes of which she was such a lively raconteuse, such as the one of when she was surprised in her bath in a hotel by a man walking into her bathroom. Before beating a retreat the stranger had the presence of mind to say: 'I beg your pardon, *sir*, for my intrusion.' Lady Randolph Churchill (who had been Jennie Jerome from New York) was less indulgent than the Duke, writing to her sister in 1880: 'Consuelo proposed herself to dinner the other night. We had old Chancellor Ball & Lord Portarlington & she being *en veine*, insisted on telling "roguey poguey" stories, which I think astonished them – they did me! Quite between ourselves I think it *du plus mauvais goût* to talk like that before men.'

In 1876 Louise Manchester's second twin, Louisa, married the 35-year-old Lord Gosford.* Disraeli told Lady Chesterfield on 9 July: 'I called on the Duchess of Manchester to congratulate her on her daughter's impending marriage to the Earl of Gosford; she is a nice girl: handsome and unaffected without, apparently, being "*fast*".' Gosford was an Irish landowner and a relation of the Manchesters with a large castle not far from Tanderagee. He was a tall, handsome, amiable sporting man whose favourite expression of approval, no doubt picked up from one of his tenants, was 'Scissors! That's moighty foine!' Gosford was very much in the Prince of Wales's set and both

---

*They had gone as partners to the Marlborough House fancy-dress ball of 1874 in the Fairy-Tales group, dressed as the Goose Girl and King, Louisa appearing 'in a shower of silver'.

he and his wife were to hold Household appointments to the Prince and Princess.

We have run on a few years to cover these weddings, but they illustrate the rosy prospects that faced Louise Manchester in 1874. Disraeli describes a dinner party at George Barrington's on 19 July which gives a view of how her affair struck the outside world. Louise was taken in by the Marquess of Bath, and Hartington was placed at some distance from her (the Duke of Manchester was also there). After dinner Louise

> retired to the end of the room with the Duke of Cambridge and never quitted him till the party broke up. Hartington . . . could not even approach her and began to talk House of Commons shop with me, which I dislike, and so I made a little party with Lady Bath's aid, and drew him into more general conversation. It was never really interesting, except to me who studied Hartington under the circumstances psychologically.
>
> I know some, in such a position, whose heart would have been in their gorge, whose blood would have turned to bile, who in the madness of their misery would have quitted the room . . . But Hartington, fortunately for himself, is not a Caduncio. But however phlegmatically, he was I am sure distrait and uneasy.

Just two days later there took place the most brilliant entertainment for many years, the fancy-dress ball given by the Waleses at Marlborough House. The guests were grouped into six themes, each of which danced its own quadrille. These were the Hungarians, Venetians, Van Dycks, Packs of Cards, Fairy Tales and Puritans and Cavaliers. Hartington led the Venetian quadrille with the Princess of Wales and was dressed in a lavender-coloured doublet and hose, with a large medallion of Henry VIII which had been given to his ancestor by that monarch; in Lady Frederick Cavendish's affectionate view he looked 'famously well and handsome – very like one's idea of Henry VIII in his youth, before he was fat'. Louise Manchester was also in the Venetian quadrille, partnered by Lord Cowper.

In November a visit to Coventry with Hartington and Louise provided the occasion for one of the Prince's most famous practical jokes. The Mayor who was conducting them round took care to show them a skittle-alley in great detail, and as Hartington's eyelids drooped he came out with the line in which he had been coached: 'His Royal Highness asked especially for its inclusion, in tribute to your lordship's love of skittles.' One of the most characteristic things about this joke is that it had taken the Prince eleven years to think it up. We may also suspect the Prince of being behind the nickname Harty-Tarty which was attached to Hartington early the next year.* It remained popular for half a dozen years, but from the 1880s ceased to be used, unless perhaps by people trying to show how 'in' they were or by historians seeking to enliven their dull trade.

In the spring of 1876 the Prince of Wales was involved in a scandal which might have been even more damaging than the Mordaunt case. The Earl of Aylesford, one of the Prince's friends, was informed by his wife that she was having an affair with Lord Blandford, the heir to the dukedom of Marlborough, and intended to elope with him. Lord Aylesford's response was to threaten divorce, but this would have meant social disgrace for both the guilty wife and the co-respondent, and Lady Aylesford riposted by handing over to her lover some flirtatious letters she had received from the Prince of Wales. The use of these was concerted by Blandford and his brother Lord Randolph Churchill, who both spent their lives demonstrating that being the son of a duke is perfectly compatible with being a complete bounder. Lord Randolph set out to blackmail the Prince of Wales into putting pressure on Lord Aylesford to withdraw his divorce plans, failing which the letters, made public, would ensure that the Prince 'would never sit on the throne of England'.

Lady Aylesford's brother, who rejoiced in the name of Hwfa Williams, was a member of the Kimbolton set, and while staying there in February 1876 he saw fit to spill the beans about the affair. Louise was therefore one of a very small circle who knew about it, and Hartington was also soon involved. Lord Aylesford proposed to challenge Blandford to a duel until Hartington succeeded in persuading him that people no longer fought duels in England in the 1870s. Thirty years later there was a story going round that he had summoned Randolph Churchill to the Turf Club, demanded to see the incriminating letters and promptly seized them and thrown them on the fire; but in fact the affair righted itself without such measures. Lady Aylesford returned to her husband and there was no divorce. But there remained the question of Lord Randolph's conduct, which had been outrageous; he had even involved Princess Alexandra by going to her with Lady Aylesford (whose reputation alone made it an affront to force her on the Princess) and threatening her with

---

*It first appears in Lord Granville's correspondence on 31 January 1875 and in Disraeli's two days later. The event which triggered this fashion has eluded record.

the consequences if the Prince failed to co-operate. A curt letter of apology sent before Lord Randolph departed for America did nothing to mollify the Prince, and Hartington was asked to send an official draft apology, which he had helped to compose, for the signature of the globe-trotting Churchill. Lord Randolph signed, but he insolently added a note that it was only 'as a gentleman' that he consented to do so. Livid, the Prince of Wales made it known that he would never set foot in a house that received Lord or Lady Randolph or meet anyone who accepted their invitations. It was to avoid this social death that Churchill, on his return, was obliged to go to Ireland as secretary to his father the Duke of Marlborough, whom Disraeli made Lord Lieutenant for the purpose, and after 1880 he embarked on his gadfly career in the Fourth Party in the hope of giving himself an independent parliamentary position.

Hartington was not the man to get worked up about such conduct, however he might despise it; but he did not grieve over the loss of Lord Randolph's society. Louise Manchester, on the other hand, was one of only two people who refused to go along with the social boycott. According to herself she told the Prince to his face: 'I hold friendship higher than snobbery.' Given that she had known the Prince far longer than Lord Randolph, this was a pretty outrageous line to take and must be classed as an example of her taste for putting her exalted friends in their places. Her effrontery enabled her to get away with it and remain as intimate a member as ever of the Prince of Wales's circle.

By these years Hartington's continuing bachelorhood had become a public phenomenon. In November 1874 Lady Frederick Cavendish trustingly hoped that he might marry his cousin Lady Florence Leveson Gower: 'Florence is a most winning creature, and we can't help a little exciting hope that Cavendish thinks of her. He certainly likes her better than other girls; and at his age one almost feels it is now or never. One evening he even condescended to billiard-battle when she was in the room, and he talks a good deal to her, and what's more *watches* her.' Lady Florence, in fact, married Harry Chaplin. She may have been the lady whom the Hon. Algernon Greville-Nugent urged Hartington to marry, only to be told: 'I would marry at once if I was certain that the Duchess of Manchester was unfaithful to *me*.' His devotion grew more dogged as the years passed by. With his incapacity for affectation, he would walk into a public gathering, make a bee-line for Louise and stand by her silently, content merely to be in her presence.

This loyalty did not imply monastic aloofness from other women. It was

Hartington's characteristic to perk up in feminine company, and he hated 'a man dinner', as he told Louise. He had a fair chance of avoiding boredom with the pretty women who flitted in and out of the Prince of Wales's set. The most famous of these was Lillie Langtry, whose beauty burst upon London society in 1877. She tells in her memoirs of going in that first season to a political reception given by Hartington at Devonshire House, which was a splendid occasion:

> On our arrival he left his place at the head of the stairs and conducted me round the magnificent rooms, pointing out a few treasures, and, on my admiring the lovely coloured water-lilies reposing in marble pools, he drenched his clothes pulling them out as an offering, as also the gorgeous liveries of the footmen, into whose arms he flung them and who strewed our brougham with such quantities of the dripping blossoms as to make the latter conveyance rather moister than was convenient; but I think 'Harty-Tarty', as he was familiarly called, did nothing by halves.

Some years later, when she was rehearsing for *Antony and Cleopatra*, Lillie sat next to Hartington at dinner and was surprised to find him brimful of Egyptian and Greek lore, from which he made helpful suggestions. Hartington was not the only man who defied respectability by consorting with Lillie Langtry; Gladstone was also interested, and he, too, helped her in his own way: she describes him coming into her dressing-room after a performance 'with his arms full of Shakespearean commentaries to prove that I was mistaken in the interpretation of a phrase'.

The 1870s were the most exciting period of Hartington's career on the Turf. In 1873 he first appeared as an owner under his own name, and shortly afterwards he set up a stud at the Polegate Farm near Compton Place. He had an early success in Rylstone, sired by Harry Chaplin's Derby winner Hermit, and won a number of races with this filly in the 1877–9 seasons. His best horse of those years was Belphoebe, which he bought from Chaplin for 650 guineas, and she gave him the only Classic victory of his life by winning the Thousand Guineas in 1877; he had high hopes for her for the Oaks but she finished only second and likewise ran into a place in four other big races of the year. Hartington emerged from 1877 with the third-highest winnings of his career: £10,200; but his racing ventures had got him heavily into debt, and he had had to turn to his father for £25,338 to clear his account. The Duke again bailed him out with a payment of £40,776 in 1881.

Hartington was elected to the Jockey Club in 1873 and in 1877 was appointed a steward, a position he resigned on returning to office in 1880. His election as party leader in 1875 obliged him to put his racing stable in the hands of a manager, and he chose Lord Westmorland, a prominent member of the Jockey Club, who did the job well. Nevertheless he was never able to spend the sums that the big owners like the Duke of Hamilton lavished on their racing, and luck eluded him throughout his career. Although he won many non-classic races, the Classics, on which every racing man sets his heart, escaped him; in particular no horse of his ever won or even came second or third in the Derby.

The Duke of Devonshire's finances were taking a sharp turn for the worse. With the depression of the middle and later 1870s the Barrow steel business ran into trouble, and the Devonshire income was crashing back down towards £200,000. Even now only the Dukes of Bedford and Westminster overtook him in wealth, as their London rents climbed. Of the former, Disraeli wrote to Queen Victoria in 1878: 'The Duke of Bedford is the wealthiest of Your Majesty's subjects; his income absolutely exceeding £300,000 a year.' The following year he was writing of Devonshire: 'The Duke is most penurious, they say; will give no general entertainments and scarcely a dinner, unless it consists of only a few persons, and those relations.' He spoke of the Duke's hatred of Chiswick House, which had been used as a dower house for Lady Granville and the Duchess of Sutherland in the 1860s and had then been rented by the Prince of Wales, being the venue for many royal garden parties. But when the Prince gave it up the Duke was thinking of pulling it down, and only Harting-ton's opposition prevented the disappearance of this masterpiece of Georgian architecture. In 1879 the Duke found an affluent tenant in the Marquis of Bute and the danger passed.

Lord Esher gives a picture of Hartington at the period when he, as the young Reginald Brett, became his private secretary.

There was a time in Hartington's career, perhaps the most troubled time, when he was smarting under the disappointment of Belphoebe's failure in the Oaks to ful-fil her early promise, that his affections were centred upon his dog Roy, a collie of that broad-browed type which, like the Whigs, has now been superseded and for-gotten. Roy enjoyed the privilege accorded to his master of breaking every social rule; whether to Buckingham Palace or to the House of Commons, wherever

Hartington went, Roy went too; and his habits, which were as leisurely as his master's, accentuated more than ever that utter disregard of time which was Hartington's most notorious characteristic.

Esher recalls: 'He would leave the card-room at the Turf Club only just in time to be late for dinner, however exalted the rank of his host.' It took a Margot Asquith, whose own manners were non-existent, to credit Hartington with 'the courtesy of a king'. Esher was closer to the mark in saying that 'His manner was a blend of curtness and courtesy.' He would walk into a social gathering, nearly always late, and ignore everybody except the one or two people whom the occasion obliged him to speak to. Yet, in his offhand way, he was a considerate superior; he did not give offence to his subordinates as a Gladstone or a Curzon could do. A request for information might be followed by the addition, 'But if you find it too much trouble, I daresay I can do without it.'

Life at Devonshire House followed the same unassuming pattern. Hartington's regular companions were Lord Edward and his growing family; they had their meals together, but probably used only for entertaining the white-panelled eighteenth-century dining-room with its rows of portraits in emphatic architectural frames. For really large occasions even this was inadequate, and Lady Frederick records in July 1872: 'Smart dinner at Dev. H. in the big square room [the Saloon]. Very splendid and stately.' In the silent vistas of the state rooms one could still see, by the doorways, the discoloured places where footmen had lolled with their powdered heads in the late duke's time.

Hartington's sister and Frank Egerton also used the house when they were in London, but Lord Frederick and his childless wife had set up an establishment of their own. The household of the bachelor elder brother and Lord Edward's family was a closely united one, and as the years passed the young Victor, who was born in 1868, looked increasingly like inheriting the headship of the ducal house, as he was to do in 1908. Of the Duke's three sons Lord Edward was reckoned the least of a typical Cavendish, but as Hartington sat at luncheon with the family one day he surveyed his three small nephews and, looking grimly at the eldest, said, 'He will turn out all right; he is the most like me.'

Hartington had fashioned a bachelor apartment for himself in one of the french-windowed ground-floor rooms on the garden front, next to the great staircase bow. It was characteristic of his disregard for comfort that his bedroom was a small space partitioned off from the main room, with a door giving access to it behind the side stairs, and he slept here on a trestle bed too short for his long legs. This was not the scene of his assignations with the Duchess of Manchester. Rising late, as was his custom, he would proceed, seldom before ten o'clock, to eat a meagre breakfast at a small table in his sitting-room. He also annexed for his use the great library on the principal floor, forty feet from end to end, working at a desk by the north window which looked out on to the garden. At each end of this cluttered room he placed on an easel the portraits of the two people who meant most to him, his father and Louise Manchester.

The domestic life of Devonshire House was a modest one. The footmen who once stood idle in the state rooms were gone; in accordance with Victorian practice a few bell-pulls had been installed, and the servants were out of sight. For most of the year the house was run on a skeleton staff. The census return for 1881, when Hartington was in residence with Lord Edward and his family, shows that their only men-servants were a valet, presumably shared by the two brothers, and a footman; although in 1871 there was also an under-butler and a second footman. On both occasions a dozen or so women served in the house. There was also only one coachman, so that Hartington and his brother must have been used to driving themselves when Lady Edward required the carriage. It was an unostentatious life with which Hartington was as much at home as he was with his modest political career.

6
The Liberal Leadership

'I CAN NEVER LOOK to Gladstone any more as a leader,' wrote the veteran Lord Russell to Hartington after the defeat of 1874. 'With great abilities he and Granville have led the Whig party of Lord Grey to destruction and dispersion.' The dominance of the political scene that Russell had known for forty-four years had been turned into a rout, giving the Tories a majority of fifty seats.

Gladstone put the blame elsewhere. He announced to his colleagues on the morrow of the defeat that he 'would no longer retain the leadership of the Liberal Party, nor resume it, until the party had settled its differences. He would not expose himself to the insults and outrages of 1866–8, and had a keen sense of the disloyalty of the party during the last three years.' That did not mean that he was resigning, however. His plan was to leave the duties of leadership to be discharged at random by his ex-colleagues until the party had learnt its lesson. From the start Hartington was one of the prime figures on whom this duty fell, and it was with a little relief that he wrote to Lord Spencer from Kimbolton on 11 March: 'Achilles is coming at all events partially out of his tent. I am very glad to be released for a time from the necessity of trying to lead our discomfited party.'

The difficulty lay in the position which Gladstone now held in the country. To middle-class Liberal opinion he seemed the heaven-sent minister. He had led a government which had carried a wide-ranging series of reforms, implementing a programme for which Liberals had been waiting for years; he had shown himself a master of the finance of retrenchment according to free-trade principles; and he had plucked at the national heart-strings with that earnest moral enthusiasm on which Victorian liberalism was largely fed. To such judgements the faults of leadership that had reduced the Liberal majority to chaos well before the election were irrelevant. Whatever the party in Parliament might think of him, Gladstone had only to speak and the country would listen and respond.

These facts meant that, as Achilles failed to come completely out of his tent, the Liberal front-benchers could not simply tell Gladstone to go; the party's tactics remained in confusion throughout the session of 1874. On one point, however, Hartington gave an unequivocal lead. The Irish members, under their new leader Isaac Butt, brought forward a motion advocating Home Rule; replying for the Liberal Party on 30 June, Hartington took it upon himself to oppose that policy in vigorous terms, forecasting that any English party would adopt it at its own peril. The Liberals *en masse* backed him in voting with the government against the motion, which received only two votes in addition to those of the 59 Home Rulers.

After a year of confusion, Gladstone consented to resign the leadership in mid-January 1875 – definitively or not, depending on how trustingly one read his message to the party. Lady Waldegrave's brother interpreted it: 'You have bad cards now; when you have a good hand I will play it.' The custom of the time was that only a former Prime Minister was regarded as the overall party head; otherwise the leaders in the two houses had equal status, and Granville would continue with his leadership in the Lords which he had resumed on the retirement of Lord Russell. The question of Gladstone's successor had of course been debated for months; there were then seven former Cabinet ministers still in the House of Commons, but significantly Hartington, despite the pair of minor posts to which he had been confined, was one of only two who were seriously considered. The other was W.E. Forster, a Bradford manufacturer known as the Gorilla for his ungainly manner. Although able, Forster had alienated his natural constituency among the Nonconformists by showing too much favour to the church schools in his Education Act of 1870 and had lost his old Radical reputation.

The Liberal defeat had thrown the strength of the party very much back to its Whig section. Sir William Harcourt reckoned the distribution of the party as 150 moderates, 70 Radicals and 70 Irish (most of these had recently become Home Rulers, but they had not yet officially relinquished their Liberal allegiance). The balance within the party pointed to the election of a moderate, and Forster's chances depended upon the fact that he was by now *not* the nominee of the Radical wing.

A devoted Whig circle was backing Hartington's claims. In December 1874 he had invited Lady Waldegrave and her husband (who was now Lord Carlingford) to Chatsworth to discuss his position. He told them he was determined to retire to the back-benches unless Gladstone made up his mind either to lead the Opposition or to resign. With that decision made, this circle of confidants turned into one of partisans. Hartington's strongest Commons supporter was William Harcourt, a nephew of Lady Waldegrave's former husband. He was a brilliant barrister and a good talker, although abrasive and overbearing; his opportunism is illustrated by the story of his reminding a fellow MP, the Hon. Henry Cowper, of a day when a cat got into the House of Commons. 'Oh yes, and I remember your waiting to see which way it would jump,' replied Cowper.* It was widely assumed that he was promoting Hartington as a front for his own influence; and this together with his unpopularity drew from his candidate the remark: 'If he is working for me, it will probably help Forster.' The prospect did not unduly alarm him, and the last thing Hartington wanted was to come in as the Whig nominee. He knew that his birth made him welcome to the Whigs and suspect to the Radicals, but it must be stressed that Hartington did not see himself as a right-winger. He realized that the next leader's task must be to unite the party, and if Forster stood a better chance of doing so he was willing and even anxious to give way to him. He also shrewdly noted that his own position would be stronger if the Radicals publicly failed to agree on Forster, obliging them to turn to Hartington.

Behind his back Hartington's women were working hard for him. Lady Waldegrave was busy drumming up support from the MPs who looked to her for their invitations. For some months Louise Manchester had been at work on Forster. She spotted that he could be got to through his vanity, and probably she was the only aristocratic hostess who bothered with this gauche Yorkshireman. Soon a strange alliance had developed between the ex-Radical and the Tory Duchess; Forster called her the most able woman he had ever come across, and Dilke was to describe his 'going and sitting with her almost every day and chuckling over her politics with his extraordinary chuckle and playing cards with her at night'. Louise's influence became so well known that Queen Victoria broke her incommunicado to write to her (through Lady Ely) when she wanted to impress a point of foreign policy on Mr Forster's attention.

---

*This was Lord Cowper's younger brother, a man much appreciated for his wit. His best reply was when he was shooting with his brother at Panshanger and another of the guests, Lord Calthorpe, was complaining to him of the way the coverts were being driven. With a shrug the Hon. Henry answered: 'Am I my brother's keeper?'

One could not say how much this had to do with the fact that a few days before the election Forster announced he was standing down. He knew, like everyone else, that he would have been the more controversial choice, that Hartington's pragmatism gave him an advantage in managing the party and that the heir to the dukedom of Devonshire could be deferred to by everyone without the personal comparisons that applied to other men. The Liberal MPs were spared a divisive contest when they met on 3 February 1875 in the Reform Club. Hartington was not there; he had spent the second half of January at Kimbolton while all the canvassing was going on and went straight on to stay with Lord Spencer at Althorp. Lord Frederick accepted the nomination in his name. John Bright wrote to Hartington on behalf of the gathering: 'I hope and believe you will find yourself supported by a strong and loyal party, with whom you will be able to render services to the country which will compensate you for the sacrifice you are now called upon to make.' Seldom, surely, can the leadership of a British political party have been transferred in so self-effacing a fashion.

His new position failed to change Hartington's ways. At the first meeting of the House after his election he arrived fifteen minutes late and was blessed with the nickname 'County Guy', after Walter Scott:

> Bird, breeze and flower proclaim the hour;
> But where is County Guy?

This remained his habit, and instead of concealing it by slipping in behind the Speaker's Chair he would enter in full sight by the main door, with one hand in his pocket and the other nonchalantly swinging his hat. For a man with a hatred of superfluous speech the task of nit-picking at a strong and popular government was repugnant, and he also earned the nickname 'Leader ohne Wörter', for his reluctance to open his mouth. It was all the more painful since he felt himself obliged to make long speeches whenever he rose; only with time did he learn to be much more effective with interventions of ten, fifteen or twenty minutes. The first response to Hartington's foibles was to call them indolence, but a week into the session Lady Waldegrave maintained: 'Dear old Hartington is taking to his work bravely, and all last week gave up his dinner and his Duchess like a hero.'

In 1874, when he was little known to the public, a journalist gave a pen-portrait of Hartington and described him as 'greatly impressed with the vast gulf that is fixed between a Marquis and a man'. Hartington was a victim of the phenonenon whereby we all recognize an unforthcoming disposition in our equals and inferiors but call it snobbery when we find it in our betters. As time went on people found that Hartington was in fact much more approachable than Gladstone had been, as he lounged in the lobbies and smoking-room. He was especially buzzed about by Radical members, who had few occasions for speaking to a duke's son and were pleased to have an official excuse for doing so.

In the 1870s the parties had not yet become regimented blocs; everyone remembered the conditions of 1846–66, when six governments had been defeated by revolts of their own majorities.* The idea of a shadow Cabinet was unknown, and although the 'Front Bench' was a colloquial expression it was thought necessary, in parliamentary diction, to wrap it in such euphemisms as 'those members of both parties who take any considerable share in the conduct of their business'. This corresponded to reality in that back-benchers did not speak as much as they do today; but neither were they used to being ordered about. That was especially true of the Liberal Party, which had always had a problem of cohesion, ranging as it did from Radical firebrands on the extreme left to young Whig aristocrats eased into respectful borough or county seats. The malaise was worse with a party smarting under Gladstone's dictatorial style and its first electoral defeat for a generation. Hartington's negligent, level-headed manner had been judged the best suited for these conditions; it also reflected his political approach, which, for better or for worse, went on the principle of listening and adapting to public opinion, rather than seeking to form and guide it.

Hartington, who confessed that he was not really interested in politics (in contrast to his brother Frederick for example), was long dismissed by historians as an indolent amateur, no more than a stop-gap in Gladstone's forceful career. More recent scholars have gone to the other extreme, have found him a hard-working, competent and shrewd politician and in some cases have even viewed his older image as a pose. Reginald Brett's estimate is called to witness: 'The mythical Hartington . . . the man who loves pleasure to the exclusion of work, who is *altogether* without personal ambition, whose mind turns away from long and serious contemplation of dull subjects. All this is fiction . . . Apart from politics he has no *real* interest in life; and cut off from them he

---

*This includes Palmerston's defeat of 1857, when he stayed in office by appealing to the country.

would be in reality as bored as he appears to be by them.' Some writers have quoted this as if it meant that Hartington was dissimulating an absorbing interest in politics; in fact all it means is that he had no parallel diversion such as Derby's or Gladstone's in Homeric scholarship. His passions for Louise Manchester and for racing hardly took the rank of an intellectual interest. Without such positive distortions, other historians make a flattering estimate of his stature; he has been called 'the ablest Whig since Palmerston' and 'certainly the best Prime Minister the country has never had'. One authority argues that he properly represented a mainstream Victorian liberalism which was diverted by Gladstone's maverick crusades, and judges that 'Had he ever been able to head the party on his own terms, Hartington might well have been its greatest leader.'

There is in these praises a certain striving to present an original view. It was certainly a merit of Hartington's that he did not form opinions until he had thoroughly sifted the facts and arguments; once he had done so, he seldom judged wrongly. He thus avoided during his leadership the mistakes which Gladstone would have made – and did make. Nevertheless his lack of genuine interest in politics is a fact, and it disabled him from doing more than respond to events, from looking ahead and formulating a vigorous party programme. That capacity as well as sound judgement is demanded in a statesman. He had no inbuilt resistance, as is often assumed, to Radical policies, but his priority was to avoid moves that would divide his party. That caution gave grounds for the dissatisfaction felt by ardent Radicals, but they were wrong when they thought him fundamentally opposed to them.

The new Liberal command had at least one strength, in the harmony between the two Whig noblemen who led in the two Houses. For Granville, who had taken Hartington under his wing from the beginning of his career, his kinsman's election was the crowning of an ideal world. Hartington would go over to Granville's house in Carlton House Terrace, and might be found stretched out on the floor playing knuckle-bones with his host's three little daughters. Granville's second wife Castalia, whom he married as a girl of eighteen in 1865, tried to maintain a political salon, and her husband spent more money than he could afford in backing her. Unfortunately Lady Granville lacked the presence for such a role, sometimes finding herself with a dozen guests at a reception to which she had asked a hundred. Nobody dared treat Louise Manchester's invitations like that.

Louise was now in the odd situation of a great Tory hostess whose lover was the leader of the opposite party; but her position was all the more powerful for that. One of its gains was a new closeness to the Prime Minister. It is only from 1875 that we find Disraeli speaking of Louise with the affectionate humour that denotes real friendship. He had known her since the 1850s, but their relations had not been easy. In 1863, when Disraeli and his wife were asked to the Prince of Wales's wedding and Louise excluded, she was so furious that she cut him for the rest of the season. But he had been Prime Minister since then, and she knew better than to ignore such a figure. If their friendship grew after 1875 it must have been because Disraeli found Louise worth cultivating; and with her hold on both Hartington and Forster, the two most important men on the opposite Front Bench, the Prime Minister prided himself on being perfectly informed about the enemy camp. An early comment on Louise in his letters is from a dinner party at Baron Lionel de Rothschild's in July 1875: 'I found a most amusing party, wh they had scrambled up – Louise, who was delightful though a little noisy, too shrieking in her merriment, and Harty-Tarty.' A year later he describes a dinner at Marlborough House: 'I was amused, sitting next to the Duchess of Manchester, who is an extremely clever woman, and very agreeable.'

From Disraeli we get a distinctive view of the carefully prepared speech which Hartington delivered on 6 August, at the close of the 1875 session, criticizing the government's record. On the Liberal benches it was hailed as his best performance, and a vindication of his election, but they were not half as pleased by it as Disraeli was by his reply. More frivolously, two days later he quoted the report made to him by the Austrian ambassador of a conversation with the Liberal leader: 'I said to Hartington, "What with whist, the Turf and what I delicately called 'morning visits', I wonder how you can find time for politics."' 'I wonder too,' Hartington had replied.

The session of 1876 was marked by the Royal Titles Bill, by which Disraeli proposed to give Queen Victoria, to her great pleasure, the title Empress of India. The measure inflamed the Radicals, who associated the imperial title with Napoleon III's recent regime. For the Whigs too this tricking-out of the English Crown in foreign tinsel was the sort of thing they instinctively disliked. Hartington, however, had no intention of spoiling his relations with the Queen by agitating against it, and he took care to inform her that he only officially opposed the measure to forestall an amendment by one of his Republican back-benchers. Granville, when he opposed it in the House of Lords, had no such excuse, and once the Bill had been passed he avoided the Queen's anger by staying away from the garden-party she held at the Duke of Devonshire's Chiswick House, then being rented by the Prince of Wales.

Disraeli was now at the summit of the royal favour and enjoying real political power for the first time in his life. Natural as this seems today, that was not how it struck his old opponent Gladstone; to him it was monstrous that this mountebank, whom he had seen wriggling through thirty years of political impotence, should have risen to such honour. When William Harcourt in 1874 supported Disraeli's proposals to curb Anglo-Catholicism in the Church of England, Gladstone fumed over his 'slimy, filthy, loathsome eulogies upon Dizzy'. But the Tory majority was impregnable. So strong did Disraeli seem in Parliament that he felt able to go to the Lords at the end of the 1876 session, accepting Queen Victoria's offer of the Earldom of Beaconsfield.

The weapon for Gladstone's counter-attack came to him from the Balkans. In the summer of 1876 the question of the Ottoman Empire's rule over its European provinces was raised by a series of massacres in Bulgaria. In his pamphlet *The Bulgarian Horrors*, published at the beginning of September, Gladstone proposed his famous solution: that the Turks be driven out 'bag and baggage' and Bulgaria restored to the self-government it had lost five centuries before. The 'Gladstone bag' became one product of this stirring rhetoric, but in Hartington it prompted other travel arrangements; in mid-September he set out for Turkey to see the situation for himself, and with him went Louise Manchester and her husband.

Travelling via Vienna and Budapest, Hartington saw the Austrian foreign minister Count Andrassy, who was a Hungarian magnate pursuing an opportunistic policy in the Balkan question. Hartington responded with caution, as he did when he went on to Constantinople. Stories of the impact of his party filtered back to Disraeli, who wrote to Lady Bradford: 'What you tell me about Louise is most interesting. Of all my solutions of the Eastern Question her capturing Constantinople never occurred to me.' He retailed a letter he had received from the Turkish capital: 'The day before there had been a grand dinner at Safvet Pasha, the Secy of State for For. Affairs, and who speaks English. The Duchess dined there, although there was no other lady. The letter-writer, who was one of the guests, says that did not seem at all to embarrass her Grace; "she lit her segar from that of Midhat Pasha, and showed the utmost *aplomb*." To the life!' After their return, on 23 October, Disraeli wrote: 'I saw Louise, who was very amusing and told me a great many things . . . She would settle the Eastern Question by making Constantinople a free Port with gambling tables!'

These jests give a pointer to Hartington's less-than-incandescent attitude; but his job was to formulate a serious policy. Lord Cowper remarked on 24 October: 'Lord Hartington is come back Anti Turk, which is more than his family anticipated.' It also contrasted with his fellow Liberal Forster, who had just come back from a Turkish visit of his own and put himself at odds with Gladstone by rejecting Bulgarian self-rule. Hartington's first public speech on 3 November avoided this pitfall and strove to present a united Liberal front. He criticized the government's policy but steered clear of Gladstone's idealism. To Hartington the Eastern Question did not offer simple solutions; he was critical of Turkish rule but was dubious about the Bulgarians' capacity to govern themselves after five centuries of despotism; he also did not want to play into the hands of Russia with its plans for expansion in the Balkans, and was aware of the fishing that Austria and Germany were doing in the same troubled waters. A more opportunistic party leader could have gone along with Gladstone's line and fashioned a meretricious policy to attack the government; but Hartington had too much honesty for this. It saved him from nemesis in 1878, when Gladstone's Bulgarian torpedo blew up in his face.

Hartington was not impervious to indignation over the Christian sufferings, but his nature reacted against gassy enthusiasm. He eyed with sarcasm the mass meetings being organized on the subject, writing to Granville: 'Why should we encourage any respectable member of the party to go and listen to, and be in some sense perhaps committed by the speeches of men like Freeman, Canon Liddon, Jenkins, Maxse, Lyulph Stanley, &c., &c., and innumerable parsons? The number of the latter on the list is quite enough for me.' It is worth making the point that Hartington was not hereby taking a standard Whig line. The Dukes of Argyll and Westminster were strongly Gladstonian on the Turkish question, and there was similar feeling from Whigs such as Lord Granville, his brother Frederick Leveson Gower, the Marquess of Ailesbury, Lord Rosebery and the Duke of Bedford's brother Lord Arthur Russell. By contrast, Gladstone's polemics found less of an echo among the younger Liberal intelligentsia, with Radicals such as Sir Charles Dilke advocating a more realistic British foreign policy. The Gladstonian view that Hartington was merely echoing the inactive section of the party must here, as elsewhere, be disputed.

Already in late 1876 it took little acumen to see where Gladstone was moving. Although he saw himself as stirring a supine party to necessary action, this did not take the form of working with Granville and Hartington; he was rebuilding a public platform of his own, regardless of the official leadership. He took to referring to Granville alone as the 'Leader' of the party, on the thesis that he, Gladstone, had conferred that mantle on him by resigning. Hartington's reaction to all this was typically down to earth: if Gladstone wanted the leadership back he should reclaim it, and Hartington would give way. He told Lord Spencer in November: 'I doubt whether he is justified in declining the responsibility which naturally follows, and in refusing the nominal, while he assumes the real leadership of the party.' But claiming it openly would have meant Gladstone's admitting to himself the personal motivation behind his campaign. It would also have meant a sort of humiliation; when he resumed the leadership it must be as a prize rightfully won, not as a gift negligently dropped in his lap by a rival.

Louise Manchester had her own sharp eye on the matter. Before leaving for Turkey she had told Disraeli: 'That gentleman is only waiting to come to the fore with all his hypocritical retirement.' Granville wrote to her on 12 November about the problem: 'Please remember that the greatest position in England is an aristocratic swell in the House of Commons, leading the whole of the popular party . . . If Gladstone were to try (which I do not believe he will do) to oust H. from the lead of the whole party, & rehabilitate himself, he would not have a chance of success.' But Granville did not rule out his trying to seize the leadership of the Radicals, and with this fear he urged Louise to cultivate Gladstone so as to gain influence over him. It was a testimony to his faith in her powers, but she did not respond. She detested Gladstone, now more than ever, and the time for such a change of front had passed.

Louise was ardently anti-Russian in the Eastern question, but she was one of the guests at the house-party which Lord Salisbury, the Secretary for India, gave for the Russian ambassador Ignatieff at Hatfield in March 1877. The Prince of Wales also invited himself and, as Disraeli told Lady Bradford, he took Madame Ignatieff in to dinner, but 'scarcely spoke to her at dinner, talking to his neighbor Lady Londonderry, but chiefly across the table to Duchess Louise who sate on my right'. As Madame Ignatieff was richly decked out, Lady Londonderry in rivalry 'staggered under the jewels of the 3 united families of Stewart, Vane and Tempest'.* As for Louise, she set everything on fire, even the neighbouring Thames; her face still flushed with the Lincoln race-course, her form in a spick-and-span new dress, scarcely finished, and her hair *à la* Marie Antoinette, studded with diamonds, who by the bye were stuck in every part of her costume. The Prince said to me: "Ask the Duchess why her hair is not in curls. Is it because it is Lent?"'

On the domestic side, Hartington's position was improved at this time by his father's decision to make over to him Hardwick Hall for his private enter-tainment, together with a part of the estate worth some £6,000 a year. The house had not been the family's principal residence since Bess of Hardwick's time and was in consequence almost unchanged since the day she left it. Lady Paget, visiting it in 1882, called it 'a dream of beauty in the old English style, utterly neglected . . .; it is literally crammed with the most beautiful tapestry and lovely things, the views heavenly'. Its desertion is often exaggerated (the Egertons were in the habit of using it in the summer), but Hartington only used it for shooting-parties towards the beginning and the end of each year. Louise and her husband were among the guests at his first party early in 1877, while Lady Frederick commented on her brother-in-law: 'He is delightful as host, even coming down in time for dinner!' From Hardwick Hartington could easily visit his father at Chatsworth, and an American who stayed with the Duke during these years describes such an occasion. After speaking of the beauty of the Chatsworth dining-room he adds: 'The most beautiful thing I ever saw in it was the light on the face of the late Duke's father as we sat at lunch, and Lord Hartington arrived unexpectedly, having ridden over from Hardwick Hall where he then lived.' Typically, Hartington's bedroom at Hardwick was in the most Spartan style, with the same original Elizabethan furniture that most of his guests had to put up with, and a later visitor, Lady Randolph Churchill, wrote of her terror in the place's lofty gloom. Assigned a cavernous bedroom near the Presence Chamber, she saw the tapestry move against the wall and, thrusting a poker through, discovered a narrow stone staircase winding down into the darkness. She was so nervous that she sat shiv-ering for hours in an armchair, surrounded by all the candles she could find, until she fell asleep from sheer fatigue.

As the Eastern controversy simmered on, there was a section in the Liberal

---

*Vane-Tempest-Stewart is the family name of the Marquesses of Londonderry.

Party which was opposed to weakening the government's policy over Turkey. Hartington was against making attacks which the whole party would not support and which would merely strengthen the government; but Gladstone followed his own line. In May 1877 he composed five resolutions urging that Europe should compel Turkey to reform. The timing was especially absurd, for war had just broken out between Russia and Turkey, and the latter had other things on its mind than constitutional change. What concerned Hartington was the party fiasco Gladstone was about to provoke, and he withheld his support. The split caused dismay in the Cavendish family; Lady Frederick wrote on 1 May: 'F is nearly wild. How can he leave Cavendish in the lurch, and yet to be driven to vote against Uncle W. seems almost inconceivable to him.' Lord Frederick bustled about to seek a compromise. Gladstone was persuaded to drop three of the resolutions and propose only the more moderate ones; nevertheless the debate fulfilled Hartington's fears when seventy Liberals refused to back Gladstone. The affair, while it did no good to the party, turned to Hartington's benefit by making him appear the safe leader against the impulsive Gladstone. The effect of the latter's position was sketched by the parliamentary commentator Henry Lucy: 'While three years ago his retirement appeared to be a calamity never to be recovered from, a proposition for his return at the present time would be voted down by a majority of three to one.'

Towards the end of 1877 the Russo-Turkish war reached a crisis as the Turks, after initial successes, were heavily defeated, and the Russians threatened Constantinople. A war fever swept the country, embodied in a music-hall song whose refrain gave a new word to the language:

> We don't want to fight, but by jingo, if we do,
> We've got the ships, we've got the men, we've got the money too.

When Parliament met in February 1878, Hartington held back from opposing the war grant which Disraeli demanded; but even so he did not satisfy the fiercer Whigs, who wanted a wholehearted support of the government in the patriotic cause. Among these, the Duke of Sutherland called Gladstone a Russian agent; Lord Fitzwilliam, one of the keenest Liberal peers, had declared long ago that it was the duty of every MP to stand behind the government; the Dukes of Bedford and Cleveland were also Disraelian. The feeling was reflected by a rumour in the clubs that Hartington was resigning after his hedging policy over the war-grant vote, and he, when he heard of it, thought he ought to do so. But from the Radicals there was never a tweet; with anti-Russian frenzy at its height, the last thing they wanted was to lose Hartington in a Whig coup. For the moment the government was riding high, and opposition was a thankless task.

The crisis of the East was resolved without a war; Disraeli browbeat the Russians into accepting a peace congress in Berlin, and there into backing down on the humiliating settlement they had imposed on Turkey. He returned from Berlin a national hero. Gladstone's crusade against his Eastern policy had rebounded against him. G.W.E. Russell gives a scent of the atmosphere this summer when he describes how a hostess begged him to come to dinner because she had invited Gladstone and no one else in London would consent to meet him. By contrast the sunny social relations Disraeli was enjoying with both Hartington and the Duchess of Manchester may be seen in a letter soon after his return. 'Yesterday's dinner was amusing, as Louise looked her best and talked her best. I sate on her right hand, and D. of Cam on her left, and Harty-Tarty not too near with Lady Westmorland, the only other lady there.' Some people blamed such influences for the mild tone of Hartington's criticisms of the Berlin treaty, which Disraeli described as 'a series of congratulatory regrets'; but in the prevalent national mood he could hardly have done more.

At the beginning of 1878 Hartington took as his private secretary, on Sir William Harcourt's recommendation, the young Reginald Brett, just down from Trinity College, Cambridge. He was the elegant and enigmatic figure who was to become, as Lord Esher, the *éminence grise* behind Edward VII's throne. Hartington's easy-going tolerance at this outset of his career encouraged a penchant for telling eminent people how to do their jobs which was nicely caught by Max Beerhohm in his cartoon ('Pertness Rebuked') of Lord Esher saying to Britannia: 'Never mind who I am. Just go and do what I tell you.' Hartington found Brett a sympathetic audience for his racing news, which he included in his official letters, and allowed his secretary to rewrite his speeches; but there is little evidence that he took Brett's freely proffered advice on political strategy. One of the first matters that Brett brought to his notice was a letter from a lady's maid whose mistress enjoyed the favours of a member of Disraeli's Cabinet; that gentleman, loose-tongued with drink, had been spouting official secrets during the lady's hair-brushing session, and Brett's correspondent was kindly offering to pass them on. Hartington rejected the suggestion with predictable contempt.

Reginald Brett was well aware of his chief's liaison with the Duchess of Manchester, and he gives us this description of her position, now more glittering than ever:

> For thirty years her ruthless beauty dominated what was then Society. Never seriously challenged, she reigned and ruled. The secret of her extraordinary success was perhaps due to a real benevolence that underlay a hardness of manner which was frequently mistaken for pride. She gambled with life, and loved to win, but she was open-hearted and invariably kind, without condescension, to young and even to absurd people. The splendour of the Duchess, of her daughters, her friends, and courtiers, was a stirring foil to the homeliness of his sisters* and brothers, and to the Cavendish simplicity that clung round the sombre glories of Devonshire House.

Was Lord Esher tacitly conscious of himself as one of the young and even absurd people to whom Louise had been kind when he first entered Hartington's service?

The year 1877 had brought Hartington a fresh party headache in the person of Joseph Chamberlain, who had come into Parliament after three years as mayor of Birmingham. This monocled, glossily dressed, orchid-sporting manufacturer with the sharp features and the businessman's hustle was a new portent in British politics. He made an alliance with Sir Charles Dilke, who, by contrast, was on good terms with Hartington. Dilke was in Lady Waldegrave's circle at Strawberry Hill; despite early republican sentiments (which made him anathema to Queen Victoria), he was also a member of the Prince of Wales's set and felt free to refer to Hartington as 'Harty'. Dilke appreciated that Hartington's aim was to hold the party together and that where this could be done he was ready to accept Radical policies, such as the further extension of the franchise which he officially adopted in 1877. He could not understand Chamberlain's dislike of Hartington, which indeed sprang from mere class feeling. He told Chamberlain: 'I as you know think Hartington the best man for us – the Radicals because he is quite fearless, always goes with us when he thinks it is safe for the party, and generally judges rightly.' Less favourable was his view of Louise Manchester, whom he described as trying hard to pick up

---

*Sic. Perhaps Brett was also thinking of a sister-in-law, Lady Edward, for whom 'homely' was a kind epithet.

information from him for Hartington: 'but her own strong Conservative prejudices and her want of clearness of head made her by no means a useful guide, and in fact the wonder to me always was to see how Hartington's strong common sense kept him from making the mistakes into which she always tried by her influence to press him'. This judgement is rather typical of both Dilke's and Chamberlain's conviction of their superior intellect, and we may set beside it Frederick Ponsonby's perception of Louise: 'a very clever and shrewd woman who pretended to be the reverse'.

Chamberlain had set up a new type of party machine on his home ground of Birmingham, and by organizing his Liberal supporters into tactical voting he was successful in capturing all three of the city's parliamentary seats. He then founded the National Liberal Federation to extend the method throughout the country. The initiative was suspect, however, to many, for the tactics of dictating political behaviour offended the traditions of British Liberalism. It savoured of the gang politics that were becoming notorious in America, and was accordingly given an American name, the Caucus. Leading Liberals such as Forster condemned it, fearing that once it had imposed voting-patterns on the electorate it would seek to impose policy on the party.

In May 1877 Chamberlain gained a boost for his cause by getting Gladstone to speak at the inaugural meeting of the Federation. The motive for the old campaigner may have been to find a body of support for his Bulgarian agitation. Chamberlain's own interest in an Eastern crusade was tepid, but (as Lord Frederick Cavendish tried to warn Gladstone) he saw the advantage of providing a refuge for the ex-leader from his neglect by the rest of the party and thus win him over to other Chamberlainian policies such as the disestablishment of the Church of England. His aim was to bring Gladstone back as party leader, and Gladstone was to all appearances going along with his plans, however much he presented himself as a simple party member speaking his mind.

Hartington wrote to Granville: 'I think that we have some right to ask Mr G. to look at the facts, as they exist . . . He does not cease to be the leader of the Party by merely saying that he will not be the leader. If, as he has done since the Autumn [i.e. September 1876], he takes the lead, he *is* the leader.' But Gladstone found it as hard to acknowledge this as to acknowledge his successor. In July 1877 the Liberal Party was to hold a dinner in Hartington's honour, and Gladstone was asked to attend to show his support for the leadership, but he told Granville a month before, 'I lean against it.' He went on leaning and dropped out. The situation was transformed, however, the following year by Gladstone's fiasco over the Eastern Question. As both he and, by association, the Caucus had the wind taken out of their sails, Hartington's hand was strengthened against the latter; in December 1878 he was brusque in refusing Chamberlain's invitation to speak to the Federation. Louise thought he should outflank Chamberlain by cultivating the other Radicals in the party, a piece of advice which historians have held up as an example of her bad judgement. But Louise had a different sort of game in her mind; she was experienced, with her card-player's skills, in manipulating the players around her. If she had been Hartington's wife and political hostess she could have won over the Dilkes and the Mundellas, freezing Chamberlain out socially and building up her husband's support. Alone, Hartington could only work with political tools, and he could not sell himself to a small section of the party for the sake of one personal victory.

In any case the need to conciliate Radicalism had temporarily passed. The initiative in the party was now with the Whiggish section which welcomed Disraeli's foreign policy and had ceased to see any need to be wagged by the Radical tail. The *Manchester Guardian* spoke of some thirty MPs who were discussing a third party, which would follow a Palmerstonian foreign policy and act in loose alliance with the Liberals. George Goschen, who had sat in Russell's and Gladstone's Cabinets, was representative of this right-wing tendency, and other ex-ministers were said to be involved. In October discussions were held by some twenty or thirty peers, principally in two of the great Whig houses in Scotland, the *Manchester Guardian* reported, with a view to reviving the old Whig party. The Duke of Sutherland (whose impulsive Radicalism of the 1860s was turning into an equally unthinking jingoism) would have been one of these plotters. The other great Scottish peer is less identifiable: presumably not the Duke of Argyll, who had acted with Gladstone over the Eastern Question. Hartington, needless to say, was careful to avoid being influenced by this disturbance on his right wing.

It was not long after its triumph at Berlin that the government began to lose its footing. Lord Lytton, Disraeli's grandiose Viceroy of India, invaded Afghanistan and, like the Russians in more recent times, he was to learn that such attempts are liable to end with a bloody nose. A massacre of the British Resident and his suite at Kabul in September 1878 obliged Lytton to send a large expedition under General Roberts to recover the country. Disraeli had to recall Parliament in December (in those days the recess usually lasted from August to February) to deal with the crisis. The Liberals had a strong hand, with an array of Whig proconsular experts on Indian affairs well qualified to make the most of Lytton's mistakes. With this backing Hartington came to life and on 13 December, in Mundella's words, 'made an entirely new departure... He smote the Government *hip and thigh*. Gladstone spoke to me in *high praise* of his speech which was really of a very high order.' The comment bears out Brett's impression that Hartington had 'pleased our extreme left amazingly'. The Liberal showing of 227 votes on the censure motion was a record in their counter-attack on the Tories. As the government tried to extricate itself over the next fifteen months the Liberals kept up the pressure, to the chagrin of the Prince of Wales, who was a strong patriot in such matters. Disraeli thus describes his visit along with Louise Manchester to Hatfield in July 1879: 'Louise has said nothing to me about politics, but I fancy she hears a good deal indirectly about Hartington's adventure. He is here, and the Prince who takes up all these questions as personal, is very short with him and says things for which Harty-Tarty seems not to care one straw. I am told last night in the smoking room this was very apparent.' The 'you-be-damnedness' of manner which one of Hartington's colleagues admired was not confined to the political stage.

The year 1879 saw Hartington's standing as leader further advanced by the opening of Devonshire House. Reginald Brett wrote in January: 'My Chief is to give Wednesday dinners followed by "drums" ... it is a politic step I am sure.' John Morley wrote after one of these events on 26 March: 'It was a brilliant affair; the place is really a palace.' The shift was underlined by a fire at Granville's house which obliged the Liberal leadership to move its meetings to Devonshire House. On his own ground Hartington began to grow more into a leader's role. In March the front-benchers met there to decide their policy on the Zulu War, where the Isandlwhana disaster had caused a fresh embarrassment to the government; yet the lack of expertise such as in the Afghan case left the Liberals feeling indecisive. There appeared to be a stalemate between the violent resolution advocated by Harcourt and the milder line proposed by Lord Granville; Hartington stepped forward and proposed his own formula, which was immediately accepted. As the party gained momentum, Hartington looked increasingly like the man in the driving-seat.

In February 1879 Louise went to the South of France to shake off a cough, and her absence was used by Queen Victoria for a bizarre intrigue, which is disclosed to us by the pen of Lady Waldegrave. The intermediary was the fat and jolly Duchess of Teck, sister of the Duke of Cambridge, and at the Queen's instigation she invited over to England Princess Frederica of Hanover, sister of the deposed king of that country. The aim was to try to arrange a marriage between her and Hartington while Louise was off the scene. Queen Victoria's concern was presumably for the dispossessed Princess, who the following year was reduced to marrying a mere baron; making her the next Duchess of Devonshire would obviously have been much more acceptable. Nevertheless the idea that Hartington was to be decoyed away from one Hanoverian lady by means of another seems most peculiar – as Lady Waldegrave commented: 'Did you ever hear of such a silly plot?' Whatever its reality, Lady Waldegrave's loyalty to Louise was now rock-solid, and it was no doubt to put a spoke in the wheel that in early March she held a dinner at which the Tecks, Princess Frederica, Hartington and Louise – by now returned – were all guests. Thus alerted, Louise would have had no difficulty in squashing whatever chances there were in the Queen's match-making schemes.

Lady Waldegrave was now in her late fifties, and Reginald Brett gives a picture of her, rouged to the eyes, sitting on a sofa in her octagon room as she received guests at Strawberry Hill. Her faith in Hartington had remained firm as she urged him not to resign the leadership in the face of Gladstone's comeback. On 23 June her husband attended the meeting of former Liberal Cabinet ministers at Devonshire House. For the remaining days of June Hartington and Louise were guests of Lady Waldegrave's at Strawberry Hill.* They left her in good health, but immediately after their departure she succumbed to a sudden illness and died on 5 July. The leading political hostess on the Liberal side thus vanished from the scene; but for Hartington it was the loss of a patroness whose help had earned his devotion for twenty years, and for Louise that of an old rival whom time had turned into her closest friend.

The same month saw the sharpest exchange between Hartington and Chamberlain. On 7 July Hartington walked late into a debate and found the House in a row over Chamberlain's attempt to get flogging abolished in the British Army. Hartington's first mistaken reaction was to criticize the Radicals

---

*Louise no doubt in the same state as when she dined with Prince Leopold at Disraeli's on the 21st: 'Duchess Louise was on my right hand, the soul of everything tho' she had a patch on her eye!'

for breach of parliamentary procedure, and Chamberlain in reply pounced on his earlier absence, calling him 'the noble Lord, lately the Leader of the Opposition, but now the leader of a section only'. Hartington, who was incapable of pretending to be in the right when he was not, apologized when he realized his mistake. As often happens, this gesture did him more good than a debating victory would have done, and when he rose to speak the next day he received a demonstration really directed against Chamberlain's bad form: 'on his getting up', wrote Sir Henry James, 'our people cheered for five minutes louder than you have ever heard them cheer . . . Everybody on both sides abuse Chamberlain, and he has lost immense way by his conduct.' Both men, however, wanted to heal the breach. In the following January Hartington accepted an invitation to Birmingham and came to an agreement over policies with Chamberlain. Even now, though, he refused to promise more than one Cabinet post between Dilke and Chamberlain in the next Liberal government, and the man he had in view was certainly Dilke, who had lately been working closely with him and flaunting a statesmanlike moderation in foreign affairs.

Hartington's intransigence towards Chamberlain contrasts with his pragmatism on other problems. It achieved its aim in getting his authority recognized, but that by itself was not its justification; his motive was that he considered Chamberlain's party machine, rather than his politics, a thoroughly bad thing for English liberalism. Tactically speaking, his stand was proved right in the short term by bringing Chamberlain to heel; in the medium term it might seem a mistake, for it sharpened the rivalry of the two men in the years 1883–5; and in the long term it proved irrelevant, since Chamberlain was forced to fall into line as Hartington's deputy in the years that followed.

With the election pending, Hartington decided not to face the country as member for his safe Welsh seat but to stand for a more challenging constituency. He chose to fight again in North Lancashire, where the Tories had held the county seats for the past eleven years. Speeches at Liverpool and Manchester in October 1879 marked the beginning of his campaign for acceptance. They were also the occasion for a rapprochement with Lord Derby, who was the most important landowner in Lancashire. Lord Derby, son of the former Prime Minister, had resigned from Disraeli's Cabinet over his Eastern policy and was gravitating towards the Whigs. He offered Hartington his hospitality at Knowsley when he came to speak at the two great Lancashire cities, and, although the rather priggish Lord Derby was not the sort of nobleman with whom Hartington was at ease, the visit converted him into a faithful Hartingtonian follower through the political vicissitudes of the next fourteen years. By the autumn of 1879 praise was becoming general over the way Hartington had consolidated his leadership. He had succeeded in raising his party from a state of disarray into an Opposition the government was beginning to fear. But there was still one wild card in the pack, and out it came when the young Lord Rosebery invited Gladstone to stand for the Scottish constituency of Midlothian, where Rosebery had his estates. In November 1879 Gladstone went to Scotland, and, in a string of speeches against Disraeli's government, galvanized the country as he had not done since his 'Bulgarian Horrors' agitation. Many who know of the famous Midlothian campaign probably do not realize that it was not an election campaign at all; it was a speaking tour to make himself known to his constituents. The seat was then held for the Tories by Lord Dalkeith, the nobleman who had pipped Hartington to the post of Lady Louisa Hamilton's favours in 1859, and he retained it until he was narrowly defeated by Gladstone in the General Election the following year.

Hartington knew the value of Gladstone's oratory, but he also knew its limitations. He had told Granville three years before, 'Mr Gladstone can never be made to understand that people who listen to him and admire his speeches don't necessarily agree with him.' But the practical point was the effect that public adulation was going to have on Gladstone's behaviour. Hartington's brother Frederick interpreted for him Gladstone's motives in going to Midlothian: 'It had flashed across his mind that the contest might place him in a very prominent position at the General Election', but his only aim was to rouse the country against the government's wickedness and then 'retire into the background'. From anybody else this would probably have provoked one of those 'great wheezy guffaws' deserved by a good jest at the Turf Club. One of the things that did not flash across Gladstone's mind was consulting the party leaders about his Midlothian campaign.

This resurgence could affect Hartington in only one way. His secretary noted his 'character pathetically proud, so conscious of his own deficiencies'. The modesty made him undervalue his own fitness for his post; the pride forbade him to continue as a figurehead while the real leader was seen to be another. He wrote to Granville on 7 December and pointed out that Gladstone 'has almost continually since his resignation chosen to act in most important matters as the leader of the party out of doors; that he has done so more conspicuously than ever during the last few weeks; that such a course renders my position intolerable'. The only possible response was resignation. A party meeting was held at Devonshire House on the 16th, and his colleagues managed to break down his resolve. Two arguments in particular weighed with him: the first was urged by the Chief Whip, W.P. Adam, when he said that Gladstone might attract Radical votes, but many moderate Liberals would be put off to see him as leader; a campaign with Hartington reassuring the moderates and Gladstone in the wings stirring up the Radicals would maximize Liberal support. The second argument was that Hartington's resignation now would be a tremendous coup for the Tories: it would show that a demagogic campaign in the Liberal camp could succeed in ousting the party's elected leader. As on so many occasions, he gave way to his friends, but he hated it, and he did nothing to conceal the fact. In January 1880 various Radicals and others devised a plan to force Gladstone to commit himself to the official leadership by inviting him to chair a banquet in Hartington's honour; but Gladstone was the one member of his party Hartington was not prepared to outmanoeuvre. He insisted on the banquet's being cancelled, even though 240 MPs had already responded to the invitation.

At this point two of the leaders of the Liberal Party had the idea of refining on the policy imposed on Hartington in December. Granville secretly proposed the tactic that Hartington should offer to stand down in favour of Gladstone, on the presumption that Gladstone's expected refusal would thereby strengthen the leader's position. Hartington viewed this as combining the worst aspects of his own continuing in place and of his actually giving way to Gladstone, and he rejected the ploy. W.E Forster must have been unaware of this exchange when he gave similar advice while staying with Louise Manchester at Kimbolton on 23 January 1880. He wrote to Hartington that 'Her Grace and I have been amusing ourselves' with composing a draft letter which he enclosed, whereby Hartington would urge Gladstone to resume the leadership. They, too, expected Gladstone to refuse, but they were cleverer than Granville and did not present the move as a trick; Forster went to some length to persuade Hartington why his withdrawal was desirable. Even if it were, that would not have been the motivation for Forster's and Louise's plot.* A Gen-

---

*Patrick Jackson (*The Last of the Whigs*, p.105) takes the proposal at its face value and cites it as evidence that Louise Manchester 'was not unrealistically encouraging Hartington's ambitions'. Perhaps not, but neither was she going out of her way to dash them.

eral Election was then expected in June, and just a day or two after this little intrigue Louise left for what was becoming her usual winter trip to the South of France. That is where she was when Disraeli unexpectedly dissolved Parliament on 8 March, and she did not get back until the 20th, to give Hartington whatever advice she thought he needed in the election contest.

Hartington flung himself into the campaign with energy and made twenty-four speeches, four times as many as any other Liberal except Gladstone, who made fifteen. But it was the latter's titanic eloquence that caught the imagination. Gladstone was given the credit when the Liberals swept back with a majority of 137 over the Tories, the Home Rulers slightly increasing their representation to 65. It is worth noting that the Whig section was not in retreat; it had actually increased its strength in the party. But the real new factor was the man whom everybody acknowledged as the architect of the victory.

7
The Phoenix Park Tragedy

WELL BEFORE THE election it was recognized that Gladstone meant to return to office, but the expectation was that he would be Chancellor of the Exchequer under a Granville or Hartington ministry. Gladstone himself in November 1879 described this idea as 'silly' (he did in fact hold the Exchequer together with the premiership for the first two years of his 1880 ministry). There was, however, no convention against a former Prime Minister holding lower office: Lord John Russell had served under Palmerston, and the Duke of Wellington had not felt that his unique national position put a seat in Peel's Cabinet beneath his dignity. Whether Gladstone had entered the election meaning to demand the premiership is impossible to say; a small Liberal majority might have made the party prefer the moderate leaders. But the triumphant victory had changed the situation.

Disraeli, before he resigned on 21 April, advised the Queen to send for Hartington. It is not uncommon for a retiring Prime Minister to advise on his successor from the same party, but nominating the leader from the other side was a piece of cheek only Disraeli could have got away with. Disraeli had lived for years with Louise Manchester's energetic hope that Granville would give way and Hartington would be the next Liberal Prime Minister. Had this wish, assumed at so many dinner tables, sunk into his mind so that he could envisage no other future? Leaving aside the unthinkable of Gladstone's return to power, the Queen's natural course would have been to invite Granville, as the senior of the two Liberal leaders, to form a government; but she took Disraeli's advice and summoned Hartington.

Hartington arrived at Windsor on the 22nd armed with a great deal of advice from his friends. The Prince of Wales had three long conversations with him at the Turf Club during these days, and on the 18th he had written to his mother urging her to choose Hartington, whom he had found 'dreadfully worried and careworn' about the matter. Reginald Brett advised his chief to form a Radical government in order to outflank Gladstone – hardly the way to encourage him to take office. Hartington, however, told the Queen that he believed Gladstone would accept no subordinate office, and no Liberal government could be formed without him. The Queen insisted that he test Gladstone's willingness to serve under him, instructing him to tell Gladstone that he would never again enjoy her confidence, a remark which Hartington wisely did not pass on. At their interview the same evening Gladstone ran true to form. A gentleman would have promised his loyalty to Hartington in any suitable Cabinet post; a great man would have thanked Hartington handsomely for his efforts over the past five years and told him that the voice of British Liberalism demanded his giving way to the preferred leader. What Gladstone did was to treat Hartington to a constitutional lecture, to which he listened with his usual patience. Gladstone confirmed that he would not serve under Hartington but would support a Liberal government from outside, although 'Promises of this kind . . . stood on slippery ground, and must always be understood with the limits which might be prescribed by conviction.' Hartington knew Gladstone's conviction well enough not to need this warning. When he went back to Windsor on the 23rd he took reinforcements with him in the form of Granville, and they told the Queen that she must send for Gladstone.

They might well have entered a hornet's nest, since the Prince of Wales, having had his mind changed by Hartington, had been tactless enough to write to his mother urging the merits of a Gladstone ministry. The Queen was furious. It was bad enough having to swallow the bolus of Gladstone's return without having it shoved down her throat by her son. She wrote to her secretary Sir Henry Ponsonby: 'The Prince of Wales may be told, but *very shortly* what the constitutional course is, which is *quite* clear. He has *no* right to meddle and *never* has done so *before*. Lord Hartington must be told, when he leaves, that the Queen cannot allow any private and intimate conversations to go on between *them*, or all confidence will be *impossible*.' But, as this note showed, the Queen was not going to let her anger cloud the official audience. As the two leaders emerged, Ponsonby noted: 'Granville kissed his hand with a smile like a ballet dancer receiving applause. And Hartington threw himself into a chair with "Ha! Ha!" Granville exclaimed – "No difficulty at all – all smooth!"'

And now Gladstone took his followers by surprise; the Cabinet he formed to lead his huge Liberal majority consisted of eight Whig noblemen and only three ministers (besides himself) who might be considered the voice of popular Liberalism. Of these Forster had once been a Radical but was steering more and more towards the right; Bright was a shadow of his old self; and only Chamberlain represented a strong Radical line. Sir Charles Dilke was fobbed off (in deference to the Queen) as Foreign Under-Secretary. It was a much more Whiggish administration than Hartington would have been able to form, even perhaps with a small majority, and certainly with a large Radical following snapping at his heels.

Hartington himself was asked to name his office and chose to be Secretary for India. With the Afghan war still going on it was the most taxing post in the government, and Hartington set himself to dismantle Disraeli's imperialist policy. He had not been converted from his Palmerstonian beliefs, but an enterprise based on rashness and bad judgement was fit only for reversal, regardless of prestige. Explaining the British evacuation of Kandahar in the House of Commons he stated baldly: 'We go away now because we do not want Kandahar, and because we have no right to be there.' Lord Lytton was immediately recalled as Viceroy (an action which Hartington had demanded while in opposition), and this caused slight embarrassment when the two met at dinner with Lord Lonsdale in December 1881. Louise Manchester was as usual on the guest list, and Lytton wrote to Lady Dorothy Nevill:

> I afterwards learned that Her Grace's devoted servant Lord Hartington was very shy of meeting me, and begged Oliver Montagu to arrange that we should not find ourselves together after the ladies left the room. Conscience makes cowards of us all. But as my withers were unwrung, I saw no reason for avoiding him, and our meeting was delightfully amicable: though I suppose that a few weeks hence we shall be disputing the veracity of each other's opinions for the edification of an enlightened public.

The India Office was almost Hartington's favourite post of the five he held in his career, because it was the least exposed to party controversy. One exception was an incident when the Viceroy's minutes on Afghanistan were held up by an Indian official's suicide, and the Tories suggested that Hartington had deliberately held them back. There was nothing Hartington hated more than charges of dishonesty thrown about to make party points, and his anger caused the slur to be withdrawn. Henry Lucy describes the reaction when in May 1881 Lord George Hamilton repeated the accusation: 'Lord Hartington down upon him in a twinkling. Takes him between his teeth and shakes him as a mastiff might shake a terrier . . . The Government should pay someone to "rile" Hartington from time to time. Very good when he is roused.' If there was one thing he did not take to at the India Office it was the vast bulk of business that the government of such a large empire entailed, for Hartington was incapable of being content, like ordinary men, with less than comprehensive understanding of his brief. Granville told Lord Spencer: 'so far from being idle, as some suppose, he hates not being able to master a matter in all its details'.

Hartington's popularity in the House of Commons was at its height in these years. The memory of his good management as leader and his prompt giving way to Gladstone won him high esteem, and there was no one who better understood the House's moods. He was now the regular party leader when Gladstone, who was over seventy, retired to bed at midnight. He had to deal with the most turbulent Parliament of the nineteenth century, and one of its disturbing factors was Lord Randolph Churchill, who formed the so-called 'Fourth Party' with Henry Wolff, John Gorst and Arthur Balfour as a ginger group within the Conservative party. Their tactics kept Parliament sitting through the sweltering August of 1880, and the Liberal leadership devolved on Hartington as Gladstone retired to convalesce in France. When at the end of the month Churchill had the impudence to criticize the government for the hold-up of business, Hartington rose and pointed out with his impassive irony that in the past four months the House had been treated to 105 speeches from Gorst, 68 from Wolff and 74 from Churchill himself. The wit and eloquence that were winning Churchill admirers did nothing to relieve the imperturbable contempt with which Hartington viewed him from the opposite benches, nor did he improve matters by threatening Hartington a few months later with a duel.

Disraeli, observing these scenes from the Peers' Gallery, lost nothing in his appreciation of Hartington, and just a few weeks before his death he describes a dinner at Lady Lonsdale's: 'Very amusing. Louise and Harty-Tarty were there – the Cadogans, H. Chaplins, Sir Charles Dilke, all very good company and talked well; Harty-T particularly, who is a clever fellow with some humour.' With Disraeli's death in April 1881 Hartington succeeded for a while to the rank of Queen Victoria's favourite politician; Henry Ponsonby found her talking of Hartington's horse for the Derby 'as if she were on Epsom Downs'. Their relations are illustrated by the well-known story told by Lord

Ribblesdale, who held a Court appointment under the 1880–5 government. He describes a dinner at Windsor where Hartington was seated at the Queen's side: 'They got on very well together. Though Hartington, like Peel and the Duke of Wellington, had neither small talk nor manners, yet he seemed to me less shy with the Queen than with his neighbours. This may be accounted for, perhaps, by their both being absolutely natural and their both being in no sort of doubt about their positions.' The Queen had the habit of eating very quickly, and the footmen practised the 'menial trick' of whisking everyone's plates away as soon as she had finished. Hartington's conversation with the Queen had held him up in his operations with a saddle of mutton, and as his plate disappeared he broke off to call out, 'Here, bring that back!' The dinner guests held their breaths, but across the Queen's face stole one of her rare unforced smiles that showed she was both amused and pleased.

The diplomat Sir Augustus Paget and his family also encountered Hartington at this time and gave their impressions. Lady Paget describes meeting 'the Devonshire House people' (i.e. Hartington and Lord and Lady Edward) in June 1880 and being charmed 'to see how cordial they are'; and four days later she went again in the evening 'to Devonshire House for a little, as they are always so nice'. Just afterwards she went to Windsor to present her sixteen-year-old daughter and was surprised to find her fall into long conversation with Lord Hartington. She told her husband: 'I asked her what she had found to talk about to him the whole evening, for you know he never speaks to girls, and she said, "Oh, we quarrelled."' She accused Hartington of writing badly in her birthday book, and that set the conversation off on the right foot with the fluent, self-possessed sixteen-year-old. She for her part said of Hartington, 'He's an old duck', finding him very like his cousin the Duke of Sutherland.

The burning issue of the 1880s was Ireland, and it was one in which Hartington could not help feeling a special interest. He had been in touch with the government of that kingdom ever since he helped his great-uncle entertain 'Uncle Morpeth' at Lismore. The 7th Earl of Carlisle had been Lord Lieutenant in 1855–8 and 1859–64 and was one of the most popular holders of his office. He had the amiable policy of acclimatizing the Irish to English habits by teaching them cricket and laid out a ground at Viceregal Lodge, where he followed the matches keenly as scorer. Hartington's father, brought up by his widowed Irish mother, also made Ireland the most conscientiously shouldered of his responsibilities once he succeeded as Duke of Devonshire, and if there was one thing that reconciled him to leaving his beloved Holker it was his annual fishing visits to Lismore. Lady Frederick gives us a picture of one of these in April 1868 when Hartington lost a fine fish after half an hour's playing. The Duke took the defeat to heart much more than his son, and on the walk back home kept breaking out at intervals with 'That scoundrel of a fish!'

His term as Irish Secretary in 1871–4 gave Hartington the occasion to form ideas on the government of the country. He believed, first of all, in law and order and already before his appointment had supported Chichester Fortescue's request for coercive powers, a demand he repeated himself when need arose. He and Lord Spencer formed a strong government partnership, but their ideas were not limited to repression. Hartington ignored *laissez-faire* economics to propose nationalizing the railways in Ireland, where some sixty small and uneconomic companies had grown up haphazard. This was a subject of which he had special knowledge, for his father at that very time was spending £200,000 on building railways at Lismore. Nationalization would enable fares to be reduced and a rationalized network to relieve rural poverty and stagnation. These plans foundered, however, on the doctrinaire liberalism of his Cabinet colleagues.

A second problem Hartington recognized was the small time the Westminster Parliament was prepared to devote to Irish measures, and the awkwardness and expense of having to go to Westminster for all legislation, however minor. By 1873 therefore he attempted a reform that would have set up county boards to handle all matters normally dealt with in private Bills. These would have included powers over police, education, railway legislation and other local matters. The plan did not spring from any abstract belief in self-government but purely from considerations of efficiency; he envisaged the county boards having some representative composition (for example, the local MPs), but essentially they were to be men appointed to do a practical job. Again, Gladstone's lack of interest in local government squashed Hartington's proposals for 1873, but in August he told Lord Spencer: 'If you had stayed on, I had quite made up my mind to make a rather more vigorous attempt next year to do something about Local Government reform in Ireland.' As it was, not only the Lord Lieutenant but the whole government went next January, and the plans lapsed.

When the Liberals returned to office in 1880, they were confronted with a situation that had been transformed by developments of only a few months' standing. One was the agricultural depression that set in from 1878 as cheap American corn flooded into the country and caused bread prices to plummet. It hit the English landowners hard, but in Ireland it destroyed the agricultural prosperity that had returned after the Famine and gave rise to mass evictions as tenant farmers found themselves unable to pay their rents; a wave of rural terrorism swept the country as the national economy collapsed in obedience to the ruling free-market orthodoxy. Parallel to this development was the rise of the Home Rule movement and in particular the seizure of its leadership by Charles Stuart Parnell. This Irish squire had imbibed from his American mother a bitter hatred of England, and riding the tide of Irish discontent he ordered his party's tactics in Parliament in a spirit of cold destructiveness towards every aspect of British rule.

Faced with the appalling surge in Irish evictions, Gladstone's response was to introduce a Compensation for Disturbance Bill in 1880, whereby tenants evicted for non-payment of rent would still have the right to be reimbursed for improvements they had made to their farms. As an emergency measure it was understandable, but economically it made little sense, and it provoked the first Whig revolt against Gladstonian policy. Hartington himself opposed it, but was persuaded to make the first of a type of speech which would be familiar over the next five years; he set out his reasons for reluctantly supporting the measure and was so convincing that he brought recalcitrant Whigs over on to the official side. Nevertheless, having passed the Commons, the Bill was resoundingly rejected by the Whig peers, failing by 282 votes to 51. The Whig defection was so large that it would have defeated the Bill even if no Tory peer had bothered to vote. The young Marquess of Lansdowne resigned his post as Hartington's Under-Secretary at the India Office and began the political journey that was to make him one of the stalwarts of the Conservative Party.

The state of Ireland made a new Coercion Act urgent, but Gladstone was reluctant to impose one without an accompanying Land Act to cure the evils from which the unrest was born. Hartington was mortified at this weakness, especially when he heard of disturbances on his father's own excellently run estates, where trouble had been completely unknown. With his itch to be on the spot he commented in December that he would rather be in Ireland 'than staying here, and not daring to look any one in the face, which is my case now'. This attitude did not imply any reluctance to redress Irish wrongs, as he showed when proposals were made by the Commission chaired by Lord Bess-borough, one of the staunchest of Whig peers. The solution proposed was to grant the 'Three Fs': Fair Rent, agreed by arbitrators; Fixity of Tenure, in place of leases held at the will of the landlord; and Free Sale, whereby a farmer could sell his tenancy to another when he wished to give it up. Gladstone wished to bring in a comprehensive measure, but he viewed it as a temporary concession to the present desperate conditions and an undesirable tampering with free-market principles; for that reason Fixity of Tenure was the last thing he wanted to grant, since it was the only one of the three which was by nature permanent. Hartington was unconcerned by such points; on 19 December he wrote to Gladstone declaring his readiness to go further, and promising con-crete proposals in a few days' time. When these came they were well received. Lord William Compton, who was the brother-in-law and private secretary of the Irish Viceroy, Lord Cowper, reported that 'Everybody is loud in praises of Lord Hartington', although Gladstone, intending no compliment, described his scheme as 'revolutionary'. Against his convictions he was nevertheless compelled to introduce the Bill with Fixity as well as the other two Fs, and in that form it became law in 1881.

This Bill, proposed in tandem with the Coercion Bill, had a rough ride in the Commons as the Irish members brought obstruction to a peak. The his-toric sitting of January–February 1881, when the House unprecedentedly sat for forty-one hours without a break, involved Hartington in an unaccustomed experience: he had gone off to bed after midnight on 1 February, and with H. Childers the only Cabinet minister in the House the sitting degenerated into chaos. Lord Frederick Cavendish hurried to Devonshire House and pulled his brother out of bed to return and take charge. The debate continued, with the deputy Speaker doing his best, until the Speaker arrived at nine in the morn-ing and against all parliamentary tradition closed the sitting on his own authority. The same morning Lady Frederick came upon Hartington walking by the Houses of Parliament with Sir William Harcourt, who joked that it was the first time in history that Hartington had been known to be in bed by one o'clock – and then he was pulled out of it. At any rate he did not repeat the experience and kept to his late hours in future while Parliament was sitting.

The Lords treated this Land Bill with more respect than that of the year before, and it became law, effecting crucial reforms in Irish land tenure. But the Whigs were mutinous; the Duke of Argyll resigned as Lord Privy Seal, his grounds being the Bill's offence against the radical free-market doctrine which he, like other Whigs at the time, was espousing in matters of land. Lord Listowel (the same who had entertained Skittles at Baden in 1861) resigned a Household appointment. And the Duke of Bedford, after rumbling for the whole of 1881, finally made his wife resign as Mistress of the Robes.

The Lord Lieutenant of Ireland in 1880–2 was Louise Manchester's old lover Lord Cowper, who attained with this office the summit of his political career. The Irish Secretary was W.E. Forster. The latter was by now viewed as belonging to the right wing of the party; his public pronouncements to mark that position had sometimes been seen as efforts to supplant Hartington but he was in fact completely loyal, and what he was aiming at was succeeding Hartington when he was raised to the House of Lords. Hartington, for his part, was Forster's Cabinet ally in his tough policy as Irish Secretary and put unusual warmth into that attitude. After a debate in March 1882 marked by captious Tory criticism of Forster, Hartington avowed a desire, so Forster's niece recorded, not so much to answer the last speaker as to throw his boot at him. Reginald Brett observed that Hartington 'for the last five years has invariably – out of some high feeling of obligation to Forster which does not exist, or desire not to triumph over him – supported him through all his difficulties'. But Hartington was more alive than his secretary to the way Louise Manchester had squared Forster and thus had a stronger sense of obligation. He backed Forster to the hilt in the bitter battles in Parliament, as Parnell deliberately tried to wreck the Land Act to prevent it from calming the crisis in Ireland on which his power was based. For this Parnell was gaoled in October 1881, with two other Irish MPs, and remained in prison for six months, while murder, cattle-maiming and other atrocities ran unchecked in the Irish countryside.

In the spring of 1882 steps were taken to resolve this impasse: an Arrears Act was to be passed to pay off the debts of tens of thousands of Irish farmers, and Parnell was to be released and use his influence to end crime and disorder. As part of this scheme of reconciliation the hard-line Irish administration was to change: Cowper and Forster both resigned and their places were taken by Lord Spencer, returning to his old post as Viceroy, and Lord Frederick Cavendish as Chief Secretary.

Hartington's younger brother had kept up his Radical reputation through a modest political career. In 1859–64 he had been private secretary to Lord Granville as Lord President of the Council, and he had sat in Parliament since

1865. In 1872 Gladstone took him as his private secretary and the following year appointed him a Lord of the Treasury, an experience which lasted him for five months. On the Liberal return to office Lord Frederick became Financial Secretary to the Treasury, a post of special importance since Gladstone was combining the premiership with the Exchequer, and the Secretary was called upon to do all the routine work of that office. Gladstone held his nephew by marriage in close affection, and with his penchant for valuing people in proportion to their admiration for himself he professed to rate Frederick's abilities higher than Hartington's. He had him pencilled in as a future Chancellor of the Exchequer.

From their boyhood a strong devotion had united Hartington and his brother. Lord Frederick's letters to 'My dearest Cavy' attest his constant admiration for his elder brother, and there was no one to whose opinion Hartington deferred more in politics; if there was one individual who kept Hartington attuned to moderate radicalism over the years it was Lord Frederick. The two brothers showed certain contrasts as well as their resemblances: where Hartington was somnolent Frederick was alive and fiery; where Hartington was level-headed Frederick was idealistic; where Hartington was casually ill-mannered Frederick was positively tactless. Lord Frederick Cavendish's impulsive generosity was covered by an aggressive oratorical style, and he pronounced with the nursery defects popularly associated with the aristocratic silly ass; a man whose threats were 'fweats' could not succeed in being impressive. Henry Lucy described his speaking style as 'singularly like an exaggeration of Hartington' and giving listeners 'the opportunity of knowing how much worse Hartington might be if he were to try'.

Although Lord Frederick had never held an Irish office, he shared all his family's love of the country and took a keen interest in its troubles. His wife describes his report to Gladstone after a visit to Ireland in October 1880:

F: got home Saturday morning; and after breakfast talked over Irish matters with Uncle W. . . . He says the panic is very great, and all the people he spoke to unanimous as to the suspension of the Habeas Corpus, on the ground that it has never been known to fail in putting down sedition. Certain landlords are said to be in danger *because* they are good ones; Parnell and Co. considering they stand in the way of their revolutionary schemes . . . F. put the black view strongly before Uncle W. that he might know the worst; but F. is as strong as Uncle W. against extra-legal measures being resorted to except as a last resource. 'What?' he said, 'are we to lock up 500 people in gaol?'

It was this charming idealist whom Gladstone chose to implement his new policy of reconciliation with the Irish people, all the stronger as a personal pledge because of their family connection and the deep affection between them. The policy was one which the Irish leaders wanted to support, but the chaos of the past few years had left bands of killers roaming about who were not amenable to discipline. One such was a group self-styled the Invincibles, who had resolved on murdering the Under-Secretary Thomas Burke, a tough Irishman who had worked for Hartington in his term as Chief Secretary and who was the most formidable enemy of the terrorists. On 6 May 1882 Lord Spencer and Lord Frederick Cavendish made their ceremonial entry into Dublin. For the latter it was just a preliminary visit; he meant to be back to join his wife in London on the following day, Sunday. He spent the afternoon talking with Burke in Dublin Castle and familiarizing himself with his new duties. Then, about seven o'clock, he set out to walk home through Phoenix Park in the fine evening to his official residence, Secretary's Lodge. A little later Burke left in an open vehicle known as an outside-car for his own residence, which was also in the park. He had not gone far when he overtook Lord Frederick and, getting down, dismissed his car and went on with his chief on foot. They followed the footpath which ran alongside the road through the park, talking animatedly, walking arm in arm as Victorian gentlemen did to show their friendship.

The Invincibles were waiting for them a little way on; they had parked an outside-car on the road along which they knew Burke would travel on his way home. Their look-out man, the only one who knew Burke by sight, saw the two officials coming and set off with two companions, with whom he climbed onto the car and drove on slowly. They pulled out white handkerchiefs, as a signal to the executioners who were waiting further on; as soon as these were alerted, two of the men on the car got down and made off, so as to be away from the scene of the crime. The assassins, seven strong, came down the footpath towards Cavendish and Burke, three of them walking abreast in front, then two armed men behind and two more bringing up the rear. The three in front parted ranks to let their victims through. But just at that moment a carriage rattled past on the road and the driver bade the walkers good day; the first two assassins, disconcerted, failed to strike. Cavendish and Burke walked past them, and to the accomplices who had made off earlier, and were watching from a distance, it looked as if the attempt had failed, like so many in the past. But the two men in the middle quickly turned round and, drawing long surgical knives, set upon Thomas Burke, aided by the two behind. Lord Frederick put up his furled umbrella and tried to fend off the blows as his civil servant was hacked to death. The assassins had no idea who he was, but they attacked him, too, stabbing him several times. Pausing only to wipe their knife-blades on the grass, the conspirators leapt on to the outside-car, which was already moving off, and left their two victims bleeding to death on the footpath.

That evening in London Hartington had gone with his sister to a reception at the Admiralty given by Lord Northbrook, the First Lord. It was past eleven when William Harcourt arrived from the Prime Minister's house, where he had received two telegrams giving news of the murders. He told Lord Northbrook first, and they took Hartington aside to the First Lord's private room and broke the news to him. He then went with his sister to Lady Frederick's house in Carlton House Terrace, where Lady Louisa told her of her husband's murder. Then others began to arrive. Lady Frederick's diary describes Gladstone's entry: 'His first words were, "Father, forgive them, for they know not what they do." Then he said to me, "Be assured it will not be in vain," and across all my agony there fell a bright ray of hope, and I saw in a vision Ireland at peace, and my darling's life-blood accepted as a sacrifice for Christ's sake, to help to bring this to pass . . . I said to him as he was leaving me, "Uncle William, you must never blame yourself for sending him." He said, "Oh no, there can be no question of that."' Lord Granville arrived, and his warm humanity brought some comfort as he went round embracing everybody. Hartington, for his part, was 'almost prostrate' and had no words to share his grief with his sister-in-law. It was he, nevertheless, who took the responsibility of sending the news to his father. By chance Lord Edward was staying at Chatsworth and Hartington was spared having to telegraph directly to his father with the terrible news; he resolved to follow up his telegram by going down to Chatsworth himself the next day. Lady Frederick spoke to him alone for a few minutes and was insistent that he should tell the Duke that it had been right for Lord Frederick to go to Ireland.

When the Duke heard the telegram's news from Lord Edward he fell on his knees at the blow. He had hated the appointment from the first, not from any apprehension of danger but because of the separation it would entail from his beloved son, whom he was so used to as his companion at Holker. Not for eight days was he able to resume his carefully kept diary, and when he returned to it he wrote:

> A most dreadful affliction has befallen me. My dearest Freddie was savagely slaughtered in the Phoenix Park on Saturday evening, a few hours after he had arrived in Dublin to undertake the duties of Irish Secretary. The dreadful intelligence reached me on Sunday morning by a telegram from Cavendish to Edward. He along with Emma arrived in the course of the day, and it has been something of a comfort to hear from him that my dearest boy is not supposed to have suffered much pain. He, along with Mr Burke, the under-secretary, were stabbed to death by 4 men in the Phoenix Park, and the wounds were of a kind to be almost instantly fatal. Cav has been most affectionate . . . We are comforted in some measure by the feeling that Freddie has fallen in the discharge of his duty.

Lord Frederick's body was brought over from Ireland, and after lying in state overnight in Chatsworth's cathedral-like chapel was buried on the 11th. Such was the profound shock caused in the country that three hundred members of the House of Commons and 30,000 sympathizers made the journey to Chatsworth to pay their respects. Of Hartington his secretary wrote: 'No one who, as I did, saw Hartington on that Sunday which followed the day of Lord Frederick Cavendish's assassination could forget the stricken face, in such contrast to the impassive countenance which his friends and companions knew.' And Sir William Harcourt, attending the funeral, saw him take a small bunch of flowers from his pocket and drop them into the open grave.

After emergency measures giving the authorities special powers of interrogation, the murderers were rounded up. One of them, James Carey, was a man of some prominence, being a member of Dublin Corporation, and he turned Queen's Evidence. On his information five of his accomplices were sentenced to death in April 1883 and three to life imprisonment. The police tried to smuggle Carey out to South Africa with a new identity, but he was shot dead by an avenger on board the ship that carried him out.

It became the rule to attach two plain-clothes detectives to the most prominent ministers, a practice unheard of hitherto. Harcourt, entering Devonshire House in February 1883 to see Hartington, when Lords Spencer and Granville had already arrived, found six detectives waiting in the hall. Hartington went further and always carried a loaded revolver with him (as did Parnell, who was afraid of his own followers). With his usual carelessness he was always losing them and leaving them behind in places – even at Balmoral when he went to stay – and after he died some twenty of them were brought to light in odd corners of Devonshire House.

The murder of Lord Frederick shocked the British public as no other event did in the tale of Irish violence and had a profound effect on political attitudes, so that years later, when Hartington was collaborating with the Conservatives and a Liberal speaker demanded rhetorically 'Since when have the Cavendish colours turned from yellow to blue?' a voice from the crowd caused an unquenchable sensation by calling back: 'Since they were dyed in the blood of Lord Frederick Cavendish.'

Louise von Alten at
the time of her
marriage to Viscount
Mandeville, later Duke of
Manchester; miniature by
Henry Thorburn (detail)

The Cavendish family; engraving by P. Baugniet, 1852. Seated centre: the 6th Duke of Devonshire; to his right the Earl of Burlington (later the 7th Duke); standing behind him Lady Louisa Cavendish; to her left Lord Cavendish (later Hartington); to his left Lord Burlington's brother George (whose wife is seated left); to his left Lords Frederick and Edward Cavendish

Catherine Walters (Skittles), whose affair with Hartington lasted from 1859 to 1862

Lord Hartington in the 1860s

A house-party at Kimbolton
Castle in February 1868.
Below, centre, standing
bareheaded is the Duke of
Manchester and to his right
the Duke of Sutherland.
Immediately above the Duke
of Manchester is the Prince
of Wales and to his right
Hartington and the Duchess
of Manchester (in riding veil).

Louise Duchess of Manchester in 1859 when she was Mistress of the Robes to Queen Victoria; portrait by Frans Xavier Winterhalter

Lord Frederick Cavendish, Hartington's brother, who was assassinated in Dublin in 1882; portrait by Sir William Richmond

Chatsworth from the south–west. On the left is the Belvedere and Sculpture Gallery range added to the seventeenth-century house by the 6th Duke. On the right is the garden with the water steps running down the hillside.

Hartington as
Duke of Devonshire
after 1891

Louise as Duchess of
Devonshire in her
coronation robes, 1902

8
Gordon and Khartoum

UNTIL 1882 HARTINGTON had approached politics with a slightly bored sense of duty; from the murder of his brother onward his attitude towards them became one of increasing revulsion. His personal pain was naturally the deepest reason, even though he fought it to carry on with his work in the India Office and the Commons; but simultaneously, because of Cabinet changes, he found himself having to struggle from an almost isolated position against the new Radical trends. Hartington has always been seen as the head of a Whig section in pre-ordained conflict with Radicalism; but it is only from 1882 that this begins to be true. Even now he fought hard against becoming a merely sectional leader and saw Radicalism as a minority movement which was being too weakly allowed to run away with the future of the party.

In a way the incentive to remain in politics became sharper at this point. From the moment he had taken office Gladstone declared his intention to retire in two years' time. An idea even penetrated his mind that he had not acted with complete generosity towards Hartington. In November 1881 he told Lord Frederick of his plan to retire next Easter, giving as one of his reasons the feeling that he was standing in Hartington's way. With all his admiration for Gladstone, Lord Frederick had enough Cavendish realism to state the objection; unless Gladstone were to rule himself clearly out of a second comeback by taking a peerage, he would make Hartington's leadership position impossible with the knowledge of that famous conviction lurking in the wings. It is worth pointing out that as late as 1896 Lord Rosebery felt himself obliged to resign the Liberal leadership when Gladstone reopened the Eastern question in defiance of his party's policy, and that was when Gladstone was eighty-six and there was no question of his returning to office.*

---

*This was the occasion for a rare sarcasm in one of Hartington's public speeches when he referred to Mr Gladstone's retirement on the score of old age, 'now happily overcome'.

Easter 1882 passed and Gladstone did not resign, but he kept saying that he was going to. Some compelling need of national importance was continually defeating his intention. In 1876 international evil had forced him to break his retirement; in 1880 he felt he must carry on until he had implemented the European settlement which Disraeli had negotiated at Berlin. Then 1882 came, and the need to solve the Irish question thrust the promised retirement out of sight. Since personal interest was never a motive, there was always a special crisis Gladstone was continually being called upon to resolve; as soon as he had grappled with this one, just a few months hence, he would go. The result was a perpetual state of expectation; no long-term policy could be formed, because the leadership was about to change, and the 1880–5 government exhibited a drift unmatched by any administration of the period.

The Cabinet change that began Hartington's beleaguerment was that of December 1882, when he moved from India to the War Office. At the same time Sir Charles Dilke (with Hartington's blessing) was brought into the Cabinet; nominally this balanced the previous departure of the old Radical Bright, but in fact it made a big difference, for Chamberlain and Dilke became an energetic pressure group, while Forster's retirement earlier in the year left Hartington as the only fighter in the Cabinet for a different line of policy.

The soft centre of the ministry was formed by Lords Carlingford, Derby, Kimberley and Northbrook, worthy Victorian gentlemen with a penchant for the line of least resistance. Hartington's strongest loyalty was to the splendid Lord Spencer, but he was virtually out of reach as Lord Lieutenant of Ireland. By contrast Lord Granville, still enjoying the Foreign Office in his late sixties, was proving a wobbly prop, who could be trusted only to go along with Gladstone on every issue. He remained on terms of confidence with Hartington, but the latter's dawningly satirical view is hinted by the occasion Granville complained of the difficulty of treating with a Turkish negotiator, 'a man of oriental reticence who spoke no French'. Hartington replied: 'I have no doubt that you spoke to him in excellent French, but I expect your reticence was quite as oriental as his.' To Louise Manchester he was sharper, and he told her in 1885: 'How Granville can go on making apologies for his blunders without proposing his resignation I can't imagine but it never seems to occur to him.'

The interplay between these different characters as they pulled the Cabinet this way and that has given a canvas to modern historians to paint their politics in colourful hues. In the Machiavellian scene they depict, some present

Hartington as playing an astute game of bluff, in which his reputation as an upright man aristocratically indifferent to politics and to personal ambition was the trump with which he was playing his way back to the leadership. This view is too much fashioned by the image-dominated politics of today and is at variance with the honesty which all who knew Hartington gave as his leading characteristic. His most recent biographer Patrick Jackson rightly resists this distortion, although he does not escape the temptation of fastening anger, glee and other exciting emotions on Hartington as he quotes his level-headed commentaries. It is certainly wrong to exaggerate Hartington's indifference to politics. He wanted to be Prime Minister and believed he was entitled to the post but not at all costs. From 1882 he was urging Gladstone not to retire, for he saw him as the only man capable of holding together the Whig and Radical sections in the party. He saw, too, that whichever section incurred the odium of forcing Gladstone out would ruin itself with the majority. As a corollary, it suited Gladstone's role as a linchpin that Liberal differences should be as visible as possible, and he allowed Chamberlain to go on an ever-widening rampage such as no Cabinet minister before had been permitted. The prospect of taking over a party on the verge of schism was enough to quash Hartington's personal ambition, and he began expressing to Granville and others a constant urge to retire. 'I am getting *more & more* sick of these beastly politics every day,' he wrote to Louise Manchester in 1885, repeating a complaint he had made many times over the past three years.

On the other side, Gladstone and Granville aired their fears of the Duchess's influence. 'His "antient Egeria" loyal to himself, is perpetually working against his colleagues,' wrote Granville in December 1883.* In a letter to Lord Derby at the end of that month Gladstone found Hartington's presence at Kimbolton ominous for his attitude to the Reform Bill; and three weeks later he told his wife: 'Hartington is gone to Sandringham: I am sorry to learn through Granville that *she* is there.' So it goes on until in September 1885, as he revolved plans on Irish Home Rule which he knew would not get past Hartington, Gladstone wrote to Granville: 'I think he has taken in poison at K as usual within the last three days.' With his brother's death and declining faith in Granville, it was easy to fear that Louise Manchester was the only con-

---

*Egeria was the Roman goddess with whom King Numa Pompilius regularly went apart to confer.

fidant who was a serious influence on him; but there was no change in Hartington's politics at this time. Louise had enough intelligence to know that trying to turn him into a crypto-Tory was not going to help in making him the next Liberal Prime Minister, and she had enough ruthlessness to subordinate policies to power. We have seen her in the 1870s urging Hartington to forge an alliance with the older-style Radicals to defeat Chamberlain, and we may be sure that her calculations now were on similar lines. However Hartington may have seen it, Louise's case against Chamberlain and Dilke was not that they were Radicals but that they were rivals. One can thus easily see her steeling him to take a tough line in Cabinet that would avoid his becoming a pushover. Hartington's views, as he pressed them at this time, did not reflect Tory influence; rather they were representative of a solid body of Liberal opinion in the country which was becoming alienated from Gladstone and the wilder spasms of Liberal policy – a constituency which was to follow Hartington in secession from Gladstone after 1886.

Confidence from Gladstone's side was not in evidence. Hartington had stepped back into line behind him in 1880; he had always treated Gladstone, in his negligent way, as a friend of his father's and virtually a family member, but there had never been rapport between them, and Hartington's jokes in Cabinet were always taken by Gladstone with deadly seriousness. It is comical to see Lord Granville corresponding with Gladstone about Hartington's opinions and probable reactions as if the latter two were separated by some linguistic chasm across which only Granville could interpret. If Hartington stood recognized as the only successor, it was not through the leader's blessing but because of the hard work and ability that lay behind his lazy manner.

The conduct of the Radicals has been reassessed in recent times by historians, who argue in revisionist mood that their aim in these years was not to force the Whigs out but to stake their own claim for a strong position in Hartington's coming administration. 'What really needs to be stressed', write A.B. Cooke and John Vincent, 'is how, much of the time, Chamberlain and Dilke were looking forward to taking their place in his government.' In view of the ease with which Chamberlain fell into the role of Hartington's lieutenant in 1886, there may be some truth in this. It is more realistic to recognize, though, that the Radicals saw Hartington's leadership as a transitional period which would end when he succeeded as Duke of Devonshire. They saw no need to oust him earlier, but from that point he and the rest of the Whigs would be yesterday's men, and the Radicals would be in control. That of course made it all the more important for them to consolidate their position while they served under him. What made the Radicals so confident was the impending franchise reform. A new Reform Bill was the one certain Liberal policy due in this Parliament; Hartington himself had promised it in 1877, and the Radicals thought they needed only one more franchise extension to sweep the country. In fact they were wrong: in 1885 they got a Reform measure tailor-made for their ends, and they failed conspicuously in the polls. If the Reform Bill and election had come earlier, Hartington's position would have been transformed; he would have been able to take the premiership in the knowledge that Chamberlain's and Dilke's radicalism would remain a minority movement for the foreseeable future and therefore in no position to dictate terms to the Whigs or the centre.

In the same line we need to note recent writers' denial of the old assumption that the Whigs were on their way out. The election of 1880 had produced, out of 346 Liberal MPs, 151 who were members of the aristocracy or landed gentry, a proportion (43.6 per cent) higher than in the 1874 Parliament. The notion that such a phalanx was about to melt away, or that the party could do without it, was another example of Radical optimism. It included a number of serious-minded young aristocrats who were keen to develop a distinctive Whig programme. Chief of them was Albert Grey, the nephew and heir of Earl Grey whose father had passed the Great Reform Act, and their links to the Chief Whip, Lord Richard Grosvenor (brother of the Duke of Westminster), put them in an influential position. Hartington steered clear of acting as the leader of this section, but privately he looked to them for support and they certainly pinned their hopes on him. As Lord Rosebery's ditty put it in 1885:

> On goose's sauce exists the gander
> And the Whigs upon the *Dish*.*

Nevertheless Hartington's refusal or failure to build up a body of support for himself either in Cabinet or in Parliament was a main factor in his difficulties at this period.

Rosebery himself was another example of rising Whig talent, this time in the Lords. Gladstone offered him the post of Indian Under-Secretary under

---

*'Dish' was a recognized levity for Cavendish. Compare the horrendous pun retailed by Disraeli when Hartington was elected Leader that whereas the Whigs had been dished by the 1867 Reform Act now they had been Cavendished.

Hartington in 1880, and although there was no one with whom he would have been happier to begin his political career he felt it would look too much of a pay-off for his stage-management of the Midlothian campaign, and he refused. That did not prevent his rise being swift, and by 1885 he was in the Cabinet. An intellectual and wit who was also a keen racing man, and a friend of Louise Manchester and the Prince of Wales, he formed perhaps the closest political friendship with Hartington and one that remained unchanged despite their later divergence.

Hartington's move to the War Office late in 1882 gave him responsibility for a problem which was to become the nemesis of Gladstone's ministry. Just before, with uncharacteristic vigour, the Cabinet had resolved to deal with a rebellion in Egypt by sending an army there and taking unofficial charge of the country's government, so as to safeguard the British investment in the Suez Canal. The Egyptian rebellion, however, had gone alongside another in the Sudan, the vast Saharan hinterland which was under Egyptian rule. The insurgent here was the Muslim visionary who styled himself the Mahdi and proclaimed a religious war against his enemies. The army sent by the Egyptian government to quell him was destroyed in November 1883. This was strictly no affair of Britain's, but the massacred commander had been an Englishman, Hicks Pasha, and national sentiment demanded at least a policy. The decision made was to withdraw all Egyptians from the Sudan and leave the country to the mercy of the rebels. But a more fateful choice was that of the man appointed to conduct the operation; this was 'Chinese Gordon', the Royal Engineer officer who had acquired his nickname in 1863–5, when he took service with the Chinese government and suppressed the Tai-Ping rebellion, winning thirty-three battles. Apart from his military genius, his choice sprang from the fact that he had just served as Governor of the Sudan in 1877–80 under the Khedive of Egypt and had had unprecedented success, restoring order and suppressing the slave trade which dominated the south of the country.

Hartington took the lead in choosing Gordon for the new task, seconded principally by Lord Northbrook, the First Lord of the Admiralty, whose cousin Evelyn Baring was the all-powerful British adviser to the Egyptian government. There was, however, a danger lurking in this appointment. The government, in opting for evacuation, had taken the course that seemed to minimize its commitment, but that was not in fact the case. It would have been perfectly feasible to hold the eastern half of the Sudan between the Nile and the Red Sea, including the capital Khartoum. To evacuate the Egyptian garrisons, officials and other loyalists was actually going to be more difficult than maintaining the status quo. Gordon was not temperamentally fitted to carry out a defeatist policy, least of all in a country that had been in his recent care. The Liberal Cabinet was later blamed for sending the wrong man for the job, but Hartington instinctively believed in a more active policy, and he at once supported Gordon in his efforts on the spot to save the situation. He met the General only briefly on 18 January 1884, the day of his departure. Gordon was summoned to the War Office and given his instructions by Lord Wolseley, who had commanded the recent British invasion of Egypt; then he went in to see the Secretary of State, who was there with Lords Granville and Northbrook and Sir Charles Dilke. Of the four, he carried away the best impression of Hartington and Granville. The General left the same evening, and Hartington went with Granville and Northbrook to see him off at Charing Cross. Gordon was a very careless man in practical matters, and the Foreign Secretary asked him before he left if he had plenty of money; searching his pockets, he found he had none at all. Granville himself could only produce about three half-crowns; so Hartington hurried off to the station-master and borrowed £30 from him just before the train left.

Gordon, on arriving in Egypt, accepted the Khedive's appointment as Governor of the Sudan and went to Khartoum, where he rapidly threw over the plans to evacuate the country. His aim was to set up an effective government that would stand up against the rebellion, and the man he chose to head it was Zobeir, one of the group of powerful slave-traders who had until recently dominated the country. Gordon had fought against Zobeir while combating the trade and had killed his son, but he saw him as a man strong enough to hold the country together against the Mahdi. When these proposals were received in England the government refused, the employment of a former slave-trader being deemed offensive to British Liberal opinion. Gladstone's biographer commented: 'To run all the risks involved in the dispatch of Gordon, and then immediately to refuse the request that he persistently represented as furnishing him his only chance, was an incoherence that the Parliament and people of England have not often surpassed.'

Almost straight away the question arose of sending a British expedition to rescue Gordon at Khartoum, but for some time it was not certain that he was in danger. Hartington, receiving unclear reports at his War Office desk, wanted to go out to Egypt to supervise the business on the spot (in the same way he had regretted in 1880 that he was not going to India as Viceroy to sort out the Afghan entanglement in person). But he consoled himself with the thought that an expedition was out of the question for the moment on climatic grounds. He firmly told Queen Victoria on 26 March that British troops could not be sent in the height of the Egyptian summer and would have to wait until late August, before the Nile began to fall, when boats could be sent up the river. Gladstone was happy at this excuse to avoid a decision, but Hartington did not want it postponed until the last moment. When Baring began from Egypt to urge an expedition, Hartington was for beginning preparations straight away, in mid-April, to be ready at the beginning of the autumn. But he was blocked by indecision in the Cabinet; after a meeting in late April he was so baffled as to what, if anything, had been decided that he had to write to Granville for enlightenment. Lord Derby's description helps us to understand this: 'Our discussion was long, and as usual in such cases, rather desultory: quite amicable, no sign of temper on the part of anyone, but much perplexity, and no agreement as to what should be done.' In mid-May Hartington addressed a circular letter to the Cabinet urging immediate preparations; but no decision came.

In other ways much of the strain of Gladstone's failing health was falling on Hartington. Besides his regular parliamentary leadership in the small hours, he took charge in January–February 1883 when Gladstone was convalescing in Cannes. Gladstone was again out of action in the spring of 1884. In Cabinet Hartington generally found himself the only minister standing up against Chamberlain's and Dilke's radical pressure and reacted by being so violent (as Reginald Brett lamented) that he sometimes forgot his own Liberal views. Lord Derby wrote in November 1884 that his 'observations are frequent, but generally mere growls of dissent. He does not like his situation, and makes the fact evident.'

A view of Hartington's habits at the War Office is given by Guy Fleetwood Wilson, the young and recently appointed assistant private secretary. Hartington was about to go away for two or three days, and to guard against his slipping out unnoticed Wilson charged a messenger to tell him the moment the Secretary of State left his room. He thus intercepted Hartington on the staircase and asked him for his address in case of urgent developments. His chief, still proceeding down the stairs, muttered the address of Holker unintelligibly into his beard, and the nervous secretary had to ask again. Hartington repeated the name in the same off-hand growl, and a third enquiry still failed to enlighten Wilson. He was reduced to sending a War Office messenger to tail Hartington to the station, where an interrogation of his valet revealed Holker Hall, Cark-in-Cartmel, as the baffling Cumbrian toponymics.

The same official describes how he had to inform Hartington of some disaster in the Egyptian conflict.* He received the news at the War Office at four in the morning, and immediately went off to Devonshire House. When he got there the servants told him that his Lordship had gone to bed only an hour before, after cards at the Turf Club, and they dared not disturb him. He was shown the door of Hartington's room and left to take the responsibility himself. Penetrating into the uncomfortable little bedroom, Wilson roused his chief from sleep and told him the news. The slow effort to shake off his drowsiness and to take in the news was painful to watch, especially as Hartington was incapable of concealing his shame and humiliation at the national reverse.

By now Gladstone was playing a cat-and-mouse game of skilful indecision. As Lytton Strachey puts it: 'He delayed, he postponed, he raised interminable difficulties, he prevaricated, he was silent, he disappeared.' Hartington, however, was a man who might be baffled but did not give up. He had given way on so many issues in the interests of Cabinet unity, but here the case was altered; in the censure debate which the Tories had moved in April he had given his pledge that Gordon would be supported. As he told Granville: 'It is a question of personal honour and good faith, and I don't see how I can yield upon it.' The inactivity frustrated him, however, and at the Derby Day dinner with Granville he was particularly depressed about the Sudan, telling him: 'We should be better there than here.' On 15 July he wrote to the same confidant: 'At the last Cabinet when it was mentioned, summoned, as I hoped, to decide upon it, I got five minutes at the fag end, and was as usual put off. Another fortnight has passed, and the end of the session is approaching. I cannot be responsible for military policy in Egypt under such conditions.' Parliament was due to rise in early August, and after that it would be too late. On 31 July Hartington cut the Gordian knot: he wrote to the Prime Minister

---

*According to Fleetwood Wilson, it was the death of Gordon, but the news of that was surely expected (*see* p. 155). Perhaps he was remembering the death of Hicks Pasha in November 1883.

and threatened to resign if the expedition was not sent. 'When Mr Gladstone read the words,' writes Strachey, 'he realized that the game was over.' Hartington was given the go-ahead to prepare an expedition almost in secret during the parliamentary recess. Four months later Lord Derby was writing in his diary: 'To this hour I do not know who was responsible for the sending of Gordon to Khartoum nor when the expedition for his relief was finally settled.' Chamberlain wrote to Dilke with sour exaggeration in September: 'Hartington is getting his own way about the Nile expedition and bang go 5 millions! This whole business is directly contrary to my advice and to the decision of the Cabinet – as far as the Cabinet ever decides anything.' On 5 October Lord Wolseley marched into the Sudan, and for four months the British public had to wait as his army fought its way up the 850 miles of the Nile to reach Khartoum.

There was a special reason why in 1884 Gladstone's mind was not on the Sudan. He was in the process of giving the country the third Reform Bill, and much of the year was taken up with controversy over its details. By early 1885, however, these had been settled and Gladstone, who was ill again, seemed definitely on the way out. On 4 January Harcourt came to Devonshire House to plan with Hartington the new ministry. Lords Granville, Derby and Carlingford were to be asked to retire; Harcourt would take Lord Selborne's place as Lord Chancellor; Dilke would become Foreign Secretary. The question was how Gladstone was to be eased out. He went to stay with the Duke of Devonshire at Holker at the end of January, and here the son of the house unexpectedly appeared, resolved on a course of killing the Prime Minister by kindness. The two got on unusually well, and Hartington wrote to Louise Manchester on 3 February that Gladstone was 'really looking forward to his retirement soon'. Life at Holker followed its peaceful tenor. On the morning of 5 February a telegram arrived for Hartington from the War Office, and as usual Hartington got up very late; it was not until after eleven that he opened the telegram. He sat down with Gladstone to decode it, and as they worked through it the details of a catastrophe unfolded. Lord Wolseley's troops had fought their way to Khartoum on 28 January, but the town had fallen to the Mahdi two days previously, after a siege of 317 days. The fate of Gordon was unknown.

Immediately Gladstone sent off telegrams summoning the Cabinet, and he and Hartington departed for London. Before they left Gladstone received a telegram from the Queen; it had been sent unencoded for any village post-mistress to read:

These news from Khartoum are frightful, and to think that all this might have been prevented and many precious lives saved by earlier action is too frightful. Express to Lord Wolseley my great sorrow and anxiety at these news, and my sympathy with Lord Wolseley in this great anxiety; pray, but have little hope, brave Gordon may yet be alive.

Gladstone thought at first he would have to resign after receiving such a public rebuke from his sovereign. But the Queen shrank from pressing the matter and took out her anger on the Secretary for War. Hartington described the experience to a friend: 'She rated me as if I'd been a footman.' 'Why didn't she send for the butler?' asked the friend. 'Oh, the butler generally manages to keep out of the way on such occasions.'

And now an extraordinary change came over Gladstone. The Prime Minister who had seemed about to leave Downing Street for a Bath chair became, in the hour of need, the man of action. The censure debate, mishandled by the Tories, proved a triumph for him. The fact that he had stalled the rescue expedition for three months was not disclosed. Hartington, who had always favoured a strong Egyptian policy, personally committed himself to wiping out the disgrace by retaking Khartoum with a new and bigger expedition. With the logic peculiar to sentimental politics, the death of one British officer was to be avenged by the conquest of a country which had been deemed useless and the defeat of a victorious rebellion which, while still in its infancy, had been judged irresistible. Thus Gladstone shone forth as the saviour of his country, and ministers who had quietly been paying court to Hartington hitched themselves back on to his bandwagon. As with the party anarchy of the past five years, the general public remained ignorant of the lofty choreography which kept Gladstone on his pedestal.

A few weeks later these plans were sidelined by an event in central Asia, where Russia annexed Penjdeh on the border of Afghanistan, threatening that country and therefore British India. War seemed to loom with Russia, a much more serious adversary than the Mahdi, and Parliament voted £11 million to face the threat. This meant that the reconquest of the Sudan had to be shelved. No other action would have been rational, but to Hartington it was a sharp humiliation to abandon a course on which he had publicly given his word. His mortification over the whole Sudan business was, psychologically, one of the strongest factors in preparing the break with his Liberal colleagues.

There was no attraction to the opposite side. Lord Randolph Churchill had embarked on a blatant policy of angling for Home Rule support, to the extent that he spoke out for Irish murderers and promised Parnell the discontinuation of Coercion. With this agreement, the Tories and Irish defeated the government on the Budget in June 1885; Gladstone had been reiterating his intention to retire in the near future, and the Chief Whip, Lord Richard Grosvenor, was suspected of having connived at the defeat by very lax whipping. The changes of the third Reform Act were not ready yet, and no election could be held until December. Lord Salisbury chose to take office in a caretaker government with Irish support, although even that did not give him a majority.

Still Gladstone did not retire. Chamberlain, with the election looming, set about pushing a Radical programme which would put himself and Dilke in the saddle after the expected landslide victory. The 'Unauthorized Programme', formulated in a series of potent speeches, was aimed as much at the Whigs in his own party as at the Tories, and attacked aristocracy and property in a way never heard of from a senior political figure; he invented the doctrine of 'Ransom', which was to be exacted of the propertied for the enjoyment of their privileges. This was at best a new departure from traditional Liberalism, in which the rights of property were the cornerstone of a *laissez-faire* system. Chamberlain's follower Jesse Collings was demanding 'Three Acres and a Cow' – the creation of small land-holdings for agricultural labourers; Chamberlain agitated for compulsory land purchase (with his town-council mind he wanted to municipalize land ownership), free public education (until then a small fee was payable even in state schools) and graduated income tax to replace the existing flat rate.

Surprisingly, this savage bark was far worse than Chamberlain's bite. In his violent way, he was throwing down bargaining counters to gain concessions from the Whigs. He went to Hartington and said that if one item in his programme was conceded he would be ready to drop the rest; he did not much care which it was, and suggested either the Three Acres or free education. Hartington was unfamiliar with this Birmingham version of the methods of the *souk* and sent Chamberlain away with a flea in his ear, confirming him in his view that Hartington was absolutely impossible. The latter was determined that Chamberlain should be disavowed. In late August he made a strong anti-Radical speech in his own constituency and wrote to Gladstone demanding that his position be upheld. Gladstone's own election address when it appeared was received by Chamberlain as 'a slap in the face', and he was obliged to retreat from his line that he would not join the government unless his programme were accepted. Nevertheless, it would be wrong to see Hartington as playing an imperturbable tactical game. In June, just before they went to the Derby together, Rosebery had found him 'gloomy and ill' and talking of impending revolution, and later in the year George Leveson Gower (Lord Granville's nephew), staying at Chatsworth, was told by Hartington that he had just read one of Chamberlain's speeches which made him feel physically sick. The Radicals seemed bent on driving the Whigs out of the party, and it looked like being very hard work to stop them.

The election results of December 1885, however, falsified both Chamberlain's hopes and Hartington's fears. There was no sweeping Liberal victory and no surge of Radicalism. Out of the 334 Liberal MPs, Lord Richard Grosvenor credited the Radicals with 101. There were 55 members from titled and 50 from gentry families, a lower proportion (31.4 per cent) than in the previous Parliament but not much less than in 1874–80. Other things being equal, the Radicals would have had to look forward to a permanent position of balance with the Whigs. But other things were about to become very far from equal.

9
The Passing of the Whigs

THE WRITER WILFRID Ward told an anecdote about a dinner-party he attended with the Prime Minister before the government resigned in 1885. Hartington arrived hungry after a day of committees and was obviously not pleased by the succession of trifling French dishes which formed the early part of the dinner; when roast beef was brought in he exclaimed: 'Hurrah! Something to eat at last', and his taciturnity thawed out. Silence fell on him again, however, when the ladies withdrew and Gladstone started to talk theology. One of the other guests was Bishop (later Cardinal) Vaughan, who belonged to an old family of Monmouthshire squires and who, while at school in Belgium, had been known as Milord Roastbeef among his more pasty-faced companions; he showed himself as uninterested as Hartington in Mr Gladstone's intelligence from the heavenly courts, and they removed themselves to the other end of the table to discuss country sports, laying the foundation of a permanent friendship. The event was still in Hartington's memory eighteen years later when Wilfrid Ward met him and reminded him of their earlier acquaintance. He looked blank for a moment and then exclaimed: 'Of course I remember. We had nothing to eat.'

The story reminds us how far Hartington still was from being a twin soul of Gladstone's, and this distance had much to do with his reaction to his leader's Irish plans. Ever since the 1881 Land Act the Liberals had been looking for further ways to remedy the discontent of Ireland, and at the beginning of 1883 Gladstone proposed four councils for the four ancient provinces of Ireland. This had a superficial attractiveness, since it granted self-government without the nationalist strength of a single body and gave scope for the separateness of Protestant Ulster. But closer thought revealed it as artificial: the provinces had no real identity and the historic Ulster of nine counties (as opposed to the six counties of modern Northern Ireland) had a Catholic majority, so that the Protestants would still not be guaranteed their haven. When Gladstone left to convalesce in Cannes in mid-January Hartington took steps to scuttle the plan. He made a public speech against it and at the next Cabinet meeting stated that he would refuse to lead the opening debate when Parliament met if it were adopted. Gladstone received a letter that there was no support for his scheme in the government.

The same year Chamberlain proposed county councils to have charge of local government. This was precisely the policy that Hartington had urged in 1873, but now he replied: 'This is not a time.' The situation in Ireland had been transformed, and he believed that any such councils set up now would simply become further organs of sedition. The essential need was to restore law and order and defeat Parnell, and only in an Ireland returned to tranquillity could such bodies be trusted.

Lord Spencer's policy of firm government alongside practical concessions received Hartington's strong support, and by 1885 it appeared to be reaping its benefits; only if both parties upheld it could there be any hope of pacifying Ireland. It therefore made Hartington angry when the Tories, in execution of their pact with Parnell, threw over Spencer's firm regime and denigrated Spencer for enforcing it. Hartington was particularly close to Spencer at this time. He went to stay with him at Viceregal Lodge shortly before the government's resignation, and he spoke warmly in his support against Tory attacks in Parliament in July.

He was not being reassured by the attitude of his own leader. After speaking to Gladstone about Ireland, on 7 August he wrote to Granville: 'I can never understand Mr. Gladstone in conversation, but I thought him unusually unintelligible yesterday.' The fact was that Gladstone had been convinced for more than a year that Home Rule must come – which was not the same as wanting to grant it himself. For tactical reasons, he hoped that the Tories would espouse the measure (they would have less trouble getting it through the Lords, and it would save Gladstone a fight with the Whigs); and with their turncoat policy in 1885 it almost looked as if they would oblige him. But this hope did not make practical sense: a Liberal landslide was expected in the December elections, and the Tories would be out. Gladstone was therefore keeping an enigmatic silence with a view to educating his party (its Whig section, supposedly, reduced to tatters) for action in the envisaged 1886–91 Parliament. His reticence, however, proved unfortunate; Parnell saw the Tories as his friends, and just before the election the nationalist leader ordered Irish voters in English seats to cast their votes for the Conservatives. There is dispute as to how much difference this made, but the election result was certainly dramatic: the Liberals emerged with a majority of 86 over the Tories and the Home Rulers with precisely 86 seats. Parnell had robbed Gladstone of what might have been a small or a substantial majority and thus of the independence which would have allowed him to change front with a disinterested appearance. Lord Salisbury chose to remain in office until Parliament met in the new year and the Irish decided whether to support him or throw him out.

By now all political leaders, both Tory and Liberal, had come round to acceptance of enlarged local government in Ireland. Hartington made a speech in Belfast on 5 November which set out his own view, declaring: 'I would not shrink from a bold reconstruction of the Government of Ireland.' His approach to the Irish question had always been a pragmatic one, and he accepted that the government was too centralized and unable to meet practical local needs. For this very reason he found little comfort in Lord Salisbury's vague promise, in October 1885, of a 'large central authority' in Ireland. As a devolutionary policy it was a step forward, but it implicitly ignored Ulster, which in Hartington's view demanded separate treatment.

In mid-December, however, while the election results were still being declared, Gladstone's son Herbert let the Home Rule cat out of the bag. Hartington challenged Gladstone, who replied that he had 'more or less of opinions and ideas, but no intentions or negotiations'. Neither Hartington nor the country was pacified by such evasions, and before the end of the year Hartington wrote a public letter making clear his rejection of Home Rule. He felt he had no choice. He had been accused of too much yielding and, as he thought, with justice. If he did not make a stand here, he might as well abandon the hope of being thought a man of principle. Moreover Ireland, although he was not given to saying so publicly, was a subject on which Gladstone's acts of statesmanship provoked mounting exasperation. In 1873 he had sought to impose an unwanted University Bill but had been indifferent to the nationalization of Irish railways and ignored Hartington's proposals for county boards. 'At that period,' Hartington remarked in a speech in June 1886, 'I was under the impression that I was perhaps more of a Home Ruler than Mr Gladstone himself.' Gladstone's bent was for dramatic acts of justice rather than practical measures. From 1853, when he first became Chancellor of the Exchequer, he had laid an increasingly heavy burden of tax on Ireland, beginning by extending income tax to that country, which had previously been exempt. With the financial pedantry which led him at one point to propose taxing charities, he refused to see that a backward rural economy like Ireland's was not ready for a fiscal system designed for the most advanced industrial society in the world. Gladstone liked to prescribe remedies for parts of the world he did not know, such as the Balkans, to which he never travelled, or Ireland, to which he had made a three-week visit in 1877. Hartington's view of Ireland was based on a lifetime's knowledge of it, and when measures of genuine benefit were proposed, such as the 1881 Land Act, he was ready to support them. What also annoyed him about Gladstone's Home Rule conversion was the way in which, springing fully armed from the great man's head, it was expected to be received without consultation or discussion by a loyal party. This was not the way in which older leaders, or Hartington himself, had formulated policy, and it was the cause of his remark, 'Did any leader ever treat a party in such a way as he has done?'

At the end of 1885 William Harcourt proposed a meeting of leading Liberals opposed to a Home Rule scheme, and this was held at Devonshire House on new year's day. Chamberlain and Dilke were there, but Granville stayed away – an omen of his growing political distance from Hartington. They resolved that Hartington should demand a declaration of policy from Gladstone before the party took any steps to unseat the Tories in the new session; but Gladstone refused to be drawn. Hartington had a difficult game to play. The party had not yet been committed to Home Rule, or against it, and if he took too strong a stand he might cause a split. He held that Gladstone must be allowed to present his Home Rule project and see it fail in Parliament; when it did so, another policy would be viable, but as he wrote to Louise Manchester: 'Mr G with an undeveloped plan in his pocket would be a terrible force against us.' For that very reason he voted on 26 January against the Liberal amendment that brought the Tory government down; by thus distancing himself from his party he ruled himself out as its immediate leader. But he told Gladstone personally that he would make no attempt to lead an opposition group or stop people joining the new Cabinet. Taking heart, Gladstone even invited him to take office on the basis of 'examining' proposals for Home Rule without committing himself to them, but Hartington sent a characteristic reply: 'I am unable to attach great importance to a distinction between examination and the actual conception and announcement of a plan.' Gladstone's third ministry was formed without him, but without souring relations, so that Gladstone was quite taken aback when Hartington opposed the Home Rule Bill in Parliament.

The Tories were licking their lips over all this, and saw their chance for the Hartington secession which they had been trying to engineer for the past three years. Knowing Hartington's mortification at having to yield so many times to his colleagues' views, Lord Randolph Churchill had played on it in a speech during the election campaign, comparing Hartington to a boa constrictor swallowing one unacceptable policy after another. If there was one thing Hartington was sensitive about, it was accusations of not riding straight (if one may shift to a more Hartingtonian metaphor). Lord Randolph was prepared to do penance for his witticism, and he wrote on 13 January apologizing to Hartington, who replied with generosity. The reconciliation proceeded gradually; Hartington and Churchill were observed to ignore each other less pointedly at the Turf Club. The moneyed men whom Hartington and Louise Manchester were increasingly cultivating were active in the matter, and the Liberals among them were Unionist to a man.* They included the Rothschilds and the popular *bon vivant* Henry Oppenheim. He brought Hartington and Churchill together over dinner, and the result was an invitation for Churchill to go down to Compton Place and see the latest improvements at the Polegate stud farm. By early March he was working politically with Hartington and was not pleased at a too-spontaneous jest made by his wife when, dining with Hartington, she asked him whether he intended to respond to the Tories' call to come over to them. 'I have not yet decided,' he said, 'but when I do I suppose I shall be thought either a man or a mouse.' 'Or a rat,' she replied, and Hartington laughed, as Lady Randolph expressed it, *d'un rire jaune.* When she repeated this to her husband he gave her a lecture: 'Those are the sort of remarks which upset a coach.'

The last thing Hartington was contemplating, however, was crossing the floor. He expected Gladstone's project to fail, and he saw Chamberlain on the verge of leaving the Cabinet. He did not want, even by taking too open an anti-Home-Rule line, to encourage him to swallow his principles and stay on as the next leader of a de-Whigged Liberal Party; Gladstone, however, underrated

---

*Louise herself was not deflected by these momentous events from her usual late-winter visit to the Continent; after staying at Hardwick in January she was at Nice in February–March 1886.

the danger from Chamberlain. His proposed Home Rule Bill was presented on 26 March; Chamberlain resigned and Gladstone made no effort to keep him. A surprisingly quick collaboration sprang up between Hartington and Chamberlain, and the former's task was greatly eased. He was able to attack the Home Rule proposals without the fear of a clash of policy from Chamberlain. On 14 May the alliance was cemented when sixty-four Liberals, drawn equally from Hartington's and Chamberlain's followings, met at Devonshire House in the early stages of the Second Reading, forming the nucleus of the Liberal Unionist party.

The 1886 Home Rule Bill was a measure prepared in a hurry and had a number of grave defects. The most fundamental was its acceptance of the nationalist myth that Parnell spoke for a united Ireland; while professing to liberate that kingdom from an alien government in London it subjected the Protestant north-east to an equally alien government in Dublin. The second was that it would have handed over the Anglo-Irish ascendancy, which still owned most of the land throughout the country, to a virtual peasant *Jacquerie* which the virulently nationalist regime under Parnell would have little incentive to oppose; hence the Bill was accompanied by another which sought to buy out the landed class almost at a stroke with the aid of a huge Treasury loan. Third, there were defects in the Bill that would have made it unworkable: Irish members were to be excluded from the Westminster Parliament to form their own at Dublin, and at first sight some English members (indeed Hartington himself), sick of parliamentary disruption, were tempted by this feature; but reflection showed that Ireland could not be excluded from an imperial Parliament which retained overall authority and in particular the right of taxation. While thus denying Ireland its due in one aspect, the Bill gave too much in others; a separate legislature and executive meant virtual independence. Gladstone, with his capacity for taking refuge in words, insisted that the supremacy of the imperial Parliament was preserved; but Hartington saw that this would count for nothing against the reality of a strongly nationalist regime under Parnell. He replied to these arguments, 'Mr Gladstone and I do not mean the same thing by supremacy.' Even an Irish nationalist can recognize that the 1886 Home Rule Bill, if it had been passed, would have been a disaster. That of 1893 would have been far safer for many reasons: it made provision for the retention of Irish members in the British Parliament; the buying-out of the landed class was well under way by then.

The country had been pacified by seven years of firm law-and-order policies; and the death of Parnell had brought the Irish Home Rule Party to a less pathological frame of mind. There was still one insuperable defect: the insistence on putting Ulster under a Dublin government. Randolph Churchill coined the slogan, 'Ulster will fight, and Ulster will be right', a prediction in which one day he would nearly be vindicated.

Since Hartington is remembered as the man who wrecked Home Rule, it is worth setting out what his positive policy for Ireland was. He considered, first, that county councils ought to be established to handle the local-government needs which the Westminster Parliament was failing to meet; but he held that such bodies should first be set up in Great Britain as a sort of trial run and should not be extended to Ireland until sedition had been quelled by a firm government policy. The executive would in any case have to retain strong powers, to prevent the councils from undermining a law-and-order administration. The county councils were in fact set up in Ireland in 1896, eight years after the English ones, by the Unionist government of which Hartington was a member. Second, he had now come round to the view that a sweeping measure of land purchase would have to be adopted. The already radical interference with property rights in the 1881 Land Act had been left behind by events, and Victorian *laissez faire* was forced to contemplate the buying-out of an entire class, with huge allocations of taxpayers' money to fund it. The Irish peasant wanted his own land, and no peace would be possible until he was assisted in buying it. Lord Salisbury's short government of 1885 had already embarked on that path; when he brought in – against factious Irish opposition – a second land-purchase Bill in 1890, Hartington supported it, and he was to take extensive advantage of it after he succeeded to his father's estates. So far from his Irish policy being dictated by landlord prejudice, it was precisely on questions of land tenure that he showed himself most radical. Third, he may already have adopted the policy of two sub-national assemblies in Ireland, one in Dublin and one in Belfast, although he did not declare himself in that sense until 1887. This was the only part of Hartington's policy which he did not see implemented by a Unionist administration before the end of his life.

Hartington's prescription kept within a firm assertion of British imperial rule; this was partly because of the patriotic grounding which he had inherited from Palmerston and partly because he refused to accept the justice of handing over the large unionist minority to a Home Rule regime. Another essential feature of Hartington's approach was its gradualism; the changes he proposed for Ireland were far-reaching ones, and he was convinced that the country would need time to adapt to them. This alone set him at odds with Gladstone's preference for a sudden measure to resolve the Irish crisis at a stroke. All through his life Hartington's interest in dramatic gestures was nil, and he absolutely refused to be stampeded into premature action. The way he looked at it was that Ireland's population was only one-seventh of the United Kingdom's,* and of that only two-thirds was supporting the nationalist revolt; the situation might look grim, but the disparity in numbers was too large to justify panic action. At one point indeed he was talking of a draconian scheme whereby an almost powerless Irish Parliament might be created, as little more than an excuse to remove the Irish members from Westminster, and the country governed virtually as a Crown colony; but he saw that only as a last resort, if every other policy were tried and failed. In 1886 he considered that that situation was far from being reached. Over the next twenty years British rule went far to justify his calm by redressing many of the practical grievances of Ireland and defusing the revolutionary situation stirring in the 1880s.

In a series of speeches on the First Reading of the Bill in April, on the Second Reading in May and in the country, Hartington set out the practical case against Home Rule. He had by now the reputation of a weighty speaker, but his oratory on behalf of the Union took everyone by surprise. Reginald Brett said of his performance on the First Reading: 'Until he sat down after his speech no one on either side of the House knew what he could do.' Harry Chaplin told him: 'If it has half the effect in the country that it has had here, it will make you Prime Minister for certain.' After his speech on the Second Reading, which was equally fine, the Ulstermen waiting in the lobbies carried him out shoulder high. Almost for the first time in his career he spoke on a subject of deep conviction – and without having to trim his beliefs to party policy; his energy took aback those inured to his lethargic manner. When the Second Reading of the Home Rule Bill was put to the vote on 7 June it was defeated, with ninety-three Liberals joining the Tories in the lobby against it.

Until then relations between Gladstone's followers and those of Hartington and Chamberlain had remained on terms of easy badinage. In May

---

*That is, 5 million out of a total of 35 million.

Gladstone gave a dinner for the Queen's official birthday, and there were so many dissentient Liberals present that (having prepared the joke beforehand) he told Hartington that if he moved a vote of no confidence against him in the dining room he would probably carry it. Later Hartington met Harcourt, Gladstone's Chancellor of the Exchequer, at Lord Londonderry's and expressed surprise at finding him in the house of the author of the Union.* Harcourt replied: 'I came to point out to you that the author of the Union ended by *cutting his own throat*, a warning which I commend to your attention.' Harcourt, as we have seen, had been the instigator of the anti-Home-Rule meeting at Devonshire House at the beginning of the year and openly proclaimed his disbelief in Gladstone's proposals; he had nevertheless accepted office from him, in the confidence that they would be defeated in Parliament. He was never a man to let a principled stand get in the way of his own career. Lady Harcourt, dining with Hartington, said to him, 'I think you would like to hang my husband.' 'No, not exactly hang him,' replied Hartington, 'only suspend him for a while.' After the defeat of the Bill, however, things turned nasty. Hartington had been expecting Gladstone to stand down at once, and was prepared to take over as Prime Minister, but Gladstone decided to put Home Rule to the test of an election. 'I was assured by experts that we should sweep the country,' he said later. With that expectation, his choice is understandable, and the parties realigned themselves for a battle on his proposals for Ireland.

The Rothschilds were still busy promoting the strategy of Tory and Liberal Unionist collaboration, and Arthur Balfour wrote to Lord Salisbury on 15 June: 'We had a coalition party at Waddesden [Ferdinand Rothschild's château in Buckinghamshire]. – Chamberlain, Hartington & his Duchess, Randolph, H. Chaplin &c.' The inclusion of 'Hartington's Duchess' alongside the elected politicians is significant. The result was a pact that the Tories would not oppose any of Hartington's and Chamberlain's followers, and with this luxury seventy-seven of the ninety-three held their seats. The Conservatives emerged as the largest party with 317 MPs; the Liberals and Home Rulers together had 276. Home Rule was decisively defeated, but the Conservatives would be dependent on Liberal Unionist votes to form a government.

In Gladstone's view Hartington's defection was a major cause of the Lib-

---

*Lord Castlereagh succeeded as 2nd Marquess of Londonderry shortly before his death.

eral defeat, such was the respect for his judgement within great tracts of the middle class. Even now Hartington clung to the belief that Gladstone would stand down, and for the first time he felt that the time was ripe for him to lead the Liberal Party; but wishful thinking deluded him. For four years Gladstone had been saying that the preservation of Liberal unity was the only motive that kept him in office; despite himself, he was indispensable. Now he had split the party but had discovered another starring role, that of the only English states-man prepared to grant justice to Ireland. Not Hartington's nor Chamberlain's nor Salisbury's proposals could be allowed any merit in that cause. The Whig MP Lord Arthur Russell (the Duke of Bedford's brother) wrote in August: 'Generally, disagreement with him produces sorrow that people can be so blind as not to see the truth, then he warms up, is shocked at your want of all moral feeling, and overpowers you with a speech which reduces you to silence.' His last apocalyptic phase as Liberal leader had begun and was to last for a fur-ther eight years until he retired at the age of eighty-four.

The Liberal Unionists did not yet believe that their schism was perma-nent, and they did not want to make it so by coalition with the Conservatives. Chamberlain told Arthur Balfour just before 24 July that he believed Glad-stone would retire, but the one thing that would stop him would be Hartington's taking office as Prime Minister with Tory support, 'in which case pure malevolence would induce him to hold on!' Hartington, although he would not have put it so savagely, was making the same calculation; his prime aim was Liberal reunion, and a formal coalition with the Conservatives would be fatal to it.

Lord Salisbury, however, laid the political world at his feet. On 2 July he came to Devonshire House and offered to serve under Hartington in a coali-tion government. His generosity was less heroic than it seemed; for years he had been trying to detach the Whigs from their party, and he now had the per-fect way to do it. He himself did not like being Prime Minister: he preferred the Foreign Office (which he in fact held concurrently with the premiership for most of his three ministries), so that personally he could afford the ultimate bid for Hartington's alliance. There was a further incentive to seek a Harting-ton government: as Prime Minister Hartington would be the leader in the House of Commons, and this would relieve Salisbury of the need to appoint Lord Randolph Churchill, whose erratic but vivid personality had elbowed out the more senior members of the Tory front bench.

From the personal point of view this was the best offer Hartington had in the whole of his career. With the ex-ministers Goschen, Sir Henry James and other able Whigs to pick from, he could have formed a strong government with the Tories; it would have meant ditching Chamberlain and his section, but even a following of only forty or fifty Liberal Unionists would have given him a safe majority. It is also worth noting that such an alliance would have been undisturbed by his succession to the dukedom, whereas it had always been assumed that his removal to the Lords would terminate his leadership of the Liberal Party. A Hartington–Salisbury coalition would have been a better government than the one which in fact held office, and might have avoided electoral defeat in 1892. But Hartington was no crypto-Tory suddenly released from his bonds; he was a Whig *pur sang*. For the heir to the dukedom of Devonshire a desertion to the Tory side would be the overthrow of a two centuries' tradition. That is not to say that he was not tempted by the offer; he gave serious thought to it, but finally he put Salisbury in alone, with independent Liberal Unionist support.

On 5 August at a meeting at Devonshire House, the Liberal Unionist Party was officially constituted. Hartington's Whigs numbered nearly fifty of the seventy-seven MPs, besides all of the 120 peers, and he was elected leader without dispute. In his speech he envisaged an early restoration of Liberal unity on the platform of keeping Ireland in the United Kingdom. The question then arose of where the party were to sit in Parliament. Although they were keeping the Conservative government in, the Liberal Unionists were not in office and did not want to sharpen the break with their former colleagues; it was therefore decided to sit with the Liberals, and Hartington took his seat next to Mr Gladstone on the front Opposition bench. His neighbour could hardly help being nettled as he saw Hartington put far more vigour into the fight against Home Rule than he had into any of the Liberal leader's causes. The idea that he was in any way indebted to his rival became increasingly irksome to him; by 1892 Gladstone had persuaded himself, and was busy persuading his entourage, that he had only come to his country's aid in 1880 after Hartington had tried and failed to form a government in defiance of the voice of the electorate.

The Whig Unionist MPs included twelve aristocrats, thirteen baronets, and seventeen men from gentry families, besides a strong representation from the worlds of finance and business, such as Goschen and the Rothschilds. It has been pointed out that they were by no means a predictable selection from either the landed branch (of which they numbered less than half) or even the right wing of the Liberal Party. The point is worth making but is overshadowed by the landslide defection of Liberal support in the Lords: out of a strength of 180 peers, a good two-thirds declared themselves Unionists. The Liberals were reduced to a mere fraction of the Upper House, and in neither of his last two administrations could Gladstone find a duke prepared to let his wife become Mistress of the Robes. This ermined secession is what has always struck observers about the Home Rule split, and it enabled Gladstone to make his 'masses against the classes' speech, in which he pictured himself as striving to grant the kind of justice which had always been refused by a selfish aristocracy.

Commentators of a left-wing disposition used to depict the Whig secession as a natural desertion by aristocrats of an already uncongenial cause, with a strong element of class fear for their Irish compeers under the threat of Home Rule. Nowadays this view is sustained in its primitive crudity only by Professor Cannadine, who has written a large book, as he tells us, to annoy the ladies who show National Trust houses to the public. Even if there had not been a single great landowner in Ireland, it is doubtful whether any Liberal Unionist peer would have been reconciled to Home Rule. The 15th Duke of Norfolk, who was perhaps the nearest the Victorian aristocracy had to a saint, joined the secession in 1886, but he had been uneasy for several years at the 'unpatriotic' strain in his party's policy; with perhaps less purity of motive, his attitude was probably the general one among the Liberal Unionists. If we are to look for class interest, we could hardly find a better example than Lord Granville, who became a Home Ruler. Lord Coleridge had written in 1877: 'Granville, who represents them [the Whigs] well, is, I think, very careless about *what* is done, so long as *they*, the great nobles, have the doing of it; and he is firmly resolved, I think, that they *shall* have the doing of it.' In 1887 Granville deplored Hartington's defection and told him: 'I still regard Mr Gladstone as a conservative force.' One can see what he meant: in 1880 Gladstone had come to power at the head of the great surge of Liberalism and had reverted to the social preconceptions of Lord John Russell, forming a Cabinet largely of Whigs; he had then stood as the main barrier against Chamberlainism. Yet to value this conservatism at the expense of the United Kingdom prompts the question, conservative of what? Granville was for keeping

Whig aristocrats in power, even if the price was abandoning Ireland to rabid nationalism. It was a sort of calculation foreign to Hartington and those who went with him.

The cleft in the Liberal governing class was nowhere sharper than at Brooks's, and into it a bomb fell in the shape of Sir William Harcourt, who had himself been blackballed when proposed many years before. A typically abrasive remark while he was dining there in January 1887 led to the blackballing of his son, and that produced a spate of mutual blackballings between Unionists and Home Rulers. It was left to Lord Granville to appeal for a truce to party differences, and to avert the threat, as it appeared for a while, that no one would ever get elected again. The Home Ruler who suffered most from the schism was Lord Spencer; he had been disgusted at the way in which his Irish regime was reviled and thrown over by the Tories during their 1885 administration, and he concluded, not unnaturally, that if Britain could not give Ireland consistent government the only alternative was Home Rule. His high character made his betrayal only the more unforgivable to his fellow aristocrats. Despite his cousinship and the close affection that had linked him with the Cavendishes the relations between the two families were broken off; and, even more surprisingly, the esteem that had developed between him and Hartington as colleagues failed to prevent an estrangement that was not healed until the later 1890s.

In the great Whig secession of 1886, the role of Hartington was central. If there had been no Hartington some Whigs (the Dukes of Bedford and Sutherland perhaps) would probably have begun to trickle out of the party from the early 1880s; but others would have remained within it even after 1886. Lord Derby, for instance, told Hartington that he regarded resistance to Home Rule as useless without him; the natural leaders in the Lords would have been Granville, Spencer and Rosebery. Hartington, however, had been seen by the Whigs as their leader at least since 1875, if not since 1866. Loyalty to him kept them in the party before 1886, and brought them out with him; it was his move that made the Home Rule schism the departure of the Whig tribe.

Another feature to note about the Liberal split is the way it defeated Radicalism for a generation. Suddenly, the attack on rank and property that had seemed so menacing was put on ice, not to heat up again until Lloyd George's Budget of 1909. With Chamberlain kidnapped into a conservative alliance, a strange hush descended as far as class conflict was concerned. It was appropriate that Queen Victoria's Golden Jubilee year was the first of this conservative and tradition-loving epoch. Hartington was to live the rest of his life in an England that had turned its back on the agitation of the mid-1880s and was ready to look on the representative of one of its great historic families with increasing reverence and affection.

10
A Time to Cancan

Louise Manchester was no longer now the captivating beauty who had astonished London society for a quarter of a century. In 1877 Princess Victoria still found her 'very handsome' in Berlin, but by 1881 Lord Lytton was writing of 'the *beaux restes* of the Duchess of Manchester'. What she had not lost was her personality and forcefulness and her capacity for making enemies. To those who were not rivals she could be all sweetness, and the awestruck young Leonie Jerome, Lady Randolph Churchill's sister, gives an example of this when she describes her kindness at a hunt ball in 1881 as Louise helped her stick her hairpins firmly in her hair before the quadrille.

Another of her young protégées was Florence Williams, whose husband Hwfa was the indiscreet brother of Lady Aylesford who had involved Louise in that affair some years before. In February 1886 Florence announced her intention of going to Nice to cure a bad cough, and Louise, for whom this was a regular expedition, annexed her as a travelling companion. In the long night journey by train from Paris to Nice Louise refused to have the beds let down in their compartment and slept bolt upright through the night. The unfortunate Florence, after dozing fitfully, was just falling asleep at dawn when Louise woke her up and insisted on her drinking the *café-au-lait* brought by the attendant. From their base at Nice, Louise would take Florence driving along the Corniche to Monte Carlo for the obligatory gamble. 'When she once sat down to play time ceased to exist, and dinner at eight meant any time after nine o'clock.'

For the 1880s a regular series of letters from Hartington to Louise is preserved, whereas hardly any survive from the earlier years. They are of faultless discretion, beginning 'My dear Duchess' and ending 'Yours very truly, Hartington'. They treat of the public affairs that have come up in Cabinet, and show that what Louise wanted was intelligent discussion of domestic and international politics; they hardly go further than giving her advance knowledge of what would soon become public. When he got back to London from Holker on 5 February 1885 the first thing Hartington did was send Louise a War Office telegram giving her the news of the fall of Khartoum. The next day, as the Queen summoned him to his footman's reprimand, he wrote: 'It is a horrid nuisance having to go to Osborne; but the Q doesnt seem to think about anybody but herself.' Hartington's furthest indiscretions are reserved for royal comments, with another example in his letter on 27 March: 'I wanted to have the Council put off till today or tomorrow, but Ponsonby said it was impossible because they are both anniversaries; one John Brown & the other the Duke of Albany.* This is the way we are governed now.'

What use Louise made of these confidences is another question. In June 1885 Lewis Harcourt (Sir William's son) notes in his diary: 'There have been some very ugly stories about lately of her having had some rather too successful speculations on the Stock Exchange and it is intimated that she has her information from Hartington.' Harcourt was not the first with this news: some weeks earlier Sir Charles Dilke had been writing of a storm 'which never burst but threatened greatly for some time, as to stock jobbing . . . One great lady (the duchess of Manchester) was perhaps guilty.' Given Louise's passion for gambling one can well believe it, and there was an additional reason: the agricultural depression had by now made great inroads into the Manchester income, and both Louise and her husband had lost a lot by gambling; she needed the money. In 1889 Lord Derby recorded the rumours that Louise's play at whist was far above her means and that her debts were being paid by Hartington, 'her liaison with whom is paraded more openly than is either decorous or prudent'. By the mid-1880s Louise was notoriously courting financiers like the Rothschilds and Henry Oppenheim, figures who begin in these years to sun themselves in the Prince of Wales's set and in London Society. Both her finances and Hartington's were receiving a boost from the advice given by such experts, which, it has to be said, seems a more probable cause for sudden profits on the Stock Exchange. It is not surprising, though, that gossips preferred the more sensational explanation. If the rumours of the first half of 1885 had got out, there is no doubt that Hartington's political career would have been finished; a combination of adultery and insider dealing would have been lethal.

---

*John Brown died on 27 March 1883; Leopold Duke of Albany, Queen Victoria's fourth son, died on 28 March 1884.

The Liberals' departure from office in June may have helped to dissipate the storm clouds, but a warning of what could happen to a politician came at the end of that year, when Sir Charles Dilke was cited as co-respondent in a divorce case. He was accused of adultery with a married woman in her early twenties, Virginia Crawford, and the scandal was responsible for Dilke's dropping out of public life, leaving Chamberlain as the sole champion of the Radical cause. The case has often been cited as an example of Victorian hypocrisy, but it had features which made it particularly shocking to public opinion; Dilke was said to have seduced not only his mistress but his two equally youthful maidservants, who were sisters, and to have taken one of them to bed in a threesome with Virginia Crawford. The headline she provided the press with, 'He taught me every French vice', would have been worthy of a tabloid sensation today. One cannot imagine any modern politician surviving such a scandal, and it provided an example of the penalties if Hartington, Louise or the Duke of Manchester allowed any lapse of discretion.

A new figure in Louise's circle in 1886 was Margot Tennant. She was the youngest of the vivid daughters of the Scottish Liberal industrialist Sir Charles Tennant who were making their impact on London society. One of them, Charlotte, had married the Liberal peer Lord Ribblesdale; another, Laura, had just died in April 1885, after less than a year of her own marriage. Margot tells how she was wandering about the London streets alone one afternoon after this bereavement and was looking at a photograph of her sister Charty Ribblesdale in a shop window when a footman touched his hat to her and asked if she would speak to 'Her Grace'. She turned round and saw Louise Manchester sitting in her carriage. As she had never spoken to the Duchess before she wondered what she could want, but they introduced themselves formally and Louise said: 'Jump in, dear child! I can't bear to see you look so sad. Jump in and I'll take you for a drive and you can come back to tea with me.' They drove round Hyde Park and returned to tea in Louise's boudoir. As they sat there Princess Alexandra came in unannounced, ran to Louise and kissed her, and Margot, who had jumped to her feet, was presented.

Louise then invited herself to dinner on a night when Margot's parents were dining alone with her and the Indian Civil Servant Sir Alfred Lyall. She handled the meeting with rare adaptability, talking little, admiring Sir Charles's pictures, being sweet to Lady Tennant and showing interest in Sir

Alfred Lyall's weighty conversation. The assertive young Liberal débutante became and remained one of Louise's firmest friends.

That was the summer of the Home Rule split, and that autumn Louise went on a voyage to India with her husband. Hartington wanted to go with her, despite the Queen's expressed disapproval, and Lord Salisbury was horrified. Having just formed a shaky minority government he did not want to lose the Liberal Unionist leader for several months. He made urgent representations to the Queen, and a letter of hers on 19 October asking Hartington in the strongest terms not to go made him resign himself to a separation. The Marquis of Huntly gives us a vignette of the Manchester party on the Ganges that Christmas:

> At breakfast in the *dak* bungalow, the duke did not sit down with the rest of us, but was flitting about, trying to find some beverage to his taste; he would not take tea. The *kitmagar* produced claret and beer, but they were rejected. At last the duchess could not stand his grumblings any longer, and in her severest tones said, 'There is water, Mandeville.' That did not quell him, however; at last a bottle of whisky was found, and, with a stiff peg, he settled down to his breakfast.

Lord Randolph Churchill, who was Salisbury's Chancellor of the Exchequer, in keeping with his new amity with Hartington, stayed with him for a shooting party at Hardwick that December. Then Hartington went abroad with Harry Chaplin, travelling in France and Italy. In his absence Churchill presented to the Cabinet his proposals for the 1887 Budget in terms typical of his hare-brained character. He had never held the Exchequer before and knew nothing of finance, but he proposed in his first Budget to destroy the system built up over forty years by experts such as Gladstone. Every existing tax was to be radically changed or abolished, and in the process a cut of some £1 million (more than 1 per cent of the entire government revenue) was to be demanded from the army and navy estimates, at a time when the fleet in particular badly needed modernizing. It was the Secretary for War, W.H. Smith, who put his foot down. Churchill threatened to resign unless Smith were overruled, Lord Salisbury replied on 22 December declining to do so, and Churchill treated his letter as an acceptance of his own resignation. He sealed his fate by leaking the news of his departure to the press before even the Queen was told of it.

This was a grave blow to the government, since Churchill's dash was one of the Tories' chief electoral assets. Once again Lord Salisbury bid high for security, and he sent a telegram to Hartington in Rome to return home, following it up with a letter asking him again to take over as Prime Minister – Churchill's departure made the Tory front bench so weak in the House of Commons that reinforcement was imperative. The weather took a hand in the political crisis: the whole of Europe was under snow and telegraph lines were down. Hartington got Salisbury's telegram three days late, on 26 December, and immediately left for England. He was at Monte Carlo when the Prime Minister's letter of 24 December reached him, supported by the Queen's own invitation, and he did not get back to London until the 28th. By that time the crisis had been resolved: George Goschen, with Hartington's encouragement, agreed to join the Tories as Chancellor of the Exchequer, a post for which he was much better qualified than Churchill. That gentleman, who had thought himself indispensable, found his bluff was called and never again held public office. When urged to entice him back, Lord Salisbury said: 'Did you ever hear of a man who, having got rid of a boil on his neck, wanted another?' The Unionist alliance held together without Hartington's having to seriously consider taking charge; nevertheless it is thought that three refused offers in a lifetime to hold the premiership constitute a record.

Lord Randolph was a good friend of Joseph Chamberlain's, their efforts to radicalize their respective parties forming a political bond, and Churchill's departure deprived Chamberlain of his direct line to the government, while Goschen's appointment correspondingly strengthened Hartington. Chamberlain was therefore keen to support Churchill's efforts for a comeback, and promoted the idea of his joining the Liberal Unionists in a so-called National Party. Lord Randolph regarded Hartington as a key man, whose judgement on political questions was almost infallible, and was put out to see Hartington virtually ignore him both socially and politically. He mobilized his wife to use her undoubted friendship with Hartington in smoothing relations. Lady Randolph describes the occasion in June 1887 when Hartington and Louise Manchester, together with other political leaders, were cruising in the Solent to see the naval review for the Golden Jubilee; without pourparlers Chamberlain drew up a deck-chair and accosted Hartington on plans for the new political alignment. Hartington, taken unawares, replied in monosyllables, which Chamberlain ignored. 'But after a time the frozen attitude of Lord Hartington began to take effect, and the conversation languished and died.' Rebuffed, Churchill started flirting with the Liberals and got the Tennants to bring Gladstone and himself together at their Grosvenor Square house, provoking a flurry of curiosity from Louise Manchester and others agog to see the outcome of this alliance. It did not work out, and Churchill remained in the political wilderness, his regard for Hartington declining year by year. It must have been about 1890 that Daisy Brooke heard Winston Churchill, then a bumptious schoolboy at Harrow, regale Hartington to his face with a ruthless spate of criticisms of his political position, no doubt absorbed from his father. Lady Randolph, with American indulgence, left the diatribe unchecked, and Hartington received it with his characteristic composure.

The year 1887 was an easy one for Hartington, the first since 1874 which had not been heavily taken up with political duties. It was the year of Queen Victoria's Golden Jubilee, and we have many glimpses of that festive summer: of the great garden-party that the Duke of Westminster gave at Grosvenor House on 27 June, with the Kings of Belgium, Denmark and Saxony, the Waleses, Prince Wilhelm of Germany and his wife, and half a dozen other royalties. But the centre of attention was the Duke's horse, Ormonde, one of the outstanding racehorses of the century, who had just run two seasons in which he had never known defeat and was about to go to stud. Lord Esher describes the scene as Ormonde held court on the lawn outside the ballroom, chomping the flowers pressed upon him by a bevy of admiring ladies and ending by snatching the carnation from Hartington's button-hole, to the delight of the wearer.

Three days later Sir Edward Hamilton describes the royal fête given at the Crystal Palace: 'The Duchess of Manchester had with her usual energy got up a party, which included R. Churchill and Chamberlain – "Masher Joe" as he may well be called now. They both made themselves very pleasant. We first attended a Concert and after a little walk in the garden proceeded to a scrambling dinner. We were given excellent places in the gallery next to the Royal box from which we saw the fireworks.' Hamilton's observation of the social metamorphosis of 'Masher Joe' continues a fortnight later with a description of a party at Louise's: in one room Princess Alexandra was dancing 'with inimitable grace'; in another the Prince and a group of gilded youths were at baccarat and Chamberlain playing with them for high stakes while Randolph Churchill kept the bank.

Archduke Rudolph, the Emperor Franz Joseph's heir, who was to shoot himself at Mayerling eighteen months later, was also in London for the Jubilee, and one night the Prince of Wales took him, with Louise Manchester,

Lady Randolph Churchill and a crowd of others, to a 'night club'.* When they had finished supper at about 2 a.m., the Prince told the band to play the quadrille from *La Belle Hélène* and danced a cancan with Louise. The mortified Archduke told Count Charles Kinsky to send the waiters out of the room so that they should not see their future King making such a fool of himself. Throughout his ministerial career Hartington had staunchly defended the proper priorities due between politics and racing. In October 1884 he insisted on changing the date of a Cabinet meeting which clashed with the Cesarewitch, and Lord Salisbury's take-over of office in June 1885 was held up while Hartington and Granville, who had to be consulted, were at Ascot. His clerks were used to finding racing tips in Hartington's official papers, and he was known to put an important document in his pocket and find it there, still unopened, at Newmarket several days later. Nevertheless government had interfered with his fortunes as an owner. The early 1880s were a disappointing period for him, although observers judged it remarkable that his trainers, the Bloss brothers, achieved what they did with so small a team. The year 1885 went better, with five of his horses distinguishing themselves, and his Sir Kenneth won three good races in 1886. The next two years marked a nadir as measured by prize money, and at this time he switched trainers to Richard Marsh, who trained for Louise's son-in-law the Duke of Hamilton, and had set up at Lordship Farm the most up-to-date establishment in the country. Lord Westmorland continued to manage Hartington's stable until his death in 1891. The following year Marsh moved with Hartington's horses to Egerton House, near Newmarket, a place where he created even finer facilities, and several leading owners such as the Prince of Wales and the Duke of Hamilton transferred their horses with him. Another big owner who employed Marsh was the Austrian financier Baron Hirsch, who had recently been taken up by English society. He was introduced to the Prince of Wales by Archduke Rudolph, whose financial difficulties he had resolved, and in the autumns of 1891 and 1892 we find Hartington and Louise at his astoundingly productive shooting estate in Austria, which was all the rage at the time. The Prince and his circle were ready to benefit from Hirsch's financial expertise even while they mocked his ignorance of the sports he patronized so lavishly. There was

---

*Presumably the Corinthian, in St James's Square, the only London restaurant of the time that could be so described.

one occasion when the Prince with Louise and others were going round Egerton House, where the residents included Hirsch's outstanding and very distinctive filly La Flèche. Louise had decided to play a trick on Hirsch and challenged him to name his horses, having arranged with Marsh to take down the nameplates from the boxes. 'Now, Baron, you must know this one,' she said as they came to La Flèche. 'Give it a name.' Hirsch thought hard but was unable to do so. After a few years the Prince tired of the obliging but dull financier, and he was heard of no more.

It was in the 1880s that a habit of snoozing at all hours of the day began to distinguish Hartington in the public mind; it gave scope for Chamberlain's anonymous gibe in the 1885 election campaign: 'It is perfectly ridiculous for any political Rip Van Winkle to come down from the mountain on which he has been slumbering and to tell us that these things are to be excluded from the Liberal programme. The world has moved on while these dreamers have been sleeping . . .' Pretending to sleep in Parliament through one's opponents' orations was often a good ploy, and it was noted that Hartington had a knack of being wide awake again when his intervention was wanted. One commentator recalled a time when a speaker was berating Hartington as he sprawled in his place with his hat over his eyes; while the orator denounced him as slumbering in the face of whatever governmental disaster flowed from his torpor, a close observer could see Hartington shaking with silent laughter. Nevertheless, taking extra naps was genuinely a growing habit of his. What troubled Hartington, oddly enough, was insomnia. He would go to bed very late and lie there devouring the fashionable novels (although he sternly resisted Gladstone's suggestions, such as *Treasure Island*). When told it was bad for his eyes he replied, 'Yes, but I can't lie awake and do nothing.'

The Hartington myth was promoted by the *Punch* political writer Henry Lucy, who created the following anecdote about him: a dinner hostess told him of a report that he had yawned in the middle of his own speech the night before; so she had been told, but she could not really believe it. 'Ah, but you did not hear the speech,' replied Hartington. Typically, when Hartington got to hear this joke he started spreading it himself. It provides an example of the way anecdotes about him developed: it began as a story of Hartington making a joke about yawning during his speech; then it became a story that he did yawn during his speeches; and finally it became a story that he yawned during his maiden speech.

Bernard Holland, who became Hartington's secretary in 1892, thus described his personal style: 'He was absolutely unassuming but every one in his presence was aware of a largeness and dignity of nature which filled much "moral space".' He would listen smoking a cigarette without much appearance of interest or attention, until at the right moment he indicated the most practical line to follow. Sir Almeric Fitzroy found that 'He never put a question which was not pregnant with meaning, nor made a comment which was not instinct with sense.' F. O'Donnell, who as an Irish Home Ruler had no cause to flatter him, preferred his speeches to Gladstone's: 'Except, perhaps, on financial subjects, there was more relevant matter and more broad thought in one of Lord Hartington's speeches than in a round dozen of the great Parliamentarian's utterances.'

Hartington would wolf down office lunches of bread and cheese and mutton chops and would travel by bus or Underground if it was handy. Such habits, as well as his casual costume, led people to say that he had no sense of his position; but when he entertained a house-party at Hardwick Hall he became the representative of the House of Cavendish, and nobody was a more magnificent host.

Shooting had become virtually an obsession of late-Victorian country-house life, and Hartington was still a keen practitioner. Long hours at government desks, however, had famously taken away his youthful skill; as early as 1864 Lady Frederick Cavendish records his dejection over a disappointing bag at Bolton Abbey. The Duke of Portland tells the story of Hartington's shooting with him at Creswell Crags on the Welbeck estate, on the Nottinghamshire–Derbyshire border. He killed an exceptionally high-flying partridge in a manner worthy of the crack shots of the day, and his friends raised a cheer. Afterwards he said to his host: 'I wonder why Harry Chaplin and the others cheered when I fired both barrels at a cock-pheasant and missed.' 'Missed a cock-pheasant with both barrels?' said the Duke. 'Why, you killed the highest partridge that ever flew from Nottinghamshire into Derbyshire!' 'Did I?' said Hartington. 'I didn't even know it was there. However, it's over now, so don't say anything about it, and let me keep my reputation.' Fifty years later they still called the place Hartington's stand.*

---

*John Pearson in *Stags and Serpents* depicts Hartington as a consummate actor who spent his life cultivating an amateur image; he interprets this anecdote in reverse and supposes that it was his false reputation as a duffer that Hartington wanted to keep.

Lady Randolph Churchill tells another story about Hartington's attachment to old and tried companions among his hats. His women friends grew so exasperated at the shabby round hat he always wore at race-meetings that some two dozen or more conspired together each to send him a hat on his birthday. For hours they poured in, every conceivable type of headgear from top hats to cricket caps; Lady Randolph herself sent a 'pot' hat. But according to Louise's grandson Hartington's response was to point a few days later to his valet, who was to be seen wearing one of the new accessories and would continue to do so for a couple of years until it had been broken in.

Early in 1887 there was a Round Table Conference between the Liberals and their separated brethren with a view to healing the breach. In a major speech at Newcastle Hartington expressed his support for reunion and for concessions to Ireland in local government; but the negotiations, handled by Chamberlain, were fruitless and necessarily remained so while Gladstone continued on the scene. Soon afterwards the Home Rule cause appeared to be discredited when *The Times* published a letter allegedly written by Parnell which appeared to implicate him in the Phoenix Park murders; but early in 1889 this was shown to be a forgery and the culprit, Pigott, shot himself. In the revulsion of public feeling Gladstone and Parnell were riding high, the government was becoming more and more unpopular, and the Liberal Unionists in particular saw themselves facing extinction at the next election. But in November 1890 Parnell was struck by the same nemesis that had brought Sir Charles Dilke down. For years he had been conducting an affair with Kitty O'Shea, the wife of one of his nationalist MPs, and the latter now sued for divorce; Parnell admitted adultery. Gladstone wrote a public letter threatening to retire if Parnell did not resign as leader of the Irish Party, and the alliance with the Liberals was blown apart. Parnell refused to resign and two-thirds of his party deserted him (the Catholic bishops threw their weight against him, and it became impossible for a Parnellite to get elected in Ireland). In October 1891 Parnell died, his mesmeric dictatorship never to be repeated by any Irish leader. On 29 November 1890, the day Parnell launched his defiance of Gladstone, Queen Victoria's diary records Hartington's saying to her in his gruff way: 'I never thought anything in politics could give me as much pleasure as this does.' He was right to be pleased, for the Liberal Unionists were saved at the polls. The Parnellites were furious at the way morality robbed them of their leader, and at one point they threatened to retaliate by exposing Hartington's liaison with Louise. That threat never materialized; perhaps they found that a 59-year-old widow would be difficult to build up into a scarlet woman. With Parnell's death ended the most dramatic twelve years in Victorian politics. They had begun with the clarion-call of the Midlothian campaign and had gone on to provide the reversal of the 1880 election, the campaign of Irish obstruction and the fever it engendered in the 1880 Parliament, the tragedy of Phoenix Park, the distant but vivid shock of Khartoum, the bombshell of Gladstone's Home Rule conversion and the fight to resist it, and the drama of the Pigott letters and Parnell's rehabilitation and fall. Two men, the unpredictable Gladstone and the ruthless Irish leader, had been the polarities between which the storm crackled, and lesser figures like Randolph Churchill, Chamberlain and even Lord Salisbury had caught the restless charge. Among them one man notably had kept his head, and his steadiness had marked him out all the more in that febrile period. The drama was about to go out of British politics to a large extent, just as Hartington was elevated to a more peaceful scene.

With Home Rule in disgrace again Gladstone was forced to look for new measures to appeal to the electorate, and he harked back to the old Radicalism of the 1870s, the Nonconformist Radicalism that had been eclipsed for a few years by Chamberlain's and Dilke's aggressive brand. In the 'Newcastle Programme', proclaimed in October 1891, he outlined a series of proposals including Church disestablishment, support for teetotalism and various democratizing measures. The Nonconformists of Scotland and Wales were happy with the idea of subjecting their Ulster brethren to a Dublin regime which they themselves would have loathed, and Home Rule continued on the agenda. The programme had the effect of consolidating Hartington's rift with Gladstone, and in November he spoke alongside Salisbury in Liverpool, declaring that he had renounced the hope of Liberal reunion.

A month earlier the death of W.H. Smith disclosed the growing rapprochement. The Conservatives did not want to appoint a new Commons leader without first securing the approval of the Liberal Unionists, but a slight hitch arose; as Lord Salisbury wrote to Balfour on 15 October: 'Hartington is at Newmarket and all political arrangements have to be hung up till some quadruped has run faster than some other quadruped.' Hartington agreed, once his horses had (in Salisbury's further comment) 'settled matters to their satisfaction', and Balfour's appointment was announced a few days later.

The political amity was reflected in the social field as the old Whig–Tory divide began to disappear. This was true of the group of younger aristocrats who in 1887 formed the witty and graceful coterie known as the Souls; most of them were the rising young Tories such as Arthur Balfour, George Wyndham and George Curzon, but they included one of Hartington's Liberal Unionist MPs, Willy Grenfell, whose wife Etty (who was to inherit Panshanger from the last Earl Cowper) was the most enchanting hostess of this circle. Hartington might seem an incongruous intruder on such a scene ('How that man does talk!' he once remarked when Arthur Balfour's name was brought up), but he was a regular visitor at the Grenfells' Taplow Court. The Souls for their part were not immune to the attractions of shooting and other traditional pursuits and were a large constituent of the society which for the next twenty years basked at Chatsworth, Bolton Abbey, Compton Place and Devonshire House.

One who straddled the gap between the Souls and the Prince of Wales's set was the naval officer Lord Charles Beresford, who had won fame in the Egyptian campaign of 1882. In August 1887 Arthur Balfour writes to Lady Elcho (another Soul hostess): 'Last Sunday I went to the Whites.* No one there but Hartington and the C. Beresfords. All in their best forms, and Charlie more amusing and more refined in his jokes than usual! Ly C. made up for any conversational restraint imposed on himself by her better half: – and, egged on by Hartington, narrated amazing anecdotes of her recent experiences at Aix with various German Barons and Brazilian Counts.' Lord Charles was at this time in the middle of his affair with Daisy Brooke, whose plump charms were making conquests throughout English society. Herself a great heiress, she had married the young Lord Brooke and entertained at her own Easton Lodge until 1893, when her husband became Earl of Warwick and she instituted an equally smart regime at Warwick Castle. In a self-revealing anecdote she describes the consequence of Joseph Chamberlain's political realignment with Hartington in the mid-1880s: 'I remember the amazement at Chatsworth when the Duke of Devonshire (*plus royaliste que le roi*) announced at luncheon that he was expecting Mr Joseph Chamberlain for the weekend. The Radical from Birmingham, one of the outer barbarians, to storm the ducal door!' The description of the shy Duke as *plus royaliste que le roi* is particularly crass, and she goes on to relate how one of her women friends, evidently as

---

*Harry White, of the American embassy, was a supernumerary member of the Souls.

snobbish and foolish as herself, asked her if the demagogue would know how to conduct himself with outward decency and prophesied that he would eat his peas with a knife. They were both proportionately over-impressed when Chamberlain arrived and behaved with perfect propriety. After becoming Countess of Warwick Daisy eventually declared herself a socialist, and having run through both her own fortune and the one she married she tried unsuccessfully to recoup her debts by blackmailing King George V over Edward VII's love letters to her. But before going into the background of this we need to look at what was happening in Louise Manchester's family.

In October 1888 Louise's last child, Lady Alice Montagu, got engaged to the Hon. Edward Stanley, nephew of the Earl of Derby. His father had remained a Tory after the Earl's defection and had just been made Governor General of Canada as Baron Stanley; he was to succeed his brother as 16th Earl, and Edward in turn became the 17th Earl of Derby in 1908, playing a large role in Conservative politics and being considered in the 1920s as a possible Prime Minister. Alice was a leading social figure in her own right, who distinguished herself when her husband was ambassador in Paris in 1918–20 and shone as a patroness of intellectual society.

Florence Williams describes Louise's next visit to Cannes in March 1889, when they went on a donkey expedition in the mountains with Hartington, who this year had been brought along, too. Louise's iron frame was beginning to age, for she found negotiating the steep hills difficult. 'Every now and again she would call a halt, always on the pretext: "My dear, do stop a minute! Really, you don't seem to have any eye for the lovely view!"' She was never too tired, however, for her gamble before dinner. It was on this visit that Hartington found Skittles out at Hyères after so many years' separation, and, in her words to Wilfrid Scawen Blunt, 'we became great friends again'.

Early in 1890 Hartington suffered congestion of the lungs and went off to Egypt until Easter to recuperate with Lord and Lady Gosford, with whom he got on very well. The Duke of Manchester, who had played host to them at Kimbolton for the last time the previous Christmas, was travelling to Naples when he fell ill and died on 22 March. Louise was at Monte Carlo and had time to get to him just before his death. Lord Charles Montagu travelled out to Naples, meeting his mother at Turin as she returned on the 23rd, and took charge of the arrangements for the funeral at Kimbolton. His elder brother had long since dropped out of being any sort of comfort to the family, although one could say that his habits only exaggerated those of his parents. After losing his seat in Parliament in 1880 he set about becoming a model for the Hon. Galahad Threepwood and those other late-Victorian good-time Charlies depicted by P.G. Wodehouse, joining the raffish Pelican Club, frequenting Romano's restaurant and moving in the sporting world of *The Pink 'Un*. He deserted his wife Consuelo and took up with the famous and jolly music-hall singer of the day Bessie Bellwood; in 1889 he was declared bankrupt for £100,000.

For Consuelo this was just one of the misfortunes she was burdened with throughout her life, and they only served to endear her the more to her friends. For a time in the mid-1880s she was the mistress of the Prince of Wales, filling a niche between Lillie Langtry and Daisy Brooke. She was said to have brought a dowry of a million dollars when she married, but somehow she managed to be hard up at this time, and her friends rallied round to provide the cuisine when she entertained the Prince at dinner. Consuelo's husband at least survived long enough to make her the first American duchess in England,* and she thought it advisable to arrange a reunion. She wrote to Bessie Bellwood asking her to give him back and promising to pay his debts and allow the ne'er-do-well Duke £20 a week. Bessie replied: 'Miss Bessie Bellwood presents her compliments to the Duchess of Manchester, and begs to state that she is now working the Pavilion, the Met., and the South London at £20 a turn so she can allow the Duke £30 a week and he is better off as he is.' The Manchester fortune was by now in serious trouble: the 9th Duke asserted that its income had sunk to between £22,000 and £25,000 by the time he succeeded; it was heavily mortgaged and a large part was tied up in providing Louise's jointure as dowager. Reginald Brett saw her at the end of 1891 and wrote: 'She is worried about Mandeville, who is dying, and whom she likes in spite of his slight deserts.' In August 1892 her son died at Tanderagee Castle. His only son, the 9th Duke, was then at Eton and was soon to show himself a fitting heir to his father's character.

Consuelo found herself edged out as the Prince's mistress by Daisy Brooke in 1889. The latter's affair with Lord Charles Beresford had hit a rock when his wife announced that she was pregnant. Given Lady Charles's looks, apart from anything else, there was no question of the father's being anyone but her hus-

---

*There had been an American Duchess of Leeds two generations before, but she was long dead.

band. Daisy was furious at Lord Charles's unfaithfulness in sleeping with his own wife and went off to enjoy more distinguished embraces. From there things only got more complicated. She sent a letter to Lord Charles not knowing that he was away; Lady Charles opened it and used it to stir up ridicule against the writer. Daisy begged the Prince to put pressure on Lady Charles to give the letter up, and Lady Charles riposted by demanding that the Prince should order Daisy Brooke to leave London for the Season, which would have been a public social disgrace. The Prince over-reacted (his fabled social sense did not, when we look into it, save him from repeated blunders); on the next occasion when both he and Lady Charles were invited to the house-party of a great hostess he crossed out her name and substituted Lady Brooke's. Charlie Beresford's Irish temper was aroused: it was one thing for him to be unfaithful to his wife, quite another that the Prince should set out to destroy her social position by ostracizing her. He had a furious row with the Prince, calling him a blackguard and a coward, and the quarrel was not made up for several years. In 1891 Lady Charles's sister Mrs Gerald Paget composed a satirical poem called 'Lady River' describing, under that pseudonym, Daisy Brooke's goings-on, and it circulated in typescript among a group of hostesses, who only had to announce a reading of it for their drawing-rooms to be crowded. Unfortunately when Consuelo Manchester permitted herself this luxury it came to the Prince's ears, and he jumped to the conclusion that she was the author. He cut her for the next ten years, and it was only after his accession to the throne that her son, leaving Consuelo's house and coming upon the King in the street, fell on one knee, kissed his hand and begged him to lift his ban. Shortly afterwards the King was a guest of Manchester's at a dinner at which the Duchess was taken back into his favour.

Her relation with the Prince in the 1880s had turned Consuelo into an arbiter of the many American ladies who were assaulting English society. The Prince was amused by her habitual reply when he asked her for guidance: 'Oh, Sir, she has no position at home; out there she would be just dirt under our feet.' In the 1890s she was the main avenue of introduction for such aspirants (whether she was doing this for money does not appear). Newly arrived mothers looking for titled sons-in-law would make the Duchess's house in Portman Square their first place of call, and if the girl's behaviour over tea or dinner was acceptable Consuelo would set the wheels in motion. Her rift with the Prince in 1891 rather cramped her, but her sister Natica was married to Sir John

Lister Kaye, who was fully in the Marlborough House circle and was able to provide the second step in the royal conquest. Late-nineteenth-century New York had invented culture as a social weapon, and American girls came to England armed to the teeth, disconcerting the more casually brought-up English men and women. One of the most accomplished heiresses to step on these shores was Consuelo's god-daughter, Consuelo Vanderbilt, whom her mother had marked out from birth for a ducal future. Sure enough, she was engaged without delay to the 24-year-old Duke of Marlborough (Lord Randolph Churchill's nephew) and married him in 1895, when she was still nineteen. Her head-first dive into the high waters of English aristocratic life was a shock she never really got over, and it was not helped when the Dowager Duchess told her: 'Your first duty is to have a child and it must be a son, because it would be intolerable to have that little upstart Winston become Duke. Are you in the family way?'

The older Duchess of Manchester, Louise, was pushing another kind of cosmopolitanism. She was related through her sisters' marriages to the aristocracies of four European countries and through her son-in-law the Duke of Hamilton to the Princes of Monaco and the Grand Dukes of Baden. How convenient, then, that those were precisely the two places most popular for the international frolics of the late-nineteenth-century upper class. Kaiser Wilhelm, who succeeded in 1888, held Louise in high respect; the fact that his mother, now the Empress Dowager, had never liked her may have given him added incentive, and he made a point of inviting her to the most exclusive feasts when she visited Berlin. She and Hartington were frequent companions of the Prince of Wales as he travelled to the annual cures that were supposed to recover him from eleven months' indulgence. An American journalist leaves a picture of the scene at Homburg, where the Prince would dine on the terrace at Ritter's or the Kursaal in a small party of a dozen or less, with the other dinner parties going on around them. The men were in dinner-jackets – at that time the height of informality – and wearing (because they were dining out of doors) the black soft hats named after the town, and the Prince was to be heard chaffing Hartington loudly across the table on the amount of champagne he was drinking.

When the Duke of Manchester died everyone was agog to see whether Louise would marry Hartington, although no one was as gross about it as Sir William Gordon-Cumming, who when the Duke was barely in his grave addressed Louise: 'When is Hartington going to make a honest woman of you?' She made no reply but got her revenge six months later in the Tranby Croft scandal, the last of those to assail the Prince of Wales before his accession to the throne. In early September the Prince went to stay for the St Leger with the ship-owner Mr Arthur Wilson, one of those moneyed men to whom his circle was becoming increasingly restricted. Gordon-Cumming, who was a rich Scottish landowner and Guards officer, was a fellow guest. He was an intimate of the Prince's and had been in the habit of putting his London house at his disposal for his amatory trysts. It so happened that just two days before the house-party the Prince had walked in and found Gordon-Cumming with Daisy Brooke in his arms. They then went to Mr Wilson's Tranby Croft for Doncaster Week, and in the evenings baccarat was played for high stakes, as was usual in the Prince's company. One night some of the guests thought they saw Gordon-Cumming cheating by moving the betting counters back or forward under cover of his hand. They confided in the Prince, and it was agreed to force Gordon-Cumming to promise never again to play cards for money. In another of his mistakes, the Prince signed his name with the other guests to the declaration which Gordon-Cumming consented to write, on the promise that the affair would be kept secret.

The house-party then, coincidentally, broke up, because of a death in the Wilson family, and the danger of anybody talking at the Doncaster races automatically vanished. The Prince, however, intercepted Daisy Brooke, who was travelling north to a funeral, and made her stop at York Station where they had a brief meeting. He did not lack incentive to discredit the man in whose arms he had found her. When the story began in the next few months to do the rounds of country houses, Daisy was blamed, and the nickname Babbling Brooke stuck to her as a consequence.* Gordon-Cumming had protested his innocence from the first, and signed his pledge only on the promise that a scandal would be averted. Now that condition was breached. Hartington and the Prince of Wales were staying at a country house in Norfolk in January 1891 when they heard news that he was suing for libel, and the Prince's signature meant that he would be involved as a witness. The grounds of the scandal

---

*M. Havers, E. Grayson and P. Shankland in *The Royal Baccarat Scandal* (an unreliable source) speculate that the 'bosom friend' to whom Daisy Brooke confided the secret 'may or may not have been Louisa Duchess of Manchester', who of course would have had every motive for spreading it. Since Louise was not Daisy's bosom friend the suggestion is especially gratuitous.

where he was concerned were that baccarat was an illegal game in England, and the public were offended at the picture of the shady plutocrats with whom the heir to the throne apparently spent his time. When the case came to trial in June Gordon-Cumming's suit failed, but the real object of disgrace in the public mind was the Prince. When he went down that summer to stay with Hartington at Compton Place, after being booed at Ascot, he was observed to be in a very bad temper.

The Tranby Croft case established cheating at cards among novelists for the next half-century as the classic social sin, which forced a man to resign from his regiment and his clubs. In fact, a less artificial attitude was expressed by Hartington when Margot Tennant asked him, apropos of the case, what he would do if he saw a man cheating in his house. 'Back him!' was Hartington's reply. People were tolerant of poorer members of society who protected themselves when forced to play for high stakes in circles such as the Prince of Wales's; but Gordon-Cumming was immensely rich, and as he was also abominably rude nobody mourned his fall. Hartington, however, was drawn into the case as he had been into the Aylesford business in 1876. ('I don't know why it is,' he remarked, 'but whenever a man is caught cheating at cards the case is referred to me.') He joined Lord Salisbury in advising the Prince on the terms in which he should write a public letter to the Archbishop of Canterbury and warned against too humiliating a statement. The Prince allayed public feeling by assuring the Archbishop that he abhorred gambling, a concept he conveniently defined as betting more than one could afford.

A postscript to this affair was provided by a young American woman, Florence Garner, who threw herself into the public sentiment for Gordon-Cumming (in reality against the Prince) and volunteered to marry him. Her parents knew nothing of the case and asked G.W.E. Russell's advice on Gordon-Cumming's guilt. Russell could think of no better answer than to refer them to Hartington, who as he foresaw provided them with an absolutely plain and unbiased statement of the affair.

11
Double Duchess

Observers EXPECTED LOUISE to marry Hartington once a decent twelve months had elapsed after her husband's death; but the date passed and no announcement was made. It was clear that the Duke of Devonshire had not long to live, and Hartington preferred not to upset his last months. But it was his brother, Lord Edward, his companion for many years at Devonshire House, who died first, on 18 May 1891. His son Victor, on whom the future of the family would fall, was now twenty-three and succeeded his father as MP for West Derbyshire. Lady Edward grew old ungracefully and would one day be known as the Slammoth (a combination of sloth and mammoth) to Victor's appalled children.

Four days before Christmas the Duke died, at the age of eighty-three. A week later Reginald Brett saw Louise Manchester and discerned her happiness: 'She will now be Duchess of Devonshire!' Brett was confident of this, but the months passed without proving him right. In July 1892 Victor Cavendish married Lady Evelyn Fitzmaurice, daughter of the Marquess of Lansdowne, and still nothing was said. A General Election had just been held, and Gladstone with his Irish allies had come back with a small majority which would force Lord Salisbury to give way to him. No one was in London except the politicians when on 16 August the new Duke and his sixty-year-old lover were married almost in secret in a church in Down Street. Outside his family, only the Queen, the Prince of Wales and the outgoing Prime Minister had been told of it, although George Leveson Gower smelt something afoot when he saw Devonshire cash a cheque for £30 that morning at Brooks's.* On the afternoon of the wedding the new Duke and Duchess of Devonshire took the train to Bolton for the usual grouse-shooting party. From there Louise

---

*Modern members may admire the fact of Brooks's being open on a Sunday morning in the middle of August.

answered Harry Chaplin's letter of congratulation: 'He is such a dear, so you may imagine how happy I am.' Reginald Brett wrote in his diary: 'It will make life easier for him. He saw her every day and never took a step without her sanction or advice.'

In September the Devonshires went to Austria for more shooting on Baron Hirsch's estate, and in October there was a house-party at Hardwick, to which Louise's sister Julie von Albedyll came with her two daughters; from there they went on to Chatsworth. In mid-November they had a large party which Lady Salisbury describes in a letter to Arthur Balfour:

> The minute we arrived here every one sat down to poker and bezique – before we took our bonnets off! & played till dinner – Afterwards we played till 12 & then went to bed – No one knows the house or has ever been in it except its master. No one either has the slightest knowledge of, or interest in its great treasures of books pictures &c . . . It is all like Offenbachs Brigands & I sing to myself 'Les Espagnolles' all day –
>
> But I think they are all very happy which is a great thing – Only they would all be so much happier at Monte Carlo & the mise en scene would fit them so much better . . .
>
> But I think it is a pity that not *one* of his family or friends are here* . . .
>
> P.S. Both the host & hostess are I think very unwell. Colds – bronchitis rheumatism &c –

Balfour, however, wrote back on the 15th: 'Hartington loves his gamblers and the Duchess is quite right to furnish them for him.' On 30 January 1893 Reginald Brett attended a party at Devonshire House and noted: 'For the first time for 80 years a Duchess of Devonshire is entertaining there. A most interesting and delightful party.'

Despite this hectic social life the Devonshire finances were beginning to horrify the Duke as his father's affairs were slowly disentangled. The 7th Duke's gigantic income had collapsed in the last seventeen years of his life. Agricultural depression caused the estate revenue to fall from £140,000 at its

---

*Lady Salisbury lists Louise's family in the party – the Gosfords and Stanleys and Lord Charles Montagu – but no Cavendishes. She mentions, however, Devonshire's cousin Lord Clifden (Leo Ellis's nephew) and others such as the Duke of Portland who could hardly be denied the title of Devonshire's friends. It is revealing of the 7th Duke's reclusiveness that she feels able to say: 'No one knows the house or has ever been in it.'

height to £65,000 in the doldrums of the mid-1890s; but whereas other landowners' non-agricultural interests, where they had them, had tended to compensate for this, the recession in iron and steel had struck an even heavier blow at Barrow; the dividend income, once as high as £170,000, was plummeting until it reached a low of £15,000 in 1896. What made it worse was that the 7th Duke had not used his huge wealth of the early 1870s to pay off a single penny of debt. The interest even on £1,200,000 seemed easily affordable out of his income at the time. This changed dramatically as income fell, and moreover the Duke started throwing more and more money at his failing industrial fief, borrowing heavily for the purpose. Despite his conscientious adherence to liberal political economy, he never learnt that economic paternalism was not the way to run an efficient business. By the end of his life the debt had gone up to nearly £2 million, and the interest was swallowing up more than half his annual income. It is instructive to compare this performance with that of the 15th Earl of Derby, who contemporaneously managed a similar great estate in Lancashire. His father the Prime Minister had left him a debt of half a million in 1869, but the 15th Earl (running a less reclusive regime than Devonshire) not only paid this off but accumulated a surplus of over a million pounds, at the same time as he raised his income from £170,000 to £240,000 before his death in 1893.

The 7th Duke of Devonshire's administration shows a total lack of financial control. A chandelier had been hired from a London firm for an event at Devonshire House under the 6th Duke, and the bill had simply gone on being paid year by year while the house was practically disused. At Chatsworth no bells had ever been installed for servants; a footman was posted outside each bedroom to whom the guest would give his orders – a system even more wasteful when there were few guests than when the house was buzzing with activity. A more common type of blindness is reflected in a story told by the trainer Richard Marsh about a bookie friend who was entertained by the 7th Duke's butler and exclaimed on the excellence of the port. 'Ah,' said the butler, 'what would the old Duke give for a glass of this!'

Hartington's early biographers depicted a case in which the Devonshire estate had been rescued by the careful management of the 7th Duke from the extravagance of the 6th and handed over to be enjoyed with lethargy by his successor and grandeur by the Duchess. It was left to David Cannadine to look into the accounts and reveal the 8th Duke as the saviour of his family's fortune.

Shattered as he initially was by his discovery, he set about putting things right with reluctant ruthlessness. The whole of the Barrow interests were disposed of, including the Naval Construction Company based there, which was transferred to Vickers, Maxim & Co. in exchange for a £300,000 shareholding; this proved a very good bargain in the Boer War, when Vickers dividends shot up and helped to boost the Duke's income to nearly £160,000. The other main resource was selling off much of the Irish estates to tenants under the government's new assisted-purchase scheme, and £660,000 was raised in this way. A further £130,000 was raised by selling part of the vast Derbyshire estate – unfortunately at the bottom of the market. By these expedients the Duke paid off £1,000,000 of debt by 1899 and another half-million by 1908, so that by the end of his life interest payments were down to 15 per cent of current income, a lower proportion than either the 7th or the 6th Duke had ever been burdened with. The ducal income of over £100,000 (leaving aside its Boer War peak) was much less than the 7th Duke had had, but at least it was almost wholly available. By most standards it was a magnificent fortune, and it was employed in a princely fashion.

For the Duke did not, even in the first dire years, allow his difficulties to reduce him to meanness. For a time indeed he was talking of selling Devonshire House (whose rates alone were £3,000 a year) and shutting down Chatsworth and Hardwick. We may judge what Louise had to say about that from her reply when a friend mentioned the rumour with regard to Devonshire House: 'Yes, perfectly true. We are proposing to live at Clapham Junction instead. So convenient a train service.' The fact was that, of his five country houses (Holker had been left to Victor Cavendish), the Duke did not sell one in the course of his tenure. Chiswick House was regrettably leased to a lunatic asylum, although its delicate classical gates were used in 1897 to replace the grim blocks at Devonshire House (they now stand on the other side of Piccadilly, at the entrance to Green Park). But otherwise the Duke followed a typical line of *noblesse oblige* in handing down to his successor the legacy which he himself had received. His choice was unconstrained, since the Devonshire estates were unusual in being completely free of entail.

In every respect the Duke was magnificent in discharging his duties. He gave £10,000 to Cambridge University after being elected Chancellor in succession to his father. In 1892 he appointed a proper librarian at Chatsworth (under his father the job had been done in a vague and non-resident way by Sir James Lacaita), choosing the young but already well-known art critic Arthur

Strong; he was also librarian to the Duke of Portland, but was dismissed about this time for smoking – a prejudice Devonshire was in no danger of falling into. When Strong died, aged only forty, in 1903, the duty was continued by his very able widow. Under their care Chatsworth became known internationally, to use the latter's description, as 'the very type of a princely collection conducted on princely lines'. No request was refused to lend treasures for exhibition, and a programme of picture-cleaning led to many discoveries. Country-house tourism, so often thought a product of our own age, was already a feature of the Victorian period, although in those days the only charge was a tip to the guide. By the end of the Duke's life 80,000 visitors a year were trooping round Chatsworth, at no gain to the owner. 'I dare say they will bring down the floors some day', he remarked, 'but I don't see how we can keep them out.'

A story was told of the Duke's visit to the Paris Exhibition when he stopped to admire a superb porphyry table in the English Section. 'This is splendid,' he said. 'I envy the man who owns this.' The friend he was with glanced at the catalogue and saw that it was lent from Chatsworth. His reluctance to show guests round the house contributed to a similar impression, and he strengthened it by such replies as to the connoisseur Earl of Crawford and Balcarres when he was marvelling at Chatsworth's treasures: 'Yes, it's a rummy old place.' The Duke did not transcend his generation, which was the most philistine the English aristocracy has produced for centuries, but he took an intelligent man's interest in his collections. He was sometimes to be surprised imparting recondite information to guests about this or that treasure. Once he walked in while some restored mediaeval tapestries from Hardwick were being hung in the Sculpture Gallery, a space otherwise monopolized by the frigid creations of Canova. After surveying the effect he pronounced: 'I can only say that to hang Gothic tapestries behind statues in the classic style is simply ridiculous, and nothing will induce me to think otherwise.'

A duty of his position which the Duke failed to relish was making ecclesiastical appointments. He was a churchman of the old Whig mould and viewed the choosing of clergymen much as Melbourne had viewed that of bishops when he was Prime Minister: 'Damn it all, another Bishop dead! I believe they do it to vex me.' With thirty-eight livings in his gift it was no negligible task, and the Duke used to have recourse to his sister's advice, his first concern being to appoint sound middle-of-the-road men with no fancy doctrines.

His own tastes influenced his stewardship, and G.W.E. Russell recalls: 'I
have seldom heard him speak with greater animation than when he was
protesting against the restrictions imposed in this country on public gambling
– "I own two towns which would be splendid places for gaming-tables. Not
Barrow – Barrow is too businesslike. But Buxton and Eastbourne – both full of
idle people and invalids. Gaming-tables are just what they want."'

Just before his marriage Devonshire was appointed a Knight of the Garter,
an honour which every Duke of Devonshire has held to this day. He also
accepted the Lord Lieutenancy of Derbyshire in succession to his father. When
offered the post he told Lord Salisbury that he 'could not even go through the
form of demurring. My father told me that he believed the office had been held
by one of our family for over two hundred years,* and I know that he hoped that
I might succeed him.' Louise, too, flung herself into her local duties as she had
when she became Duchess of Manchester. In London she might set the pace of
the fastest set, but in Derbyshire she took to tenants' dinners and agricultural
shows like a perfect Lady Bountiful. The first Duchess of Devonshire for
eighty years did much more than fulfil expectations. It was the same when the
Duke was elected Mayor of Eastbourne in 1897. The residents were thrilled at
the garden parties their glamorous mayoress gave with a zeal quite beyond the
graciousness of the conventional great lady.

Louise is said to have made the Duke cut down on his racing expenditure,
and he may have been forced to do so in the middle 1890s. The early years of
the decade had been a good time for him, with two notable horses, Morion and
Marvel, winning a string of races. In 1892 the Duke leased the Prince of
Wales's horses while he was in mourning for his eldest son the Duke of
Clarence, and in November of that year he moved his own twenty-one horses
and eight of the Prince's to Marsh's new training establishment at Egerton
House. Marsh wrote of him: 'I liked and admired him so much because he was
so very fond of his horses, and especially in the breeding of them. So fond was
he that he hated selling them privately, and still more had he a dislike of getting
rid of the bad ones through the medium of selling plates.' He mentions the
Duke's refusal of a splendid offer of £15,000 for Morion from Count Lehn-

---

*From 1660 it had always been held by the Earls and Dukes of Devonshire except in 1685–9
(when James II excluded the 4th Earl), 1711–14 (Queen Anne's pure Tory interlude) and 1764–6,
when the under-age 5th Duke succeeded; he was nevertheless appointed as soon as he reached
eighteen.

dorff. He still kept Beaufort House in Newmarket High Street and remarked after his succession, 'I have six houses, and the only one I really enjoy is the house at Newmarket.' Lord Esher wrote: 'I often saw him tremble with excitement as the horses began the final rise of the Rowley Mile at Newmarket and his straw jacket was seen to be in the van.' But he pronounced the Duke not a fine judge of racing, lacking quickness of eye. He had the reputation of playing the strictest game, running his horses whenever they were fit to race, even when their chances were slim. The assiduous Leach totted up that Devonshire won about £90,000 in prize money in the twenty years 1884–1903, but it was far less than he spent, and the three or four years after 1892, when he was cutting down expenses, were particularly fallow, with only one horse, Balsamo, doing him credit.

If the Duchess made him trim his costs it was not from lack of interest on her part. She was still a familiar figure at the races, and in the early years of her marriage was running after other pleasures as merrily as ever. Florence Williams describes giving a fancy-dress dinner-party at the then fashionable Niagara ice-rink, south of St James's Park. As usual when she gave a party she turned to Louise for advice, and that lady was inspired to borrow a black domino of Florence's and go with her to Niagara. During the after-dinner dance Sir John Leslie, disguised as an organ-grinder, came up to Louise and, recognizing the domino, addressed her: 'Now then, Firenze, it's no good mimicking the old Duchess, because I know it's you.' Luckily Louise neither saw through his disguise nor knew of Florence's taste for mimicking her friends.

Louise's marriage earned her the nickname of the Double Duchess, although no one would have used it to her face. It also promoted her to an even grander position than she had enjoyed as Duchess of Manchester; the Devonshires' great possessions obliged them to make an annual progress like a medieval court. The year began at Chatsworth with an enormous house-party, as Louise's friends were gathered from their own celebrations over Christmas. The house would be packed at this time, to the bewilderment of the Duke, who once told his secretary, as he surveyed the company assembled in the Library before dinner: 'This is all very well, but I should like to know who all my guests are. Do you know the name of that red-faced man over there?' The Duke of Portland tells the story of a friend of his who arrived rather late one evening and had to be given a bed in the hall porter's room. Early next morning he was roused by a rain of letter-bags on top of him and the voice of the postman: 'Get up, you lazy young devil! You've overslept yourself again!' Arthur Balfour describes one of these parties in January 1895, when he played ice-hockey, and noted: 'There are 14 bicycles in the hall.' Cycling was the very latest craze and therefore strenuously adopted by the Duchess in her sixties, who started practising it in the carriage court of Devonshire House, behind the privacy of its enclosing wall. Another new fashion was bridge, which the Prince of Wales had turned to when the Tranby Croft scandal made him give up baccarat, and it immediately became the smart game. Louise took it up with such energy that she was nicknamed Grand Slam; the Duke, who had played a good game of whist all his life, found it difficult to adapt to and played with irritating slowness. The story was told, in illustration of his hatred of unfair dealing, that one evening his partner, as she waited for his declaration, said: 'Of course you will make no trumps.' He immediately proceeded to make a different declaration and to lose every trick, growling at her at the end: 'I shall do this every time if you are not careful.' That was not the Duchess's approach, for she was notoriously out to win by fair means or foul. When her poorer guests lost to her, though, they noticed that their cheques remained uncashed.

Shooting was a big occupation at Chatsworth, and Devonshire showed the Duke of Portland a gate where he said he must have made a record shot. He fired at a wounded cock-pheasant which was running past the gate, killed it and also killed a retriever which was running to pick it up; with the same shot he hit the owner of the retriever in the leg and also the Chatsworth chef, who was watching. 'I asked him, "Which did you most regret having hit?"' writes Portland. '"Why, the chef, of course," he replied; "for if he had been badly wounded, all our dinners might have been spoiled."'

Late winter was traditionally Louise's time for gambling at Monte Carlo, where Daisy Princess of Pless said that she was followed by detectives and watched by the croupiers in case she tried to snatch any money. As for the Duke, he was known to allow the spinning wheel to disturb his usual calm, much as when he was watching his straw jacket take the lead at Newmarket. In early spring they went for a few weeks to Lismore, which had not lost its charm despite Ireland's troubles. Here Devonshire fished in the Blackwater beneath the castle's walls, and Louise accommodated herself to this rural pursuit. Daisy Brooke's husband, who became the Earl of Warwick in 1893, wrote of the Duke: 'He thoroughly enjoyed his fishing, and was so pleasant a companion that we were always delighted at any success he obtained.' After Easter the scene was Devonshire House, which awoke from its long sleep in 1893 for a London season such as it had not known since the 6th Duke's time. No invitations were more coveted, and the grim wooden gates that had scowled on Piccadilly for thirty-five years opened to the smartest carriages of that cheerful thoroughfare, while flower-boxes sprang into colour on the plain brick walls. The Duke moved upstairs to take full possession of the main floor; the two square corner rooms overlooking the carriage court were appropriated for Their Graces. The south-east one became Louise's boudoir, and that on the south-west was the Duke's bedroom. It adjoined the long Library, which remained his den as it had been when he was Lord Hartington. By the north window, which looked on to the garden, was his desk and next to it a table neatly covered with the thirty or so cigar and cigarette cases that people had given him in the course of a long smoking career.

During the summer the Devonshires went down for week-ends at Compton Place, where there was much political society. It was a pleasant, sunny early Georgian house of modest proportions. According to Florence Williams, there was nothing to do there but play bridge, but others no doubt took an interest in the adjoining Polegate stud farm where the ducal horses were bred. Compton was the scene of a famous exchange when a guest who had been climbing round the ruins of Pevensey Castle sought to please his host that evening by praising this notable part of the Cavendish property. 'Pevensey?' said the Duke; the name rang a bell. 'Whose is Pevensey?'

The twelfth of August found the Devonshires inescapably at Bolton Abbey for the grouse season. The house was merely a shooting box attached to the old abbey gatehouse, with the monastic ruins adjoining. To Lady Frederick Cavendish Bolton had always been 'Happy Valley' during her husband's life, and he had been foremost of the shots who enjoyed its superb moors. 'Swarms of birds,' Sir Henry James noted after shooting there in 1886, and Sir Augustus Paget found the same in 1893: 'Anything like the number of birds here I never saw before, and everything connected with the chase most beautifully managed.' Sir Augustus was charmed by Louise's making him take her in to dinner although noblemen of higher rank were present, and he gave his wife a glowing picture: 'We breakfast at 9, the Duchess being almost always the first down. She appears to me since I have been here to be quite different from the idea I have always had of her – quite natural, so friendly and amiable without any sort of swagger or pretension, and doing the amiable hostess in the most perfect manner. She and the Duke quite on the footing of an old married couple.' The party would go up to the moors in the morning on ponies, the Duke following on a cob. Luncheon was served at half past three or later, and they were home any time after eight. One night the Duke, when fully dressed for dinner, fell into the bath in his dressing-room and in the hurry of changing appeared in a coloured shirt. 'Great merriment!' reported Sir Augustus. 'After dinner,' he adds, 'everyone sets to work at cards, and I take the newspaper or a book and go to bed when I like.'

Pheasant shooting in October required a visit to Hardwick, where things ran in similar fashion. The New Year parties Hartington had always held at Hardwick since 1877 were now replaced by those at Chatsworth. Here, Louise held a string of house-parties throughout the winter and ruled them on autocratic lines. Margot Asquith recalled: 'I have heard her reprove and mildly ridicule all her guests, both at Compton Place and at Chatsworth, from the Prince of Wales to the Prime Minister.' And her grandson Manchester described her taste for snubbing everybody and for making people sit up. The languid Balfour was a great offender, his habitual posture being described as seeking 'to discover how nearly he could sit on his shoulder-blades'. Louise would call out to him at dinner: 'Sit up, Arthur! Sit up, immediately!' – orders which Balfour took with complete good humour.

For Christmas Louise used to have a tree specially brought over from Germany and loaded with presents for the guests. Florence Williams describes coming to Chatsworth a week before Christmas with her daughter Gwenfra, who had been given a jack-in-the-box at Claridge's before they left London. They arrived at lunch-time, and the little girl took the box to the Duke's place at the head of the table and presented it to the eminent elder statesman. The Duke's reaction when he unwrapped and opened it more than fulfilled expectations, but when he had recovered he asked to borrow the jack-in-the-box and played the same trick on successive guests as they arrived over the next few days.

Under the Liberal government, two political issues principally stirred Devonshire's concern. The first was the Irish Home Rule Bill which Gladstone got through on his Commons majority in 1893, and the Lords had to resort to an autumn sitting to deal with it. It was appropriate that the man who had done most to wreck the first Home Rule Bill should be on the spot when the measure was at the mercy of the Upper House. The Duke led the Bill's rejection in a weighty speech on 5 September, and it was thrown out by 419 votes to 41, most of the minority being government office-holders. The virtual extinction of official Liberalism in the House of Lords was thereby signalled. Although some of the defects of the 1886 Bill had been remedied, Devonshire pointed out the insistence on imposing a Dublin government on Ulster as one of the continuing features that damned it; in words that echoed Lord John Russell's Whig historicism he upheld the right of resistance which in 1914 came to the verge of being exercised: 'Who can say – how, at all events, can the descendants of those who resisted King James II say – that they have not the right to resist the imposition of a government put upon them by force?'

Ireland was no longer the seething cauldron it had been under Parnell's leadership, and the failure of the Home Rule Bill stirred little reaction. In England it was received with relief. The fact that it had spoken for the nation placed the House of Lords in a strong position, and it set about using this to maul the government's other Radical measure of the same year, the Parish Councils Bill, which aimed at setting up a local democracy. Devonshire made a strong plea for moderation, realizing that partisan action would in the long run damage the Lords. Under his leadership the gap between Liberal Unionists and Tories in the House widened once more, and the Bill eventually went through comparatively unscathed.

In March 1894 Gladstone finally won his battle with his duty, and Lord Rosebery took over as Prime Minister. This was personally welcome to the Duke of Devonshire, and his sporting sense was pleased by Rosebery's feat of winning the Derby in both the summers he held office, 1894 and 1895. What charmed the Duke less was the Budget produced in 1894 by William Harcourt as Chancellor of the Exchequer. Harcourt had for twelve years before 1886 promoted himself as a loyal Hartingtonian, but now he was bidding for Radical support with a view to succession to the Liberal leadership. He imposed swingeing death-duties aimed at whittling away the estates of the landed class, with a progressive tariff rising to 8 per cent on estates above £1 million. His policy has since been taken so much further that we treat such a tariff as ridiculously mild; yet at the time its unfairness was manifest. The measure came at the depth of the agricultural depression, when wheat prices had fallen to only half their level of twenty years before, and sound policy would have pointed to an easing of burdens on landed property. Moreover, real estate unlike personalty was already burdened with rates, which the depression had made unrealistically high on agricultural land, and was thus being attacked twice over. One can trace the discriminatory drive of this tax by the experience of the past hundred years, when large landownership alone has been penalized while business conglomerations, even under socialist finance, have grown bigger and bigger. It was easier for democratic politicians to target the declining nobility as the privileged rich rather than the Rothschilds and Liptons who were the real plutocracy of the period.

To the Duke of Devonshire this blow came just at the time when the full extent of his father's debts became known, and the impact was devastating. He told Sir Edward Hamilton that his surplus income for keeping up all the family houses was only £30,000 and that his nephew would be saddled with death duties of £600,000 – twenty years' available income. We of course know the answer to this: that ducal estates ought not to exist and that the business of government finance is to destroy them. Lewis Harcourt, on hearing the Duke's complaint that it would be impossible to keep up Devonshire House and Chatsworth, remarked that this meant they had hitherto been subsidized by the tax-payer, an early airing for the socialist doctrine that a citizen's property is what the State chooses not to confiscate from him. But the Duke was assuming the old Liberal principle that taxation was imposed on sources fully capable of bearing it. He could not bring himself to believe that the government intended a new aim, of making it an instrument of confiscation. So strongly did he feel on this that his usual good judgement deserted him and he wanted to oppose the Budget in the Lords, but Lord Salisbury pointed out what a godsend this would be to the ailing Liberal government. The death duties went through, and ten subsequent years of Conservative rule failed to dismantle them.

12
Elder Statesman

IN JUNE 1895 Lord Rosebery resigned as Prime Minister after a weak government of sixteen months, ended by a minor defeat in a Commons division. The accession of this Whig magnate to the leadership might have seemed the chance to bring the Liberal Unionists back to their fold, but the political will was absent. Only if the Liberals had swallowed their pride and jettisoned both Home Rule and the Newcastle Programme of 1891 could Devonshire have contemplated reunion; and parties seldom see their plight as desperate enough for such surrenders. Besides, the personal atmosphere had been soured by Joseph Chamberlain, who had led the Liberal Unionists in the Commons since 1892 and whose adversarial sharpness rankled in a way Hartington's leadership never had.

The Liberals' ten-year eclipse could not be foreseen, and to the Unionists the priority was to prevent the recurrence of a Home Rule government. They therefore espoused the formal coalition rejected in 1886. There had been talk of a ministry under the Duke of Devonshire, but the Liberal Unionists were no longer the key floating element they had been in 1886 and were in a weaker position as a permanent and minor centre party. Lord Salisbury therefore took the premiership on Rosebery's resignation. He brought five Liberal Unionists into his Cabinet, a share reflecting their weight in the House of Lords rather than the Commons. Devonshire was offered the Foreign Office but judged that his French was not good enough and opted for the near sinecure of Lord President of the Council; with this came the presidency of the Committee of Defence which had earlier been recommended by Hartington's own Parliamentary Commission to co-ordinate the two services. The other Whig grandee to enter the Cabinet was the Marquess of Lansdowne, whose daughter had married Victor Cavendish. Lord Salisbury, in making him Secretary for War, gave the specific reason that as an intimate of Devonshire's he would work well with him in the Committee of Defence. The Admiralty went to

Goschen, who had already served with the Tories in 1887–92. Sir Henry James, now ennobled, became Chancellor of the Duchy of Lancaster, and Chamberlain was Colonial Secretary. Among the Tories, a promotion that must have pleased Devonshire was that of his old racing friend Harry Chaplin as President of the Local Government Board.

Sir Frederick Ponsonby relates that at the hand-over of office care was taken to keep the outgoing and incoming ministers apart, given the unusual situation that some of the latter were Liberal turncoats. The Liberals therefore waited on the Queen at Windsor at eleven, and the Unionists, whose appointment was for twelve, were kept hidden in a room apart. The Duke, however, was very late, having driven over separately from a place near Windsor. 'As he came up the stairs he met all his old colleagues who had just given up their seals and who, of course, chaffed him on his joining the other party. No face was, however, more suited to a difficult situation like this and he was quite unperturbed and passed through them with his mouth wide open and his eyes half closed.'

It was the Duke's task as Lord President to supervise the swearing-in of the new Privy Councillors. This was the fourth Cabinet in which he had taken office, and yet as he stood reading out the list of Councillors his hands were seen to be trembling so badly that he nearly dropped the sheet of paper.

It proved lucky that the government was formed before the General Election, which was immediately called, for the Tories emerged with at ten-seat overall majority and might otherwise have taken office alone. With by-election losses, however, the 71-strong Liberal Unionists became by 1900 a necessary partner in the coalition. The Duke of Devonshire found himself for the first time serving with Lord Salisbury, and popular opinion thought them ill-assorted colleagues; certainly few great aristocrats had less in common. Salisbury was a devout, subtle, scholarly man, shy of society and uninterested in sports or amusements. But there was less distance between them than between Hartington and Gladstone. Salisbury's was a realistic and unbombastic intelligence congenial to the Duke, who also formed a hearty audience to the witticisms the Prime Minister liked to scatter about him. Some of these were at Devonshire's expense, such as his allusion to the priority the Duke gave to the racing calendar. When suggesting a date for a Cabinet meeting he would turn to Devonshire and enquire: 'Does that happen to be a sacred day, Duke?' On being asked by somebody whether he played bridge Salisbury said no, but he thought of learning, as he then might get to know the Duke of Devonshire.

The Duke also had his fun, and in the circles of the Liberal Unionist Association he liked to indulge in simple humour against his Tory colleagues. The Vice-Chairman of the Association was his nephew Victor Cavendish, whose political apprenticeship left him with a lifetime's conviction of the separateness of the Whig tribe. He was abetted by other Whigs such as Lord Lansdowne, and years later when the two were caught by a shower in Pall Mall and Victor suggested their taking refuge in the Carlton Club, Lord Lansdowne looked at him aghast and insisted on battling through the rain to the safety of Brooks's. Harold Macmillan recalled shooting with Victor, by then Duke of Devonshire, well after the First World War and hearing his host complain, 'These damned grouse; they won't fly straight – like a lot of Tories.'

The Duke of Portland tells the story that Lord Salisbury in Cabinet once turned to Devonshire for his opinion on a subject, only to find him asleep. He was woken up, and the whole argument pro and con was repeated for his benefit; he then gave his opinion, which was immediately adopted by the Cabinet. One suspects that Ben Trovato, rather than a Cabinet informant, was the source of this story. A similar impression is given by Arthur Balfour's reply when rebuked for ignoring a Cabinet vote: 'I was quite unaware of any such decision, but our decisions are very often unpalpable and perhaps I ought to have been able to construct one from materials afforded by Devonshire's yawns and casual interjections round the table.' Lord George Hamilton, who was Secretary for India in that Cabinet, describes the Duke's habit of reverting to a discussion that had been long closed with some new objection or suggestion; his rumination, however, usually proved so apposite that his colleagues had no choice but to go back and reopen the topic.

The Duke of Portland tells of another occasion when Devonshire walked into the House of Lords and, finding the ministerial bench full, casually walked over and sat next to Portland. In two minutes he was asleep. When he woke with a start he looked at the clock and said, 'Good heavens! What a bore! I shan't be in bed for another seven hours!' Devonshire's own humour contributed to this narcoleptic legend. Once when conversation turned to the question of dreams coming true he cited a case from his own experience: 'I had a horrid nightmare. I dreamed that I was making a speech in the House of Lords – and I woke up and found I was actually doing so.' Growing deafness was making him vaguer and more remote, and it is from this period of his life that date the comic anecdotes which built up posterity's idea of his character and which tend to obscure his commanding political stature of the 1880s.

The Duke of Devonshire had attained a unique national standing, compounded of his position as head of one of the great historic families, his popularity on the Turf, and the trust inspired by his now familiar character. Among many, his record as the man who had saved the United Kingdom from disruption gave him special honour. He became 'the Duke' as no one had been since the Duke of Wellington. His friends continued to call him Hartington, while to Victor and his growing family he remained 'Uncle Cav'; but as we lack that intimacy we shall know him by his public title.

The seven years 1895–1902 were one of the two political high points of Devonshire's career, and for his wife they were certainly her apogee. It is only with her second marriage that she comes into her own as a political hostess, for the Duke's position gave her a real power base as well as great houses from which to dispense patronage. Being a political hostess was a job to be worked at; it meant, first of all, having the skill to orchestrate large social events, and that had never posed a problem for Louise. She gave the big dinner at Devonshire House every February before the parliamentary Session, and this remained for seven years the leading party event; but she knew how to avoid making such things mere official functions. A hostess had influence because her invitations were desperately coveted, especially by the women who provided the domestic half of a politician's life. That Louise could ruthlessly exclude was as much a part of her power as her catholic readiness to woo and welcome.

One of the Duke's Cabinet colleagues called the Duchess the most powerful person outside the government. Several ministers were established members of her circle; first of these was Arthur Balfour – a major asset as the Prime Minister's nephew and Conservative leader in the Commons. The Salisburys, by contrast, were never to be seen at Devonshire House or Chatsworth if they could avoid it. Then there were Lord James and Harry Chaplin as old racing friends of the Duke's. Lord Lansdowne could not really be classed as a Devonshire House man, partly perhaps because his wife was a rising hostess of her own. The oddest among those very much included was Joseph Chamberlain – odd because Louise did not really like him; but she was ready to suppress such feelings in view of his position in the Liberal Unionist party and in the Cabinet.

The Devonshire House circle also contained several leading Liberals. Sir William Harcourt (Liberal leader 1896–8) clung to his friendship with Devonshire like a limpet but never won cordial acceptance from Louise. On the other hand, Rosebery's long-standing friendship was as warm as ever; although he resigned the party leadership in 1896 he remained the ablest Liberal in the Lords, and right up to 1905 there were thoughts of his coming back as Prime Minister. It was this subtle and world-weary statesman who paid Louise the compliment of calling her the wisest woman he had ever known. A surprising habitué of her set was Herbert Asquith, whose connection came through his marriage to Margot Tennant in 1894. He refused the Liberal leadership on Harcourt's resignation because he could not afford to give up his career at the Bar, but he became with Rosebery, Grey and Haldane one of the group of Liberal imperialists who dominated the party's councils. His liking for the social fleshpots was one of the more curious traits of this slightly pedantic Yorkshire lawyer, and he and his wife were at the heart of the smartest set in the country.

The presence of these politicians made the Devonshire House circle important especially to diplomatic society, and it was frequented by some of the best-known diplomats of the period. Among these was Count Albert Mensdorff, First Secretary at the Austrian Embassy and Ambassador from 1904, who took pride in being a cousin of the English Royal Family both through the Saxe-Coburgs and through Queen Victoria's mother the Duchess of Kent. Another camp-follower was Baron von Eckardstein, who married the daughter of a well-known English racing owner and from 1899 virtually ran the German Embassy as First Secretary. The most celebrated was the Marquis de Soveral, who returned to London in 1897 as Portuguese Ambassador after a short stint as his country's Foreign Minister. What gave him prominence was his close friendship with the Prince of Wales and his social ease ('what perfect manner – what risqué stories!' recalled Lady Warwick). His nickname 'the Blue Monkey' derived from his six o'clock shadow and his skill as an entertainer.

A major source of influence was that the Devonshires were among the three or four hosts who entertained the Prince and Princess of Wales (from 1901 the King and Queen) year after year. Of the other leading hostesses the closest to the Prince was Lady Warwick, followed perhaps by the willowy and artistic Lady De Grey, whose husband was ubiquitous in country-house society as one of the legendary shots of the period. As a strictly political hostess Louise's main rival was Theresa Marchioness of Londonderry. Her husband had been Lord Lieutenant of Ireland in 1886–9, and although he did not reach the Cabinet until 1900 he was, next to Lord Salisbury himself, the most important peer in the Tory ranks. Theresa Londonderry was thus the leader of Tory society, while Louise Devonshire took her place at the head of the Whig camp. If there was any aptness in this it was in the freer manners that marked the Devonshire House circle, in keeping with the older Whig tradition. Lady Fingall identifies these two ladies as the dictators of the social scene, saying: 'If you were Lady Londonderry's friend or the Duchess of Devonshire's, no one would dare to say a word against you. It was an equally bad thing to be the enemy of either.'

Lady Londonderry's social regime was distinguished by its hauteur – Sargent indulged his gift for character in her ineffably arrogant portrait – and she was known for the pomp with which she received her parades of guests at the top of the grand staircase at Londonderry House. She was a strong partisan, described by E.F. Benson as 'a highwaywoman in a tiara', and her violent influence is said to have been behind some of the Tory political imprudences of the coming twenty years. Margot Asquith, who detested her, once angled for a judgement on this domineering figure, 'whose arrogance and vulgarity had annoyed us all', and gave Louise Devonshire's reply: 'I dislike her too much to be a good judge of her.' This was an example of the restraint that Margot noted when she described Louise as 'the last great political lady in London society as I have known it. The secret of her power lay not only in her position – many people are rich and grand, gay and clever and live in big houses – but in her elasticity, her careful criticisms, her sense of justice and discretion. She not only kept her own but other people's secrets; and she added to considerable effrontery and intrepid courage, real kindness of heart . . . She was powerful enough to entertain both the great political parties which few can do.' Elsewhere she remarks: 'Louise Devonshire was a woman whose social ascendancy eclipsed that of anyone that I have ever seen or heard of in London society . . . She had distinguished children, an intimate knowledge of men and affairs, amazing courage, a perfect profile, and unrivalled personality. She was intimate with every King, Courtier, Commoner, and Prime Minister, and there was no one in London who did not covet her invitations.'

Lady Angela Forbes writes in very similar terms: 'To be invited to Devonshire House in those days, or not to be invited, was a question of burning importance. The old Duchess of Devonshire was a personality neither preceded nor succeeded. Her approbation counted for success, and her approval secured perquisites, in the way of invitations, for many who might otherwise have remained in comparative obscurity. She had the strength of an eagle, the wisdom of the serpent and an intimate knowledge of the frailties of human nature.'

The great scene of Louise's social dictatorship was Chatsworth, and in those late-Victorian and Edwardian houses-parties which she assembled we see the epitome of the aristocratic luxury which the Prince of Wales's sybaritic tastes had brought to a peak. Such was the extravagance that a smart weekend probably cost twice as much as it had fifty years before. For men it was *de rigueur* to change one's clothes three times a day, for women four times; nor could a woman appear twice in the same outfit in the course of her stay. Where once dinner had been the only full meal of the day, now breakfast was a riot of little silver dishes, luncheon was a meal of several courses, and for tea the bloated guests were thought capable of taking in poached eggs in addition to the tea-cakes, sandwiches, cake, scones and other delicacies that had become traditional to the occasion. But it was at dinner that the serious business of eating got under way: a dozen courses elaborately prepared by a highly paid chef succeeded each other on the table, and, in case anyone felt underfed after this diet, hospitality now required that a plate of sandwiches or cold chicken be provided in each guest's bedroom at the hour of retiring. In all this Chatsworth was at the head of fashionable practice. It is true that Lady Warwick, always willing to put in a critical word, describes the food at Devonshire House as 'beyond words', and there were many English chefs in those days for whom the eminence of their establishments was sufficient cover for the mediocrity of their performance; but certainly expense was not spared. It was known for turtles to be ordered to Chatsworth from London at £24 a head to make turtle soup and to be thrown out to rot if not needed. When Vita Sackville-West wrote *The Edwardians* she attributed this practice to her ducal household as a supreme example of the extravagance of the period.

The utmost prize of a country-house party was to entertain the Prince and Princess of Wales. Chatsworth was, with two or three other places such as Warwick Castle, at the top of the royal visiting list. For all its splendour it was not the most convenient of places to stay. There was only one bathroom in the house, and it was reserved for the Prince when he was there. The other guests had their baths brought to their bedrooms and filled from immense cans of hot water. The house was always kept very hot, so that guests were at least spared the common country-house experience of shivering into and out of their baths in the spartan bathrooms of the period. The Prince's taste for practical jokes found a reflection at Chatsworth, and there was a tree in the grounds whose branches had been hollowed out and filled with water to deluge unsuspecting guests. As with the Duke and the jack-in-the-box, no one ever thought of blabbing the secret and each victim was only too eager to lure some other newcomer to the spot.

Etiquette at Chatsworth followed the semi-formal rules that applied when the Prince and Princess were among friends. One bowed or curtsied only to say good-morning and good-night. Another piece of royal influence was the high level of polished adultery that went on behind the scenes. The Prince's mistress at the beginning of this period was Daisy Warwick and, although she was not on the best of terms with Louise, outward courtesy ensured a series of mutual visits. In her own houses Lady Warwick positively encouraged her guests' liaisons; her later advocacy of the redistribution of property was backed by long experience in the redistribution of spouses. Louise Devonshire did not quite go so far, but she was expert in that tactful allocation of bedrooms from which she and Hartington had for so long benefited. It was during a house-party at Chatsworth early in 1898 that Daisy Warwick sent letters to the Prince and Princess of Wales to say that her relations with the former were now merely platonic. Any relief the Princess may have felt was clouded by the fact that her husband was just then taking his last mistress, the smart and racy Alice Keppel; she was just the kind of person Louise Devonshire took to and was even more of a regular Chatsworth visitor than Lady Warwick. The Prince did not ration himself to these ladies and once attempted at Chatsworth to persuade Daisy Princess of Pless to be 'nice' to him. When she evaded the invitation he called her a humbug.* We should note, finally, the role of Chatsworth in altering a custom that served in the pursuit of these amenities: the late-night plate of sandwiches, placed outside a bedroom door, had been

---

*Daisy's mother 'Erin' Cornwallis-West had been the Prince's mistress as one of the Society beauties of the late 1870s, and her brother George Cornwallis-West was widely thought to be the Prince's son. The possibility that Daisy too might be his daughter does not seem to have constrained the Prince.

used as a signal that it was safe for the beau to approach his belle. One night Baron Eckardstein, coming upstairs and spotting one of these snacks, found himself a little peckish and polished off the sandwiches; the invited gentleman arrived to an empty plate, which he supposed must be some warning whose exact meaning escaped him; and the Countess waiting beyond the signalled door spent the next hour or so in a state of painfully unresolved suspense. She and her imitators were obliged for the future to devise a less edible semaphore. It should be understood that all these activities were kept under a veil of strict discretion. Publicly the decorum of the house was absolute, and on one occasion when a beautiful Russian came down to breakfast in a blouse that revealed too much of her willowy charms she scandalized the whole party, not least the severe hostess; *she* had not got where she was by being transparent.

An invitation to Chatsworth introduced the guest to one of the stateliest and most finely sited great houses in England. The house stands on the slopes of a long hill in a park of great beauty, which has not lost the rugged drama of the Derbyshire hills. The west front looks down on the valley through which the river Derwent winds; a classical bridge spans the river at an angle that shows to good effect from the house and provides from the river itself, when the house on its wooded hillside is seen beyond it, a composition of picturesque perfection. The west front, with its pedimented centrepiece, is the grandest of the four. That on the south sports a majestic monotony, with twenty-four tall windows on two storeys overlooking a formal garden, where an immense canal-like pond, with the Emperor Fountain in the centre, stretches out into the pastoral landscape. From the east the famous water-steps ripple down the hillside. The house is built round a square courtyard. By rights the west front should be the entrance front, through which one would drive into the courtyard and thus reach the huge Painted Hall in the east range; but in fact that arrangement has never obtained. The 6th Duke put the main door in the north front, in what cannot escape the appearance of a makeshift side entrance. Arriving in a low square hall the visitor has to turn into a short stretch of corridor to reach the Painted Hall, which is the true introduction to the building. Rising two storeys in height, and measuring an approximate double cube of thirty feet, it is dominated by the vast frescoes of Laguerre on the walls and ceiling. At the end a monumental staircase leads to the first floor. Unusually, one has to go on to the top floor – following the Elizabethan arrangement – to reach the state apartments, which stretch in an enfilade along the south front. These are marked by a heavy seventeenth-century splendour, with richly carved panelling and sumptuous red-and-gilt wall hangings. The inconvenience of these rooms made them little used in the 8th Duke's time, and entertainment largely went on in the beautiful eighteenth-century rooms on the floor below. The long northward extension to the house built by the 6th Duke includes the elegant dining-room, where Louise's large house-parties were feasted in splendid array, the sculpture gallery and finally the theatre in the north pavilion, which now came to life again after a sleep of forty years.

The great estate in which Chatsworth was set matched the resources of the house; the shooting was particularly praised, with excellent high-flying birds and bags of a thousand head regularly recorded. As time went on the Duke's oversight of these arrangements became increasingly vague. Sir Frederick Ponsonby, writing of a time when the Duke had passed seventy, declares that he only chose the guns late at night, so that the list was not known until next morning. If he was feeling sleepy he would simply say, 'The same guns as today.' Lord Rosebery once came down to breakfast in his shooting clothes, not having shot the day before, and was met by his valet who said: 'You had better take those clothes off, my Lord, as you are not on the shooting list.' Rosebery was furious and promptly left for London, provoking an apology from the Duke. This was not the only drawback of large numbers. Lord Rosebery wrote to Daisy of Pless after a party at Chatsworth: 'Unfortunately in a great Vanity Fair of that kind one only sees those or converses with those whom one shoots with or golfs with or Bridges with or sits next to at dinner.' Daisy herself felt during her first visits: 'It is not really a "happy" house to stay in; it all breathes "society" and nothing else.' By 1907 she seemed to be more reconciled to 'all the usual Court set and a nice mixture of people with brains'.

Louise Devonshire, for all the grandeur she had reached, was not without family troubles. Lady May Montagu, one of her beautiful twin granddaughters, died in March 1895 aged only sixteen; the other, Alice (known as Nell), was to die in 1900, to the added grief of the family. Sir Shane Leslie wrote: 'The Manchester twins were the two most beautiful and delicate girls imaginable. They both died before the world of men or worry could add a line of sorrow to their angel faces.' Their brother the 9th Duke of Manchester went on from Eton to Cambridge in 1894, being sent there with the adequate though not splendid allowance of £400; by the end of his first year he had run up debts of £2,000, and the experience was not repeated. He was sent out to East Africa for nine months and on his return spent his time trying to find a rich bride. In 1897 he was pursuing May Goelet, who belonged to one of the best families of old New York society and had just been launched with great success into the London scene. But the Goelets knew better than to entertain such a match, and in May 1898 Manchester was engaged to Joan Wilson, of the Tranby Croft family (her cousin the beautiful Muriel Wilson was a popular visitor at Chatsworth and regular actress in the private theatricals). The marriage was put off twice, however, and after a year she dropped him.

A similar scene was found in the family of Louise's second daughter. Lord Gosford was running up racing debts that forced him to sell the library and finally the whole contents of Gosford Castle. The heir, Lord Acheson, who came of age in 1898, was also obliged to turn fortune-hunter and ended by marrying an American heiress in 1910. His three sisters, Alexandra, Mary and Theo, began to be launched in society at the turn of the century and inherited the good looks of the women of the family. They were painted by John Singer Sargent at Chatsworth in 1902 in one of his most superb group portraits.

One success Louise Devonshire had not attained: that of vanquishing Queen Victoria's disapproval. Nevertheless, now that she was an 'honest woman' the Queen could not positively refuse to receive her, and Louise eventually stormed even this bastion. In May 1897 Lady Salisbury was ill, and her task of presenting diplomatic ladies to the Queen at three levées was passed on to the Duchess. We can imagine the triumph with which she returned to the field of her forty-year-old glory, and she is described as looking 'very regal in a lovely costume of violet velvet'. The royal attitude did not stop Louise from choosing the Queen's Diamond Jubilee as the occasion for the high point of her social career, the fancy-dress ball she held at Devonshire House in July 1897. It was the event by which she demonstrated to the full the splendours of the house, her own skill as a hostess and the position she had won that made her ball, in a year of pomps and ceremonies, the *ne plus ultra* of the 1897 season. She was wise to wait five years to work up to this climax.

The ball was fixed for 2 July 1897. Although the invitations were not sent out until the end of May everyone knew about it well in advance (and had even ordered their costumes – some with an over-optimism betrayed when their invitation failed to arrive); no one even dreamed of holding a rival entertainment on that night. It was to be a fancy-dress ball such as London had never seen. Memories remained of the great Marlborough House ball of 1874, which until then had been perhaps the touchstone of splendour, and Lady Warwick had held an eighteenth-century ball at Warwick Castle in 1895; but generally hostesses fought shy of requiring fancy dress of Victorian manhood. Such fears did not deter Louise Devonshire. The chance of passing a night in the glittering rooms of Devonshire House, and at the request of the Double Duchess, tempted dukes, statesmen and savants to lay aside their gravity. Seven hundred invitations were sent out, and inclusion or exclusion stirred emotions to which only the *Paradiso* and *Inferno* could have done justice.

Thus, there was poor Lord Charles Beresford, who was still at odds with the Prince of Wales and could not be invited to a function graced by the royal presence. After six years of estrangement, that year's Ascot witnessed his desperate manoeuvres. He accosted the Duke and Duchess of Devonshire in a hail-fellow-well-met manner and exclaimed how glad he was to see them again. Louise described this strange behaviour to the Prince and said they had been so taken aback that they did not know what to do. But before the end of Ascot Lord Marcus Beresford asked if his brother might be allowed to congratulate the Prince on the success of his horse Persimmon, which he did very humbly. Thus the rift was healed, but it was too late; Louise's list was closed and Lord Charles did not come to the ball.

Lady Fingall tells how the previous year, as a young and unsophisticated visitor from Ireland, she committed the sin of sitting on a bench at Newmarket that was reserved for the Prince and a select few of his lady friends. As Louise Devonshire approached she drew her skirts aside and said, 'Do come and sit down here.' The Duchess simply glared at her and sat down at the other end of the bench. The Prince, however, was charming and the next day made her sit on the bench with him. Louise was furious and when the time came did not invite Lady Fingall to the ball.

One feature of Louise's circle in London was its cosmopolitanism, which marked it out at a time when few English people thought that anything beyond the Channel could matter a great deal. We thus see a large number of foreigners, some of imperial or royal birth, among the guests at the ball.* A well-connected American tells the story of one foreign lady who moved heaven and earth to get herself invited, finally appealing to her country's ambassador.

---

*Princess Alexandra was reported to have been 'horribly bored' by the number of foreign guests; a Danish Princess's prerogative, no doubt.

'If I am not asked to this ball,' she said, 'my position in Paris, in St Petersburg, in Vienna, will be ruined.' His Excellency waited on the Duchess and expounded the international crisis looming; but Louise was like flint: her list was closed. Then, after a pause, she added: 'If she likes to come without a card she may come.' Our informal age needs to understand the humiliation mixed with the mercy of this reply.

The invitation sent out in May stipulated 'allegorical or historical costume before 1815'. The guests threw themselves into the task of finding interesting and *recherché* costumes, and the Print Room at the British Museum gaped at the sight of smart ladies and gentlemen competing with scholars in their researches. The idea developed of forming five courts, each led by a prominent lady, to which most of the revellers attached themselves. The Court of Queen Elizabeth was headed by Lady Tweedmouth (whose husband was one of Lord Rosebery's late Cabinet), that of Maria Theresa by Lady Londonderry, that of Queen Guinevere by Lady Ormonde, that of Marie Antoinette by Lady Warwick and that of Catherine the Great by Lady Raincliffe. Louise herself, by who knows what Freudian logic, chose to represent Zenobia Queen of Palmyra, the potentate who nearly brought the Roman empire to its knees in the third century AD, and was attended by a host of Orientals. Finally there was an Italian procession. The servants were put into Oriental and Elizabethan costumes, and the footmen wore the Devonshire livery of the eighteenth century.

As the intricate plans grew, the tension mounted lest anything should happen to wreck the ball. Two days before it the 64-year-old Duke was overturned in his carriage returning from Newmarket; but he was merely shaken, although one of his companions was put into hospital. On the very day of the ball the death of the nine-year-old Marjorie Cavendish, daughter of Lord Chesham, threw eight of the intended guests into mourning and decimated the Arthurian procession. But the fine July day smiled on the Duchess's ambitions.

The zeal shown in confecting the costumes surpassed all precedent. Louise had hers made by Worth of Paris, as did several other ladies – and not only ladies: the Duke of Marlborough ordered an eighteenth-century ensemble of dazzling sumptuousness. Louise's and Monsieur Worth's fancy flowered in a robe of cloth of silver, covered with an over-dress of gauze shot with green and gold and with a train of turquoise velvet falling from the shoulders; every part of this costume was studded with precious stones, and great ropes of pearls hung from her diamond head-dress. The Duke was more sober, although very fine, as the Emperor Charles V (the Cavendishes and Habsburgs were said to resemble each other with their jutting jaws), and the Prince of Wales had lent him his genuine Collar of the Golden Fleece to complete the costume. The Prince took inspiration from the office of Grand Prior of the Order of St John in which he had succeeded the Duke of Manchester and stirred piquant memories of the husband whom his hostess had cuckolded for thirty years.* The Princess, resplendent in almost as many pearls as Louise, was Queen Marguerite de Valois. All over London ladies had their jewels reset against time, and the day of the ball itself saw a famine of hairdressers in the capital, every minute of whose day had been bespoken to conjure the strange coiffures that were to converge on Piccadilly.

The invitations were for half past ten, and a series of separate dinners, like that of the Souls at Lord Cowper's house, gave a preview of the costumes. As the guests' carriages began to turn into the Devonshire House courtyard, a staring crowd, including many less favoured members of Society, and even, it was said, a relation of royalty, thronged at the gates. The costumed figures began to alight under the *porte cochère* and to climb the swirling crystal stair-case to where Louise and her husband stood to receive them. At a quarter past eleven the Prince and Princess of Wales arrived. The Duke and Duchess took them across the ballroom to the Saloon, where a dais had been set up from which they were to watch the processions. Carefully rehearsed, the Eliza-bethan, Austrian and Russian courts filed in; then came Louise as Zenobia, borne upon a palanquin, with slaves holding huge fans, and followed by the rest of the Orientals. Next came the Italians and the Court of Marie Antoinette and finally the 'allegorical costumes', full of goddesses and other mythological figures. The display was a dazzling one. There were a few absurdities, such as the beautiful Lady Westmorland (daughter-in-law of the Duke's late racing manager), who came as Hebe, with a large stuffed eagle perched on her shoul-der for the duration of the evening; but most of the guests had been at pains to achieve beauty and splendour. The splendid breeding of the English aris-tocracy was on display, and some of the guests, such as the Duchesses of

---

*His costume was variously described as that of a Chevalier of Malta or of a Prior or Grand Master of the Knights of St John (or of Malta). Since it was quite unhistorical, there is no point in trying to resolve these discrepancies.

Sutherland and Portland and Lady De Grey, were among the most beautiful women of their time. Consuelo Duchess of Marlborough was a ravishing sight in an eighteenth-century dress that successfully disguised the fact that she was seven months pregnant. As these figures danced and walked through the glittering rooms of Devonshire House they transcended the make-believe of a fancy-dress party. 'It seemed', wrote a contemporary, 'as if all the glories of the Renaissance, all the beauty of the French Court, and something of the barbarous magnificence of other places and periods had been dragged back from their flight into the ages, and held by some subtle charm in the keeping of the Cavendishes for the six hours of a summer night.'

After the processions the guests were offered champagne, and the dancing began in the ballroom, where great banks of flowers had been set up, as they had in all the splendid rooms. Each court opened with a quadrille of appropriate style, which had been previously rehearsed; one account recalled: 'Nothing more harmonious could well be imagined than these slow dances walked through by magnificently dressed men, and by women whose beauty and jewelled costumes set off one another with all the charm of something strange, exceptional and unique.' A programme of fifteen dances followed through the evening, but most of the guests were too absorbed in admiring each other's costumes or managing their own. After midnight supper was served in the marquee that had been set up in the garden, and which was one of the miracles of the night. A stately staircase had been built from a window of the room adjoining the ballroom, and the descent was so decorated that many guests were not even aware they were leaving the house. The same deception reigned in the marquee, where Louise must have been recalling her own wedding-ball at Wilkenburg forty-five years before. Thick crimson carpeting covered the floor, crystal chandeliers hung from the ceiling, and the walls were hidden by huge looking-glasses, tapestries and a gigantic display of gold plate from Chatsworth. The room was filled with twelve tables, each with a palm tree rising from the centre, and tiny electric lights hidden in the fronds and in the flower groups all round the marquee gave the place a glittering, fairy-like appearance. There were two sittings of supper with place cards, and then the rest of the seven hundred guests came in at will to savour the refection of sixteen dishes.

The great garden of Devonshire House had three acres to spare after accommodating the marquee, and guests strolled about in the mild night air along walks that glittered with the light of twelve thousand lamps. A veranda had also been built round the house, roofed with crimson and cream awnings and provided with chairs for those inclined to sit out, amid banks of flowers and ferns. As the splendid night wore on, alliances were forged and wars declared. Lady Randolph Churchill, who had been widowed two years before, met the man she was to take as her second husband, George Cornwallis-West. Her seventeen-year-old son Jack (brother of Winston) found cause for disagreement with a Crusader over a certain young lady. They both lost their tempers and decided to fight it out in the garden. As Jack Churchill, however, was armed only with a rapier to go with his eighteenth-century costume, he was at a disadvantage against the double-handed broadsword of his opponent and soon retired hurt with a nasty cut in his pink silk stocking.

Few guests wanted to take their leave early from this scene of enchantment, and dawn was breaking when the carriages began to be called. Consuelo Marlborough walked down through Green Park to Spencer House, where she and her husband were then living, and she leaves a glimpse of the other England surrounding the luxury of Devonshire House: 'On the grass were the dregs of humanity. Human beings too dispirited or sunk to find work or favour, they sprawled in sodden stupor, pitiful representatives of the submerged tenth. In my billowing period dress I must have seemed to them a vision of wealth and youth, and I thought soberly that they must hate me. But they only looked, and some even had a compliment to liven my progress.'

For the rest of the Season people spoke of little else than the Devonshire House Ball, and it remained a memory passed down to the next generation. It has been said that nothing like it was seen again until Charles de Beistegui's Ball at the Palazzo Labia in Venice in 1951. None of Louise Devonshire's contemporaries even attempted to emulate her, and she had done the thing just in time. Within a few years of her death the way of life in the great London houses which the ball had epitomized was extinct.

Writing thirty years later, Lady Augusta Fane passed judgement on Louise as one who instead of raising Society's tone had lowered it, for her passion for gambling and such frivolities nullified the good influence which her high position could have exercised. One could hardly disagree that the years after she became Duchess of Devonshire show Louise von Alten at her worst. It is true that she still measured swords only with worthy adversaries. The way she could charm Sir Augustus Paget at Bolton showed how she still behaved to one who was neither a rival nor a satellite; but otherwise the discipline of seeking power had yielded to a shameless indulgence in it. A woman who had impressed eminent men by her intelligence and had won those closest to her by the loyalty of her friendships seemed to be modelling herself more on the Duchess in *Alice's Adventures in Wonderland*. Her outrageous behaviour at the card-table shows an impulse to push her position to its limits, to test what she could get away with. It is not surprising that rivals such as Lady Warwick disliked her.

Despite figures like Rosebery, Asquith and the Souls, Louise's circle was not distinguished by intellectual interests,* and she could show surprising limitations. While touring the Chatsworth treasures one day she pointed at a dove in a picture of a saint and said, 'What is that extraordinary bird that's got into the cathedral?' 'Oh, my dear,' mumbled the Duke into his beard, 'even *I* know that is the Holy Ghost.' We should not conclude, though, that Louise was not a woman of clear religious convictions – or at least one. Talking to Margot Asquith she said: 'We have both married angels; when Hartington dies he will go straight to Heaven, and when Mr Asquith dies he will go straight there, too; not so Lord Salisbury.' And her finger pointed straight down to the floor.

About the Prime Minister's mortal sin there can be no doubt. He was three years older than the Duke and in 1898 his health and his grip on affairs seemed to be failing. It was widely expected that he would retire, and the assumption was that Devonshire would succeed him. The Tories of course would have wanted Arthur Balfour, but to Queen Victoria he was just a young whippersnapper, and there can be little doubt that she would have sent for the Duke, to whom she had already looked three times in her reign to be her Prime Minister. Devonshire, however, was doing nothing to make that choice inevitable, and when Salisbury's illness in 1898 left it to him to make a statement on Far Eastern affairs in the Lords he made a poor show of it. He was again typically vague the next year when the Queen confided to him her intended visit to Ireland. She asked him to convey the news in strict secrecy to the Prime Minister, but on returning he forgot all about it. When Lord Salisbury next visited the Queen she asked him what he thought of her plan and was surprised when he had no idea what she was talking about. In any case Salisbury did not retire,

---

*She was not, however, the Duchess of Manchester to whom it was news in 1896 that Arthur Balfour was a philosopher (J. Ridley and C. Percy, *The Letters of Arthur Balfour and Lady Elcho*, 1992, p.153). Consuelo Manchester appears twice in this book and is both times misidentified, on this occasion as her mother-in-law and on p. 117 as Consuelo Vanderbilt.

and the Queen was not called upon to stir the Duke from his easy inactivity.

The years preceding 1902 were the time when Britain was forced to abandon 'splendid isolation' and make up its mind between a French and a German friendship. The Triple Alliance of Germany, Austria and Italy had been answered by a rapprochement between France and Russia, and the alignments were ready which were to lead to the First World War. Each bloc had its partisans in English Society. The Prince of Wales was strongly Francophile, and his visits to Paris as King were to cement the *Entente Cordiale*. Louise Devonshire by contrast headed the Germanophile set and included many Germans in her circle, such as Prince Henry of Pless and the Duke of Teck (brother-in-law of the Duke of Cambridge and father of Princess May, who had married the Duke of York and was to become Queen Mary). A further connection was provided by Lady Edward Cavendish's brother Frank Lascelles, who was British Ambassador in Berlin from 1895.

Other factors helped the Duke on the same path. In the European scramble for colonies Russia seemed to be poised for a carve-up of China, where the Lancashire textile industry had a large market. The manufacturers were terrified of seeing this disappear into a protectionist Russian empire and believed that only a German alliance would help Britain resist destabilization in the Far East. The Duke's lifelong connection with Lancashire was not severed when he left his Rossendale constituency, and he responded loyally to the pleas he was getting from the manufacturers in the late 1890s. Another advocate of the German alliance was Joseph Chamberlain, who subscribed to the racial-supremacy doctrine being peddled by Cecil Rhodes at this time and believed that if the three 'Germanic' powers, Britain, Germany and the United States, got together they could control the world. His zeal was a reason for increasing chumminess with Louise Devonshire.

One of the habitués of the Chatsworth circle was Baron von Eckardstein, who was working his way to being the most important force in the German embassy. As early as February 1898 he attended a dinner given by Alfred Rothschild, with the Duke of Devonshire, Chamberlain and Harry Chaplin, aimed at promoting an alliance between Britain and Germany. Eckardstein then spoke to the Kaiser, whom he thought favourable, but his hopes were dispelled. The trouble with the Kaiser was an inferiority complex towards England and a bombast that made him incapable of pursuing a rational policy. Thus in 1896 he had quite pointlessly angered Britain over the Jameson Raid, to such an extent that he had to suspend his annual visits to the country and was not even invited to the Jubilee celebrations; and his famously prickly relations with his uncle were also the product of his tactless behaviour.

In 1899 it was hoped to heal this rift by inviting the Kaiser back to England. But a new fracas was created by Admiral von Senden, one of those ambitious sailors whose pressure for a rival navy was about to wreck Anglo-German relations; his contribution had been to repeat some unflattering remarks the Prince of Wales had allegedly made about the Kaiser, thus fanning the fires between them. That summer, the Prince was saying that he would not tolerate Senden's coming to England in the imperial party, and Eckardstein went to Germany to convey this; but the Kaiser replied: 'If I go to England at all this autumn I shall take who I like with me.' The situation became grave when the Boer War broke out in October. Britain, without allies in Europe, was seen as a bully trying to conquer two weak African republics. As a series of humiliating defeats up to the end of the year made the British plight blacker and blacker, the danger of foreign intervention loomed. If Germany had placed itself at the head of a European combination, Britain might have faced a disaster comparable to the War of American Independence.

Returning from Germany, Eckardstein discussed the Senden affair over luncheon at Devonshire House. The Duke told Louise that she must get the Prince to give up his ban, and she promised to speak to him at Newmarket. Eckardstein wrote of Louise: 'The Duchess was one of the cleverest and most capable women that I ever met in my life. And she consequently had not only a social but a political position such as few women have enjoyed in modern times.' She was successful at Newmarket, where the Prince was charming, demanding only an apology from Senden, which Eckardstein arranged. The Kaiser's visit went ahead in November, and Germany remained neutral over South Africa. When the Boer President Kruger made a tour of Europe the following year the Kaiser, unlike the French President, refused to receive him, and Britain fought the war to its clumsy end without intervention. For the moment it looked as if the cause of Anglo-German friendship was winning.

The year 1900 saw further international troubles. The Boxer Rebellion in China pinned the European residents in their Legations in Peking until colonial troops arrived to raise the siege. When the crisis was over Russia wished the other powers to withdraw their forces, leaving its own with a free hand. Germany was aghast, not wanting the situation to slip into Russia's grasp before it had time to send its own troops half-way round the world to stake its claim. At Eckardstein's request the Duke of Devonshire promised to move heaven and earth to keep the British troops in Peking. Russia's move to tighten its grip on China confirmed his worst fears, and he became quite excited about the danger. Other disturbances came from the Pacific; Germany aggressively proposed to annex Samoa, against the opposition of Britain (more accurately of Australia) and also of the United States. Lord Salisbury cynically told the Duke of Devonshire that summer: 'I am waiting daily for Berlin's threatened ultimatum about Samoa.' With hindsight we can regret that Germany did not provoke a war at that point. The United States and Britain, even with the latter distracted by the Boer War, would have easily stripped Germany of every foot of its colonial possessions; the militaristic regime in Berlin would have been struck a mortal blow; and the future history of Europe would have been very different. Naturally that was not the aspect that occurred to the Duke of Devonshire, and he would have looked on such a development with horror.

At the beginning of 1901 the Duchess invited Eckardstein to Chatsworth for the big January house-party, telling him: 'The Duke has several urgent political questions to discuss with you.' Joseph Chamberlain was going to be there, and with a party of fifty or so in the house they would have no difficulty in finding a room to disappear into, away from the curious eyes of Asquith and other Liberals. Louise's solicitude shows in the comment: 'The Duke makes a great point of your coming as he is again much worried about the Eastern Question and it is so good for him to have someone to talk to about it.'

The Prince of Wales was casually informed by the Duke of the German talks, and this was a rare case of his being better informed than the government, for the negotiations did not go through the Foreign Office. After dinner on 16 January Eckardstein, the Duke and Chamberlain withdrew to the Library and concerted plans for a *démarche* to Germany. Eckardstein urged the need to bypass the sinister official at the German Foreign Ministry, Baron von Holstein, who consistently worked against Britain. For this purpose the approach would be made direct to the German Chancellor and would be represented as coming from Chamberlain alone. A draft convention was composed that May, but the German Foreign Minister Bülow was doing his best to wreck it; he asked Sir Frank Lascelles not to mention it to the Kaiser, who therefore remained in ignorance. When Lascelles confided this to the Duke in June a picture began to emerge of the cat-and-mouse game being played by the German government, and the hopes of any relation of trust were soon dissipated. The Anglo-French *Entente* was signed in 1902, all alternatives having been exhausted.

Still in January 1901 the Devonshires were involved in a minor eddy of this negotiation when Queen Victoria died, and the avaricious King Leopold of Belgium was one of the many crowned heads who came over for her funeral. The King was running in the Belgian Congo, as his private concern, the most exploitative colonial regime in Africa, and he wanted to extend his financial interests to the Far East, where they would lean on French and Russian support. He proposed himself as a guest to Chatsworth, where he wanted to discuss China with the Duke; but Eckardstein was also busy putting a spoke into this wheel, and Louise told the King that she feared the house would be so full that she could not find a suitable set of rooms for him.

As Lord President, the Duke was responsible for the proclamation of King Edward VII and presided at his first Privy Council. Next came rehearsals for the Opening of Parliament, which was to be held with a state unknown since Queen Victoria's widowhood. Lord Salisbury passed on the duty of holding the Sword of State in the procession to Lord Londonderry, and Balfour wrote to Lady Elcho: 'The last chance of comedy is thus dissipated, unless Devonshire drops the crown which he is quite likely to do!' As far as history records, this mishap was averted.

About this time Louise went to France, no doubt for her annual flutter at Monte Carlo, and Consuelo Duchess of Marlborough gives a picture of their encounter at the races. She had gone to Longchamps with her father, and as she hated mourning she had relieved her black with a pair of white gloves. 'As ill luck would have it, the first person I met . . . was the old Duchess of Devonshire, in the deepest mourning . . . Rumour had her beautiful, but when I knew her she was a raddled old woman, covering her wrinkles with paint and her pate with a brown wig. Her mouth was a red gash and from it, when she saw me, issued a stream of abuse. How could I, she complained, pointing to my white gloves, show so little respect to the memory of a great Queen?'

Louise was an elderly woman now, but she refused to accept old age. She would have looked much more distinguished with her own white hair, but she insisted on covering it with a wig and had begun to paint herself heavily. An older custom had banned any sort of make-up for respectable ladies, and only a few eccentrics such as Lady Charles Beresford, trying to keep hold of her roving husband, had used it.* Not everyone was displeased with the effect; Daisy Pless, at one of the Chatsworth parties in January 1903, wrote: 'The Duchess of Devonshire is marvellous and *looks* marvellous for her 74 years [she was just short of seventy-one]. Always very décolletée in the evening with dresses that only a woman of thirty should wear; and yet she does not really seem dressed too young; she generally has a wreath of green leaves in her hair (or rather wig!).' With her indomitable spirit, the only things Louise was afraid of were decrepitude and death. When she went driving she always ordered that her carriage should not pass a funeral if it could be avoided. For some years now she had assumed a sort of totemic mask. Sir Almeric Fitzroy commented at Chatsworth in December 1898: 'The strange personality of the Duchess. Has she any desires, feelings, or reminiscences? What is hidden under that impassive mask? At times she gives you the impression of a somnambulist, almost an automaton . . . She is not, I think, an unkindly woman, but there is something mechanical about her to the verge of insensibility. No very particular friend of hers was included in the party, but even to those she knew best she wore the same impenetrable air, which seemed to admit very little distinction between pleasant impressions and the reverse.' Lady Warwick gives the same view of her: 'She never relaxed, never revealed any emotion. She appeared neither angry nor pleased nor vexed, although at times she would be strident, emphatic or persistent. As a hostess she was correct, cordial upon occasion, outspoken, but always unperturbed.' An American friend linked this mask to her policy of high discretion, citing her maxim: 'Listen to everything; answer nothing.' It must be said that these were the impressions of people who were not close friends; nevertheless it was a strange persona for the woman who only a few years before had danced a cancan with the Prince of Wales and gone rushing off to a fancy-dress dance in a young friend's borrowed domino.

Another intimidating example is an incident at a shooting-party at Bolton Abbey. Two young men (presumably Lord Ribblesdale's son and a friend) had come over to lunch from the neighbouring Gisburne Park and are the sources of the story. The Duchess took them out driving and after savouring the view was getting back into the waggonette when one of the horses moved on a step

---

*Max Beerbohm contributed an article, 'The Pervasion of Rouge', to the first issue of *The Yellow Book* (1894) in which he reported the statement of a cosmetic-maker that business had multiplied twenty-fold in the past five years. But he denied the right of men to criticize: '"After all," as a pretty girl once said to me, "women are a sex by themselves, so to speak."'

before being checked by the coachman, throwing her forward onto her knees. Without a word she hit the coachman smartly over the back with her stick, then took her seat and resumed her conversation as if nothing had happened. We may remember, though, that even the charming Princess Alexandra had been known to strike her maid of honour in public with her umbrella.

The Duke was also growing old, and there is the well-known story of his forgetting that the King was coming to dinner. Lord Dudley went to dine at Devonshire House in April 1902 and arrived casually dressed in a smoking-jacket over his evening shirt. He was alarmed to see himself preceded into the entrance court by the King's carriage and to find the King in the hall, received by surprised servants, for the Duke was not at home. As messengers were sent out to find him, the King took out his annoyance on Lord Dudley. The narrator may have been embroidering when he adds that it took thirty-five minutes to run the Duke to earth in the Turf Club, since a nippy footman could have got there in about thirty-five seconds.

The King had endured a lifetime of such casualness and cannot have been too surprised on a similar occasion when he attended a ball at Devonshire House. He waited until it was time to wish the Duke good night and to congratulate him on the 'magnificent manner in which everything had been done', before telling him confidentially that there was one thing that was not quite right. What was that, the Duke asked anxiously. 'You have got your Garter on upside down.'

One thing age had not worn down was the Duke and Duchess's devotion to each other, and Lady Warwick recalls an incident at Chatsworth. The Duke had gone out shooting with the guns and they did not return for tea as expected; the ladies had tea by themselves, and afterwards Lady Warwick happened to walk into the entrance hall.

> To my surprise, I found the Duchess pacing up and down in a state of great agitation.
>
> 'Is there anything wrong?' I asked, and there was a note of real distress in her curiously guttural voice . . . as she told me that she could not imagine what had happened to the Duke.
>
> Naturally I suggested that it was some ordinary delay that had kept them, but she still strode restlessly to and fro and I could see tears in her eyes. At last the guns came in, the Duke leading them, and shaking the snow from his ulster.

'Why, what on earth is the matter?' he inquired tenderly, and went on to explain that they had turned aside on their way to look at some new buildings on the estate, and then had waited awhile, thinking the snow would clear.

To all outward appearance both the Duke and Duchess of Devonshire were devoid of normal human sympathies, but there was no other man in the world for her, and there was no other woman for him. They were not prepossessing people, but their love for one another was a very beautiful thing.

Florence Williams adds a lighter picture of a time when Louise went away on a cure and asked her to amuse 'the sweet thing' in her absence, with the result that Florence invited the Duke to dinner. One of the other guests was the Russian ambassador De Stael, a very courtly gentleman. After dinner the brandy was passed round and the ambassador exclaimed: '*Le parfum, le parfum; comme c'est bon!*' From the other side of their hostess came the Duke's gruff voice: 'Hang the *parfum*, I want some more.' After rising from the table they all played 'puff-ball' together, prompting Louise, when she returned, to tell Florence that she had made the Duke far too frivolous.

13
Resignation

The new reign meant the ultimate triumph of the Fast Set over which Louise had for forty years been the acknowledged queen. Fat cigars were now smoked openly at Windsor, and the shiny motor cars emblematic of the new plutocracy were seen rattling in and out. Louise was a devotee of the motoring fashion, as of every fashion. Her mania for bridge was undimmed by old age. Where once she had been 'Grand Slam', a wit now dubbed her 'Ponte Vecchio'. She still cheated as shamelessly as ever, and everyone indulged her. Lord Crawford found a few years later: 'much animosity shown to Balfour, which arose from his detection of the Duchess of Devonshire in her customary cardsharping'. When in January 1902 the King and Queen gave their first dinner-party at Windsor, at the close of their year's mourning, with the Devonshires among their guests, the suggestion was made after dinner that they should walk through the state rooms. 'It then got quite cheerful and informal – but the old Duchess of Devonshire seemed much put out, running about in the cold; she wanted to play bridge with the King,' relates Sir Lionel Cust. She got her way, as she always had.

The Duchess of Sermoneta gives a picture of Louise at race meetings: 'She was very old when I knew her and always very stiffly corseted. She always sat on a bench like a stone image, quite immovable and stupendously dignified. One day I was rewarded by seeing her pull up her skirts and produce a purse from a bag secreted among her petticoats. "Put two pounds for me on Cream Tart," she said to one of her satellites. It sounded like the voice of an oracle.' George Lambton adds: 'The Duchess took the greatest delight in betting, and would back three or four horses in one race for small sums. She had an extraordinary knack of picking out long-priced winners. I remember once having to back four horses for her. I forgot one of them and it turned up at thirty-three to one.'

The Devonshires' and the royal household's routines were now intertwined as no others were. In 1902 a ritual was instituted which continued until 1907. On Derby Day the King gave a dinner at Buckingham Palace for the Duke and other members of the Jockey Club, while Louise entertained the Queen and the members' wives at Devonshire House; after dinner the men went on to Devonshire House for a great ball. It was part of an unchanging ceremonial which included the yearly January visit to Chatsworth, the shooting parties at Bolton Abbey, Sandringham and other great country houses, and the trips to Homburg and similar places of healthful recreation abroad.

The Duke's racing fortunes continued on their disappointing lines. In 1898 there was a flutter of excitement when his horse Dieudonné won an unexpected trial just before the Derby, and the Duke and Duchess had high hopes of his winning the race itself. They confided this to Harry Chaplin, who went round urging the other members of the Cabinet to back Dieudonné, but he came in fourth. In 1901 the Duke was again asked to lease the King's horses after Queen Victoria's death, but he suffered the same jinx as throughout his Turf history; the stable included the Prince's Derby winner Diamond Jubilee, but he defrauded hopes by making a surprisingly bad finish to his racing career. The Duke was so disappointed that at the end of that season he took his horses away from Egerton House, pointing out to Marsh that with some eighty horses there he had more than any trainer could fully attend to. Characteristically he added that the horses were too far away there, and he wanted them back at Beaufort House where he could go and see them easily. His trainer for the next three years was W. Goodwin, and later S. Darling. The year 1902 was made successful by a complete fluke, when Cheers won the Eclipse Stakes, starting as a twenty-to-one outsider, and bumped his owner's winnings this year to the highest figure of his career; but the rest of the Duke's life saw few successes. This lack of obvious triumphs did not stop him from being regarded as one of the key figures on the Turf and one of its most popular personalities.

Devonshire's political role in the 1895–1903 government was of more solid quality. Besides his Cabinet office as Lord President of the Council he held the presidency of the Committee of Defence, which was intended to establish co-ordination between the War Office and the Admiralty. In this the Duke is not judged to have been a success. As First Lord of the Admiralty George Goschen showed a spiky opposition to interference, and the Duke may be blamed for not having imposed a real plan of co-operation. Nevertheless he was hardly responsible for the War Office deficiencies which led to the early disasters of the Boer War, although that did not prevent him from taking them hard. Sir Almeric Fitzroy, the Duke's secretary at the Privy Council, found early in December 1899: 'Poor man, he feels these reverses in his impassive way rather heavily.' The committee was not put on an effective basis until it was reconstituted as the Committee of Imperial Defence in 1902, and then Devonshire's presidency of it only lasted a year, until his resignation from the government.

A different case is the Duke's responsibility for national education, which was then subject to a Department of the Privy Council. In this capacity he was responsible for the 1902 Education Act, which ranks with those of 1870 and 1944 as one of the major landmarks of British educational history. It is characteristic that this achievement of Devonshire's has gone virtually unnoticed, and that is partly because he did not hold the explicit title of Minister of Education. We even find confused historians stating that the Duke had a 'nominal' responsibility for education; nominal was precisely what his responsibility was not. It is also common to see Balfour given the credit for the Act. Given that as Leader of the House he had the task of piloting this large and controversial measure through the Commons, there is some justice in that. Nevertheless, it was the Duke who saw the need for a comprehensive measure, guided it into its final form and got it adopted by the government. As Leader of the Lords in autumn 1902 he also took charge of the Bill's passage through that House.

The objective of the 1902 Act was to create a network of secondary education for the country, for the 1870 Act had only set up primary schools. The measure was rendered urgent by an appeal-court decision in 1901 that the Board Schools could not legally provide secondary education, as some had quietly been doing. The man who was active in trying to reform the system was Sir John Gorst, Devonshire's Vice-President of the Council, a pushy and awkward man, although well-meaning. It was due to his tactless handling that several attempted Bills on the subject, starting in 1896, had failed in the House of Commons, and the last of these ran into fresh difficulties in June 1901. The Cabinet decided to withdraw it, and Devonshire was asked to break the disheartening news gently to his Vice-President. The Duke went to Gorst's office, stood for a while with his back to the fire, and then said, 'Well, Gorst, your damned Bill's dead.' Gorst was also the hero of the anecdote told by Leach that ministers were wondering how they might get rid of this troublesome colleague, and one suggested that he be given a colonial governorship. 'Well,' said the Duke, 'we don't mind losing Gorst, but we don't want to lose a colony.'

The Duke's tolerance enabled him to get on without friction with this subordinate, and equally creditable was his acceptance of the advice of his admirable Civil Servant, Sir Robert Morant, to whose vision the 1902 Act was due. It was to the advantage of this measure that at Cabinet level responsibility for it fell to a man with a long record of thoroughness and doggedness and one with no time for the sectarian squabbles which had bedevilled English education. Although a solid Churchman, Devonshire was the reverse of a bigot, and he constructed a measure which balanced the interests of the church schools and Dissenters. The Act abolished the old school boards and put both primary and secondary schools, the church schools included, under the county and borough councils. With all these schools now on the rates there was a marked rise in standards, as well as a great increase in the number of pupils in secondary education. In 1902 a separate Board of Education was created with Lord Londonderry as President (personally not an improvement on Devonshire's control) and with Morant in charge to implement the system which he had fashioned.

The great drama of that year was King Edward's Coronation, which had been fixed for late June. In the weeks leading up to it he was complaining of increasing abdominal pain but did not want to have the ceremony put off for surgery. His determination turned against him, for on the very day before the Coronation had to be cancelled for an emergency appendectomy. Lord Salisbury, whose own health was failing, had intended to retire after the Coronation and did so as soon as the King's recovery was assured, on 11 July. It did not occur to the King to send for anyone but Balfour, and this is singular on three counts. Some, like Victor Cavendish, felt that it would have been a fitting tribute to the Duke to allow him a brief premiership. More cogently, as one who had been asked three times to be Prime Minister, he was the kind of senior figure who was customarily consulted when a new Prime Minister was selected. But there was also a constitutional point: the ministry in office was a coalition, and a consultation of the leader of the second party was definitely called for. The convalescent King, who had been denied constitutional training throughout his mother's reign, cannot be too much blamed for overlooking these facts, but Balfour ought to have pointed out at least the third of them. Instead, he went to get the support not of Devonshire but of Joseph Chamberlain, who was in bed after a cab accident in which a pane of glass had smashed on his head. He then went to the Duke and discussed the Education Bill with him. As the Duke was leaving the room, according to Lord James, he said, 'Oh, by the way, the King sent for me this morning and asked me to accept the Premiership, which I have done.' The Duke said, 'Oh,' and left the room. In his own account to Lord Lansdowne, the news had been put 'in a sort of interrogative way', but the Duke was told that Chamberlain had already given his adhesion. Balfour had acted in character as one whose graceful charm concealed an underlying callousness. What troubled the Duke was not his own loss of the premiership or the constitutional solecism, but the fact that his lifelong friend the King should have passed him over without even consulting him. Almost for the first time in his life, he was offended. Two weeks later the King held a council on board his yacht in the Solent, and before it he saw the Duke privately. He asked, 'I hope you think I did right in sending for Arthur Balfour. I really could not do otherwise – do not you think so?' The Duke's assent was cold, and only now did it strike the King that he had been remiss. After luncheon, therefore, he gave him another private audience and made a point of thanking him for having supported Balfour. That support had in fact been more than ungrudging; when Balfour held the first meeting of his followers, Devonshire had sat at his side and tendered his allegiance in generous words that touched everybody.

The rescheduled Coronation took place in August, and a feature of it was the special enclosure set aside for some of the King's lady friends; these included Mrs Keppel and Daisy of Pless, and it was nicknamed 'the King's loose-box'. The peeresses of course attended as of right, and provided a moment of balletic unison as they all donned their coronets when Queen Alexandra was crowned. Before the ceremony, however, Lady Londonderry had a mishap in the peeresses' lavatory and was heard calling from her cubicle for a forceps. There was consternation at the thought that a little Vane-Tempest-Stewart was about to be delivered in such inopportune circumstances, but no: her tiara had fallen into the pan, and she was not prepared to retrieve it without an instrument.

Louise Devonshire was one of the queue of peeresses that built up in vain as a result of this contretemps and suffered accordingly during the ceremony. The moment the royal party had processed out at the end she left her place and dashed out in search of relief, but her haste undid her; she tumbled head-over-heels at the foot of Sir Michael Hicks-Beach, and her coronet flew off and went rolling against the stalls. The Marquis de Soveral helped her up, Margot Asquith recovered her coronet, and she galloped off again, apparently none the worse. A foolish story went round that she had tried to join the royal procession in disregard of proper precedence.

The following year was thrown into turmoil by Joseph Chamberlain's espousal of Tariff Reform. The policy of abandoning a free trade system in favour of preference for colonial trade was one fostered by the dominant imperialist ideology, and Britain's relative commercial decline gave a protectionist incentive for it. Other countries moreover had been giving up what little attachment they had to free trade over the past twenty years, and hostile tariffs invited retaliation. The Colonial Conference of 1902 gave voice to the colonies' wish for tariff union, and Chamberlain as Colonial Secretary was keen to accept it. He believed that an imperial system would revitalize the British economy. The problem was that an imperial tariff would be meaningless without duties on food, which were the colonies' main produce. This would prove an emotive issue in Britain, with memories of the agitation against the Corn Laws; but Chamberlain believed that the country would accept a small duty on corn, and was under the impression that the Cabinet had actually accepted this for the 1903 Budget. The Chancellor of the Exchequer, however, C.J. Ritchie, was an out-and-out free-trader and proclaimed his refusal to make any departure from the system. Chamberlain riposted by declaring publicly for Tariff Reform in a speech of 15 May 1903, and the breach was open.

For four months Balfour tried to evade any sort of decision, but several members of his Cabinet had definite views on the subject. As it happened, the Duke of Devonshire had longer experience than anyone in answering renascent protectionist arguments. His opponent in his Lancashire constituency in 1880 and 1885 had been W. Farrer Ecroyd, who has been treated by the Duke's biographers as a maverick of absurd views but who was in fact the leader of the Fair Trade movement which had emerged even then as mid-Victorian prosperity flagged, and Hartington was obliged to spend much of his election campaigns expounding the arguments for a free market. Economics were not his subject, and he had always been happy to go along with Gladstonian orthodoxy, but, although predisposed, his mind was not closed in 1903. Nevertheless we should note two personal reasons which added their weight for free trade. First, a Tariff Reform system would have proved especially harmful to Germany, which would have been horrified to see the British Empire turn into a protectionist bloc; and with the pro-German policy which the Duke and his wife were still promoting this was a consideration. Second, Tariff Reform was opposed by the traditional manufacturers and in particular by the Lancashire textile industry, which as we have seen was worried at the loss of its Far Eastern market and especially afraid of that region's being carved up into a jigsaw of protectionist colonial possessions. The Far East had by now become a special hobby of the Duke's, and as a staunch Lancashireman still he would have taken a lot of persuading to throw over this unofficial constituency of his.

The widespread feeling against Tariff Reform was reflected by the King. Lord James describes an opera performance at Covent Garden in July in honour of President Loubet of France, at which the King went between the Acts into an ante-room where several Cabinet Ministers were, and said: 'I will never give my assent to a Bill taxing necessary food, and I do not care who knows that I have said so.' As he walked away the Duke murmured to Lord Balfour of Burleigh: 'Very good. We must send him on the stump.' Two weeks earlier he had given a dinner at Devonshire House for some thirty peers and Privy Councillors for the King's official birthday.* After it Joseph Chamberlain's agricultural sidekick Jesse Collings, elevated by the excellence of the vintages, buttonholed his host and started expatiating on the benefits of Tariff Reform. The Duke listened in silence, while he steered Collings towards the grand staircase. When they reached the top of it, he said firmly, 'Good night, Mr Collings; take care of the first step.'

The effect of these dissensions was to put Balfour's premiership in question. As early as 3 July the Liberal Sir Edward Hamilton, who was Permanent Secretary to the Treasury, was opining that Devonshire should resign with the other free-trade ministers and place himself at the head of a Liberal coalition, thus bringing down the government; he believed that Lord Rosebery, who by now had semi-detached himself from the Liberal Party, would be willing to join the Duke's government as Foreign Secretary, while Lord Spencer had made open efforts to lure him over. Hamilton urged this policy on Louise, whose ambitions for her husband he recognized. She for her part told him that

---

*Harry Chaplin, who sat on the Duke's left, told him at the end that he had never had a better dinner, but there was just one criticism he asked him to pass on to the Duchess: the grapes with the ortolans were not stoned.

Chamberlain had declared in 1902 that he was willing to serve under Balfour but not under the Duke. Here she had got hold of a psychological if not a literal truth, and it made her all the keener to press her husband into an anti-Chamberlain stance.

It did not escape Balfour that the free-traders in the government were hoping to oust him and replace him with Devonshire, and his next actions were designed to split them. By September he had concocted a policy which was intended to straddle the gulf between the free-traders and tariff reformers; he rejected food tariffs and any sort of imperial union but declared his willingness to consider retaliatory tariffs against dumping by foreign countries. Armed with this doctrine he proceeded on 14 September to dismiss in summary fashion the two most hard-line free-traders in the Cabinet, the Chancellor of the Exchequer Ritchie and Lord Balfour of Burleigh (no relation, nor any sympathizer). At a meeting of these with Devonshire and Lord George Hamilton, the latter two agreed to resign in support of them, which they did on the 15th. Balfour had thus failed in his aim of splitting the four, but he had a card up his sleeve. Joseph Chamberlain had written to him a week before offering his resignation, which he now decided to accept. In a meeting with the Duke on the 16th he sprang this news upon him and asked him to retract his resignation. As the government had thus, apparently, repudiated Tariff Reform, the Duke agreed to his request. Balfour appeared triumphant. He had shed the extremists on both wings and kept the Duke (whose adherence, it will be noted, he valued more than Chamberlain's). But his victory lasted only a few days.

The Duke, as he and everyone rapidly realized, after a lifetime of sound judgement had made the most prodigious mess of things. It should have been obvious that if he were to remain in a free-trade government he ought to have insisted on the reinstatement of Ritchie, Lord Balfour and Lord George Hamilton; but he failed to make this condition. His confusion at the sudden news of Chamberlain's departure was partly responsible, but there were two particular reasons. First, he was aware of his own special position in the Cabinet; he was not just any minister but the leader of the second party in the coalition. If he went, it was tantamount to the break-up of the alliance, especially once the other Liberal Unionist leader had resigned at the same time. The second reason was that, characteristically, he was leaning over backwards to be loyal to Balfour. The very circumstances in which Balfour had taken over made Devonshire all the more anxious to avoid the slightest appearance of vindictiveness. The thought that, as observers like Sir Edward Hamilton saw, he was the figure whose loyalty would do most to save the tottering government may or may not have occurred to him.

At a personal level there were other things going on. At this crucial juncture Louise happened to be away in Scotland. If she had been in London she would certainly have fought tooth and nail to stop her husband withdrawing his resignation and would have gone on to try to steer him towards the premiership. In her absence members of her family were involved in the affair. Her son Lord Charles Montagu and her son-in-law Lord Stanley had lunch together and Lord Charles urged Stanley to go and see the Duke, who as usual when his wife was away was feeling lost and lonely. According to a story that Stanley told Winston Churchill years later, when he was Earl of Derby, he actually contributed to the Duke's withdrawal of his resignation, which is the last thing his mother-in-law would have prescribed; but his account does not tally with other versions of the events. Behind the scenes, recently retired ministers like Lords James and Goschen were also urging Devonshire to stand firm for free trade.

Lord James had pointed out to the Duke before the crisis that the King might invite him to form a government if Balfour fell, and he had replied: 'Too old – too old.' But he said it with a smile that suggested he was not ruling it out. As for Louise, she came back from Scotland and set about undoing her husband's retraction. According to Stanley, she got Ritchie to write to him reproaching him for his lack of solidarity, and he more than fulfilled her hopes, accusing the Duke of dishonesty and breach of faith. The Duke was distraught: 'To think I have gone all through my life and then at the end of it to have these sort of accusations levelled at my head!' Late in September Almeric Fitzroy knew that Louise was egging him on to resign. Balfour, however, was doing everything to placate the Duke, consulting him closely over the reshuffle necessitated by the resignations and appointing Lord Stanley Postmaster General and Victor Cavendish Financial Secretary to the Treasury. Then, on 1 October, Balfour made a speech in which he set out explicitly his fiscal doctrine, including the commitment to retaliatory tariffs. To Devonshire this was a denial of the free-trade assurances he had received, and with huge relief he sent in his resignation the next day. Balfour fought to keep his victory and accused the Duke of 'inquisitorial subtlety in detecting imaginary heresies'. The accusation, from such a source to such a victim, was laughable, and Devonshire replied: 'This the first time that argumentative subtlety, whether controversial or otherwise, has ever been imputed to me.' He did not rise to Balfour's bait again.

Thus passed the Duke's last opportunity of attaining the premiership. His vacillation over resigning robbed the free-trade secession of the force it would otherwise have had; but even done decisively it is hard to see that it would have brought Balfour down, as sympathizers hoped. That would have taken the Duke's concerted effort (not necessarily in his own interest) to bring it about, and that is what he conspicuously refused to do. As Balfour's government staggered on, however, Louise did not give up. Lord George Hamilton found the following April that her one idea was to push her husband somehow to the leadership. 'What an unreformable old campaigner!' exclaimed Lady Paget when she heard it.

Devonshire's successor as Lord President of the Council was Lord Londonderry, and as the King had been invited to shoot at Wynyard he decided to make the change-over there, holding the first Privy Council in a subject's house since Charles I's time. The Duke had to be there as outgoing Lord President ('He will assist at his own funeral with the greatest good humour,' said the King to Sir Almeric Fitzroy), and they travelled down on the King's train on 19 October, with Louise and various other guests including Count Mensdorff. After dinner the Privy Council was held, which the King dated in antique style: 'At Our Court at Wynyard.' When this ceremony was over, however, the Edwardian age reasserted itself, and the King sat down to bridge with Louise Devonshire and Mrs Keppel, while the rest of the party played poker. The following day Lord Londonderry treated his guests to one of the big rabbit-shoots that were a feature of life at Wynyard, and they shot three thousand; the Duke, however, got bored with such tame shooting and annoyed his host by laying aside his gun and lighting a cigarette.

Consuelo Manchester made the rather risky decision to give a dinner on 7 November for both the Prime Minister and the Duke of Devonshire by way of social reconciliation, and it almost failed. The Duke at least felt that Balfour showed constraint, although Joseph Chamberlain's son said they were cordial. Louise made a point of inviting Balfour to the usual post-Christmas party at Chatsworth, and he stretched his luck by replying with his characteristic banter, by which she failed to be amused.

Tariff Reform wrecked the Liberal Unionist Party. The Duke objected to

Chamberlain's trying to commit the party to the policy, but Chamberlain out-manoeuvred him, representing his objection as an effort to keep hold of the presidency for himself. The Duke was defeated, and in May 1904 he resigned, with the majority of party members henceforth following Chamberlain's lead.

There remained a need to give body to the Duke's stand for free trade without deserting Unionism. Most of the hot free-traders were in fact strong Tories, like Lord Salisbury's sons, who hated the commercialism of Chamberlain's crusade for imperial union. Another young rebel was Winston Churchill, who had been elected a Tory MP in 1900, and he came to lunch at Devonshire House a fortnight after the Duke's resignation from the government to discuss with him the formation of a Free Food League, of which Devonshire shortly accepted the presidency. For a while the Duke was appearing on the same platform with the young firebrand, and at the Manchester Free Trade Hall he gave him an insight into his oratorical method. He said: 'Do you feel nervous, Winston? I used to, but now, whenever I get on a public platform, I take a good look around and as I sit down I say, "I never saw such a lot of damned fools in my life," and then I feel a lot better.' But in 1904 Winston Churchill crossed the floor, opening the way for his joining the Liberal government in 1905.

That the Duke had indeed achieved a sovereign unflappability in public is shown by an anecdote told by his first biographer. In one of the early Free Food meetings he began his speech, 'I am not going . . .', then stopped, looked at his notes, took a drink of water, perused his notes again and showed no signs of relieving his audience's suspense; such was the respect he commanded that only one voice called out, 'Buck up!' from the crowd. This serenity did not prevent the Duke from surprising his friends by the vigour with which he took up the free-trade campaign. Balfour got the same sort of surprise as Gladstone had in 1886, as his somnolent colleague came to life to oppose him. The Duke presided at a two-hour party meeting at Devonshire House in December, and soon he was deep in collaboration with Lord Spencer and trying to negotiate an electoral pact with the Liberals. The Free Food League, however, fell between two stools and wilted for lack of financial support, while followers like Winston Churchill deserted it.

Balfour's fiscal compromise had failed to keep his government together, but more seriously it failed in convincing his party. Retaliatory tariffs alienated those attached to free-market orthodoxy, but they left the dearest aims of the tariff reformers completely unsatisfied; they did nothing whatever for imperial unity or for the redirection of British agriculture and industry. The device was a typical product of Balfour's nimble but abstract brain and exemplified the severe judgement that his colleague Lord Curzon gave of him years later: 'sheer intellectual indolence, a never-knowing his case, an instinctive love of compromise, and a trust in the mental agility which would enable him at the last moment to extricate himself from any complication however embarrassing . . . The truth is that Balfour with his scintillating exterior had no depth of feeling, no profound convictions, and strange to say (in spite of his fascination of manner) no real affection.' It is probable that in the years 1903–6 either a firm free-trade stance or a bold tariff-reform policy would have given strength to the Unionist Party. By trying to avoid both, Balfour only let the party tear itself apart and earn the contempt of the electorate. In December 1905 he resigned, instead of dissolving, in the absurd hope that the reality of a Liberal government, after the lapse of ten years, would make the voters draw back from the abyss. Instead, the Prime Minister Campbell-Bannerman went boldly to the polls in January 1906 and emerged with a majority of 377 to 157 over the Unionists, with a further 83 Irish Home Rulers and 63 Labour members adding to his overwhelming position. It was the most crushing electoral victory since that of the Whigs after the 1832 Reform Act. Balfour himself lost his seat and had to find one hastily vacated by a loyal supporter.

Balfour's political secretary, analysing for him the causes of the defeat, gave as one of the reasons: 'The defection of the Duke of Devonshire . . . The Duke's influence was *always* enormous with a class which is mainly Conservative – viz the well-to-do middle and upper classes.' With hindsight, we can say that a Devonshire premiership in 1902–5 would have been much better for the Unionists than Balfour's. With the Duke in charge, it is probable that Chamberlain would not even have dared to make his tariff-reform attempt, since he would have known that it had no chance of acceptance; and if he had made it he would have been firmly repudiated, and the party would have gone into the election with a clear and simple policy. Whether Devonshire would have been able to defeat the swing of the pendulum is not so predictable, but his weight and reliability counted for much, and he would have avoided the effete and hair-splitting style which under Balfour's leadership made the Unionists seem a force of the past, to be swept away by the great surge of Edwardian social idealism.

14
The Closing Years

For the first seven years of King Edward's reign, Louise Devonshire continued to wield a formidable power in London Society. We have a picture of this situation in Vita Sackville-West's *The Edwardians*, where the Duchess of Devonshire and Lady Londonderry appear as the two awe-inspiring guardians of the social proprieties (this was equally ironical in the latter's case, for she had been guilty of an affair which, it is said, made her husband refuse to speak to her except in public for twenty years). Lady Roehampton, who has allowed her reputation to be clouded, finds herself invited only to the larger parties at Devonshire House, and not to the more exclusive occasions of twenty or less. In real life one *habituée* left a description of the latter as the Duchess and a group of her friends discussed what gift they would choose for a young girl at the outset of life: beauty, wealth or brains? They decided on brains, because that was the one advantage that could remedy the lack of the others. The anecdote gives a glimpse of how these smart ladies passed their time and of the competitive and alert world they took for granted.

The Devonshire House circle exhibited the capriciousness of Edwardian social inclusion noted by G.K. Chesterton in *The Queer Feet*. People were mysteriously in without necessarily being aristocratic or rich or brilliant. The Duke on his side refused to bow to certain social rules. One of his younger friends was Sir Charles Hartopp, 5th Baronet, whose wife was a Wilson of the Tranby Croft family, and they stayed at Chatsworth several times. But in December 1902 Lady Hartopp sued her husband for divorce on the grounds of adultery. The Duke agreed to appear as a witness for Hartopp – who simply hoped thereby to impress the jury – and when the divorce was granted refused to drop him as convention demanded, continuing to invite him to stay. The court appearance provided a touch that amused Max Beerbohm, who much appreciated Devonshire ('my favourite Duke, the most natural and monumental'); he cited the following exchange from the report:

Counsel: 'I think it is a fact, Your Grace, that the petitioner and the respon-
dent and the co-respondent were among the party of guests entertained by you
and the Duchess at Chatsworth House last year from January 12th to January
17th.'

The Witness: 'What?'

These January parties, besides giving the guests scope for getting into the
wrong beds, were celebrated for their private theatricals, which Lady Warwick, although not given to praising Chatsworth, acknowledged as the best she
ever remembered. They were put on by a bevy of keen amateurs who included
Daisy of Pless, the lovely Muriel Wilson (who had energy to spare to conduct
an affair with the Marquis de Soveral), Mrs William James (one of the social
leaders of the period and occasional mistress of the King), Lady Maud Warrender, Leo Trevor, Frank Mildmay and Captain Philip Jeffcock. The
rehearsals were long and exacting and the costumes and scenery of the most
elaborate. Daisy Pless describes her first appearance in the 1902 party, when
they acted *A New Year's Dream*, specially composed by Leo Trevor, and she
sang a duet with Lord Hyde.

The 1903 visit is described by her in some detail. On Twelfth Night

we all danced round the Christmas Tree, Soveral leading the Duchess; then the
girls [the Duke of Connaught's two daughters] and I ducked for an apple; I could
not get it. And we cut a cake containing charms: little Princess Beatrice of Coburg
cut the ring, and the Prime Minister, Mr Balfour, got a little gold heart – perhaps
to make up for the one that he missed years ago! [a reference to his bachelorhood]
After that we danced in the long passage which, however, is really much too narrow for the purpose. I cannot think why they do not use the rooms upstairs [i.e.
the State rooms, immediately above], or take the table away from the billiard-
room, which is never used as everyone plays bridge; and there are always a lot of
girls who want to dance.

On 10 January she records: 'Three days rehearsing, while we ought to have
had a week.' She did a twenty-minute musical monologue called *The Eternal
Feminine* but broke down, and the prompter lost his place; 'Some of them say
that I stamped my foot and said, "Damn the man," but I am sure I didn't.' She
then played a ghost in a one-act play, *Shades of Night*, appearing with Muriel
Wilson, Frank Mildmay and Leo Trevor.

Later in her stay she describes a discussion with Soveral and Lord Gosford over the minor foreign crisis, where Britain and Germany had decided to blockade Venezuela and ran into a fierce American response. 'Lord Gosford says the Government, as usual, was caught napping, "and if you consider its representatives can you wonder?" And while he spoke he looked towards Mr. Balfour and the Duke of Devonshire.' After most of the guests had gone, Daisy Pless notes: 'I walked with the Duchess in the afternoon and told her all about Germany and her old friends; she was quite amused and interested, although generally she is not easy to talk to.'

The year 1904 was the first that the King and Queen visited Chatsworth after their accession. The play on that occasion was a special *Cinderella* written by Harry Trevor. Queen Alexandra, who always enjoyed Chatsworth enormously, liked to slip into a back seat to watch the rehearsals, and the actors would pretend not to see her. Coming in for the play was attended with a little more ceremony than was usually observed at Chatsworth. The King would enter first with the Duchess, then the Queen with the Duke, and they would take their seats in armchairs in the front row; then the rest of the party came in more or less in order of precedence and sat where they pleased. Daisy Pless and Muriel Wilson were a great success that year as the Ugly Sisters. Towards the end of the visit Daisy writes: 'The King has his bridge with Mrs Keppel who is here – with lovely clothes and diamonds – in a separate room, and in the other rooms people are massed together, also of course playing bridge.' In case that entertainment palled, the Duchess had gambling chips permanently available in every room. 'Generally, to amuse the Queen, I am made to go and sing and dance in the corridor where the band is, with Muriel Wilson, Maudie Warrender, the Duchess's grand-daughters (the Acheson girls) . . . The last evening there was very cheerful; the Queen danced a waltz with Soveral, and then we each took off our shoes to see what difference it made in our height. The Queen took, or rather kicked hers off, and then got into everyone else's, even into Willie Grenfell's old pumps. I never saw her so free and cheerful – but always graceful in everything she does.'

The following April the Duke and Duchess were in Rome, and they spent much of that summer abroad, as he tried to shake off recurrent ill health; in September they were at Homburg. That December was marked by a visit to Chatsworth of King Carlos of Portugal, who was to be assassinated three years later. King Carlos dignified the occasion by starting a snowball fight among the guests, and he sought to honour his host by investing him with the Order of the Tower and Sword. The Duke was no lover of 'badges and chains and things', but he felt obliged to wear it at dinner. Afterwards, as he struggled at the bridge table, he complained: 'I believe this damned Elephant and Castle is bringing me bad luck. If I have another poor hand I shall throw the wretched thing into the fire.' Soveral was standing right behind him, but he joined in the laughter with the others.

This house-party seems to have eclipsed the normal one at Twelfth Night, for no account of the latter appears. The early spring of 1905 was spent by the Duke and Duchess in a two-month visit to Egypt, and when they returned he told Almeric Fitzroy that Louise was suffering from chronic pain in the side, although it had not stopped her from enjoying Monte Carlo on the way back – or from corseting herself as tightly as ever. That year the Duke began to show signs of heart trouble, and if he had still been in office he would probably have had to retire now. In October Louise had a sort of stroke at Aix-les-Bains, and, so Fitzroy reported, looked desperately ill at Newmarket. Despite such setbacks she continued an active social life for nearly another six years.

The fall of the Conservative government in December brought good news at least for Louise's grandson, the 28-year-old Duke of Manchester. He declared himself a Liberal, rather improbably, and as the only Duke left in that party received a Household appointment. He had found his rich bride in November 1900 in the form of Helena Zimmerman of Cincinnati, and his financial troubles appeared to be over. His father-in-law enabled him to buy Kylemore Castle in Ireland, where he entertained Edward VII in 1904.

In January 1906 the King came again to Chatsworth, although he had been ill and had to shoot from a chair. A farce, *Time Is Money* was acted, and Daisy of Pless sang a musical fantasy of her own devising called *The Lotus*, suggested by a Burmese love song, for which two friends wrote the lyrics and music. It took an hour to perform and involved Daisy changing her costume three times, but the Queen liked it so much that she asked her to repeat it. Not everyone had the same reaction; Louisa Gosford wrote to her sister Alice Stanley: 'Princess Pless sings more than ever – she unfortunately has no rival to check her – she is much more amiable and contented.' After dinner one evening, while the ladies were waiting for the gentlemen to come out of the dining-room, Daisy performed tricks balancing a glass of water on her head and showing how high she could kick, 'which is higher than my own head a good bit. Princess Victoria held up her fan for me to kick.' Her judgement on this year was: 'I never had a greater success at any Chatsworth party.'

The last Twelfth Night party at Chatsworth was that of 1907 and is described for us also by Sir Frederick Ponsonby, who was there in attendance on the King:

Before dinner the third night the King told me that he intended to give the Duke the Grand Cross of the Victorian Order. Knowing how little the Duke knew or cared about such things and nervous lest he should make disparaging remarks about the King's personal Order, I determined to prepare him for the honour. I went to his writing-room where I found him at his writing-table, and after discussing with him some letters he had received I told him of the King's intention to confer the Victorian Order upon him. He asked in a sleepy way what he was expected to do with 'the thing' when he got it. I replied that he must wear it and certainly that night he should wear it instead of the Garter. Anyone less anxious to receive an Order I had never seen, and I had to explain that the King looked upon his personal Order as a high honour, but the Duke seemed to think it would only complicate his dressing. Before dinner the King sent for him and handed him the Order when I believe he suitably expressed his thanks, but he straightway came to my room and asked me to put the Order on properly for him. He said that he presumed that if he wore the Victorian Order, he should not wear any part of the Order of the Garter. I was not prepared for such a difficult conundrum but I told him that I had always understood that Knights of the Garter should always wear that Order on all occasions. I therefore suggested that he should wear that night not only the Riband and Star of the Victorian Order but also the Garter Star and diamond Garter on his leg. He said all this was complicated and tiresome but he followed my advice and the King seemed to approve as he made no comment.

Ponsonby describes the general ambience of the house: 'Everything was managed in the most princely way, and the dinners were a wonderful sight. All the women wore tiaras and jewels, while the men wore Orders and decorations . . .' In the theatricals, 'Lady Maud Warrender sang, but she seemed too big for the tiny stage and certainly her voice was too powerful for the room.' Daisy of Pless came on last, and sang three songs, with acting and cinematograph in between to give her time to change her costume. 'My first song was out of the Mikado,' she writes, 'and I wore a brown wig and looked much nicer than with my own stupid yellow hair. Then an American coon song in a beggar frock and big pale-blue felt hat, and a short dance with a red cotton umbrella. And for the last, a French song, "Il Neige", by Bemberg, in a new white tobogganing dress from Fürstenstein [her husband's country house], a white hat with a bunch of red holly on it, some mistletoe on my white fur muff, and high red boots.' Ponsonby adds that she looked lovely and sang in a shower of artificial snow.

Lady Maud Warrender took the part of an Eastern character in a play with Muriel Wilson and wore a costume of gorgeous green and gold, with a helmet and a fine steel spear. The King made up for his inactivity of the previous year by seizing the spear and with the words 'Now we'll do some pig-sticking' pursued a terrified guest at full speed down the long gallery.

For the last evening Ponsonby describes the scene, when he sat next to the Duchess at dinner:

> She was in a delightful mood, most amusing and witty, and she told many stories of the old days. It was Twelfth Night and we had a sort of Christmas dinner with crackers and paper caps. Queen Alexandra was wonderful at this sort of thing and made everyone play up so that the fun became fast and furious. Arthur Balfour, who had good-naturedly worn a paper cap and helped to play the fool, had had enough after a short time, and asked me to come and play bridge again with Lady Elcho and Mrs Grenfell. We went off in high spirits to the bridge room, where we found three silent and serious rubbers of bridge going on. I told Arthur Balfour that we were too sober for the revels but too drunk to play a solemn game of bridge, which amused him very much.

That March Louise was at Monte Carlo with her son Lord Charles Montagu and the Keppels, and Daisy Pless met her there, 'poor old dear, very cheerful and very rouged', for dinner and an opera. Later that spring the Devonshires were hosts to the King and Queen at Lismore, and Ponsonby noted the Duke's technique as a host of ignoring anyone who might prove tiresome. 'At the same time he was one of the most delightful of men to talk to and could, when he chose, be the best of company.'

The accession of the Liberal government still left the Duke some political work to do. He was by now sitting on the cross-benches, with Lord Rosebery as a companion, but he gave an eve-of-session dinner to some of the free-trade Unionists in 1906. The House of Lords now embarked on the folly of trying to wreck the government's legislative programme, in pursuance of Balfour's intention that 'the great Unionist Party should still control, whether in power or whether in Opposition, the destinies of this great Empire'. It was a fatuous pronouncement, and he was equally astray in looking for precedent to the 1892–5 ministry, when the Lords' opposition had undermined and then brought down the government. The Liberal government of that time had a weak majority and a central policy, Home Rule, which was highly unpopular; now, Campbell-Bannerman had a huge majority and a clear mandate from the country. A partisan use of the House of Lords was a policy that would have required great judgement and discipline to make it effective, and Balfour was too frivolous a politician to provide them.

The political scene, especially from 1908, when Asquith succeeded Campbell-Bannerman as Liberal leader, was developing into a curious penumbra of the social world that Louise Devonshire had created a dozen years before. Balfour may have looked upon his House of Commons sparring as an extension of the drawing-room rivalries at Chatsworth, when he had faced Asquith across so many bridge tables, but in playing the House of Lords against Asquith's Commons majority he bid on the wrong suit. One of the first Liberal measures to earn demolition was a Bill of 1906 aimed at amending the 1902 education system in the Nonconformist interest. The Duke of Devonshire made a strong speech defending religious education, but he was not out to be confrontational. He approached Augustine Birrell and asked him to explain a section of the government's Bill and on hearing the answer said, 'Umph! Then it is not the damned nonsense I thought it.' The Education Bill, or its role in the partisan use of the Lords, seems to have been the subject of a surprising interview he had with Victor Cavendish in December, when the Duke was in an ungovernable temper and ended by kicking over the fender. Victor was quite shaking as he walked home afterwards with Lord Crawford but was unable to explain exactly what happened.

By 1907 the Duke was concerned at the departure of the House of Lords from its proper function as a revising chamber and was pressing with several other leading peers for reform. In May Lord Newton proposed a Bill that would have given comprehensive reform, introducing life peers and restricting the rights of hereditary peers to those who had first qualified by public service. The Duke supported this in a speech which in Almeric Fitzroy's judgement raised the level of the debate. In the event the proposals were referred to a committee, which was chaired by Lord Rosebery and also recommended reform, but the policy was never implemented.

Instead the fate of the House was decided by its catastrophic action over the 1909 Budget. This was a radical measure, increasing death duties and introducing a graduated income tax, besides incorporating provisions for land registration which ought never to have formed part of a Budget. The Lords seized upon the last feature to reject the Budget, or as they said to refer it to the decision of the people. Unfortunately constitutional points of that sort tend to lose distinctness in the political battle; and, while the Lords objected to land registration clauses in a Budget, what the people saw was their objection to the land tax which these would enforce. The Lords chose to test their constitutional powers on the worst possible tactical issue: the taxation of the rich. The timing was also foolish; the 1906 Parliament had only a couple more years to run. The Liberal Party was losing support (even as it was, it only managed to tie with the Conservatives in the 1910 election); and a policy of patience would probably have allowed the Conservatives to win the next election and repeal the Liberal measures. There were members of the Lords who saw the folly of rejecting a Budget, a thing the House had never done in centuries. Lord Lansdowne appealed for moderation, but he lacked authority. Diehard Tories remembered that he was only a Whig who had turned his coat, and he was not listened to. Perhaps even the Duke of Devonshire, if he had been alive, would have found the same neglect, in spite of his unique prestige. The two General Elections of 1910 confirmed the Liberal government in power. The Parliament Act abolished the Upper House's power of veto; Balfour was obliged to resign his party's leadership, and Asquith had comprehensively won the rubber.

The Duke, however, did not live to see those reverses; in the summer of 1907 his health was showing real deterioration. On 5 June the Devonshires held the usual Derby Day dinner and dance; they went to Windsor for Ascot week in mid-June, but the Duke was taken ill and was unable to go to the races. He was brought back to Devonshire House on the 20th 'suffering from acute heart weakness complicated with a considerable settlement of water on the lungs'. But the Duchess, inviting Lady de Trafford to dinner the next evening, was able to give her a favourable report. When he recovered, they went down early to Compton Place for the summer. That September Lady Louisa Egerton died, the last of the three younger siblings all of whom the Duke had survived. His own life had begun to take on an autumnal tinge, while Louise kept up her lifelong insistence on exercise. Walking into the Library at Chatsworth one day, the Duke found his librarian, Mrs Strong, arranging some rare books. He sat down with a copy of *Paradise Lost* and began to read aloud from the first line. After a while he paused to remark: 'How fine this is! I had forgotten how fine it was.' Then the Duchess came in and, poking her parasol into the Duke, said: 'If he begins to read poetry he will never come out for his walk.'

On 24 October they set out for Egypt again for the winter. Writing from Helouan on the Nile on 24 January, one of their companions described the party. The Duke was taking regular strychnine for his heart. 'Louise looks ten years older . . . What they have all been through these last five months. It must have been hell! There is only one description possible of Their Graces. It is a d——d cantankerous old couple. Her Grace is very cheery though. She has been into Cairo to have luncheon with Cassel.' *

In March 1908 they were on their way back to England, but while staying at the Hotel Metropole in Cannes the Duke fell ill with pneumonia. As his mind wandered, he seems to have thought he was playing cards and muttered, 'Well, the game is over, and I am not sorry.' He died on the 24th.

His body was taken back to Chatsworth for burial. As she entered the house on the 27th, Louise suffered a bad fall, but she insisted on coming to Edensor church on the following day and on accompanying her husband's coffin to the graveside. She was wheeled up the steep ascent in a Bath chair and then stood leaning on the new Duke's arm as the burial took place, with Lord Charles Montagu and Lord Stanley on her other side. It was left to Sir Almeric Fitzroy, who had been devoted to the Duke, to strike a heroic note as he wrote: 'It seemed as if the storied pride of a great line had reached its culmination in the life and death before us, and, as the hills on all sides inclined towards the Duke's last resting-place, I felt the force and grandeur of the epitaph which the Greek historian places in the mouth of the Attic orator:

Ἀνδρῶν γὰρ ἐπιφανῶν πᾶσα γῆ τάφος†

The 8th Duke of Devonshire was almost the last head of one of the great families of England to play the public role that had historically belonged to

---

*Sir Ernest Cassel, one of Edward VII's financier friends; also a notable contributor to Louise's favourite charities, to which he gave tens of thousands of pounds.

†'For the whole Earth is the sepulchre of famous men.' From Pericles' funeral oration in Thucydides, Book 2, Chapter 43.

them. Of his successors, only Lord Lansdowne and Lord Curzon achieved a comparable prominence, and neither of them imposed himself so strongly by his character on the consciousness of his countrymen. Among statesmen who never achieved the premiership, the Duke attained a stature equalled only by a few figures such as John Bright and Joseph Chamberlain; that is the estimate that contemporaries would have given, although a later preference for democrats over aristocrats may find it less apparent.

The Duke of Devonshire was often called the last of the Whigs. He embodied the last generation in which Whiggery had a distinctive political presence, but just as significantly his was the last period in which the Whig style was possible at all in British politics. In the last two decades of the nineteenth century changes took place which turned the parties into well-drilled blocs and which were to lead in the direction of state power, of politics by slogan, and of popular mandates deemed to override opposing interests. Leaving aside the question of class or of conservatism, the virtue of Whiggism was that it provided the country with a body of public men who were in politics not out of zealotry or ambition but from a sense of tradition which was rational, cultivated, respectful of differences and public-spirited.

The 8th Duke of Devonshire also stood at the very end of a social era. Even within a year of his death the Radical attack began to make the life of the great London houses an anachronism. Devonshire House remained almost disused by his successor. In 1920 it was sold and soon afterwards pulled down, as were virtually all of the private palaces in which so much power had been wielded. Louise Devonshire and Theresa Londonderry were almost the last hostesses who were able to entertain in the grand traditional style and certainly the last to dominate Society with such formidable control; the latter helped to dig the grave of the old order by backing the die-hard peers in the crisis of 1909–11. Louise would never have done anything so unintelligent, but even before her death she must have realized that her own kind had had its day.

Within a few days of the Duke's death Skittles, now a respectable old lady in South Street, often to be seen going in and out of the neighbouring Jesuit church, was writing to Wilfrid Blunt: 'It is a terrible unhappy thing for me the Duke of Devonshire death.' Any idea that she was heartbroken over her old lover was dispelled by the succeeding correspondence. The Duke had died just before the quarter-day, when her £100 ought to have been paid as it had for the past forty-four years, and the cheque had been withheld with striking promptness. 'I am in a dreadful state of mind and at my wits end what to do . . .' she wrote on 5 May; 'I counted on the money to pay my rent and taxes and other things.' She contemplated an appeal to the heir, but 'I am told the present new Duke is not a nice fellow and of course the old Dowager Duchess would be dead against me.' What happened was that the nasty fellow ordered the allowance to be continued, and Skittles received it until her death in 1920. This was despite the furious opposition of Victor's wife, a prudish memsahib to whom even more innocent pastimes than fornication were anathema. The 9th Duke also tried to get his uncle's love-letters back (how did he know of their existence – had Skittles attempted blackmail?), but Skittles insisted that Hart-ington had been her closest friend and she could not bear to part with them. She bequeathed them instead to two later lovers, Wilfrid Blunt and Gerald de Saumarez, and the latter collection is now back at Chatsworth.

The Duke left Louise £8,000 a year in his will, in addition to her continuing jointure from the Manchester estate, and offered her the option of taking Compton Place as her dower house; but she preferred to take a house in Grosvenor Square, where she lived until her death. She enjoyed the devoted support of her second son, Lord Charles Montagu, who had never married, and in December 1908 we find Queen Alexandra sending him a beautiful little Fabergé box (now at Chatsworth) to take to his mother as a Christmas present. Louise was on one of her trips abroad, which were frequent. In May 1910 King Edward died, the second of the trio who had been the ringleaders of such a merry life for half a century. Sir Almeric Fitzroy found Louise at his funeral and at the luncheon helped Lord Charles Montagu provide food for his mother, 'who looked as if her last hour was not far off'. Despite her social energy, she had been hampered for years by ill health, including rheumatism and other ailments. While in Cannes in February 1911 she fell ill again and was not able to return to England until late April . On 14 July she went to Sandown races and the hot day brought on a seizure. She was taken unconscious to the nearby Esher Place, the house of Sir Edgar Vincent, and there she died early on the 15th. According to her sister Julie, 'death came with so mild a hand that she hardly noticed its coming'. After attending her funeral, Arthur Balfour told Lady Elcho: 'I thought the atten-dance at the service unexpectedly small; especially as few went to Chatsworth. But after all I suppose that death had greatly thinned the circle of her intimates, and I did not particularly notice the absence of any expected faces.'

NOTES

These notes are chiefly intended to indicate the bibliography available, and sources are not usually cited more than once, references being added to the other pages quoted elsewhere in the book.

CHAPTER 1: LOUISE VON ALTEN

Louise's early life is described by her sister Julie von Albedyll in *Lebenserinnerungen aus Hannover und Preussen*, 1914, pp. 1–34 (other ref. p. 334).

p. 14 Lady Augusta Fane: *Chit-Chat*, 1926, p. 106 (other refs pp. 107–9).

p. 15–16 Francis Cavendish on Louise: F.W.H. Cavendish, *Society, Politics and Diplomacy*, 1913, pp. 222 and 239.

p. 16 Princess Radziwill: *My Recollections*, 1904, p. 84.

p. 19 Louise wins promise from Derby: Count Albrecht von Bernstorff, *Im Kampfe für Preussens Ehre*, 1906, p. 384 (other ref. p. 399), and Sir Shane Leslie, *Long Shadows*, 1966, p. 48: 'She had made Lord Derby, when young, sign a promise that he would give her that office in the unlikely case of his becoming Prime Minister which he did.' This is evidently a family tradition from Col. Charles Leslie, but it shows at least two inaccuracies: Lord Derby was nearing sixty and had already been Prime Minister once when the promise was made.

p. 19 Louise impresses Lord Carlisle: Susan Oldfield, *Some Records of Harriet Countess Granville*, 1901, p. 247. The author is the Susan Pitt mentioned on p. 56.

pp. 19–20 Louise in Paris: Earl Cowley (ed. F.A. Wellesley), *The Paris Embassy During the Second Empire*, 1928, p. 142.

p. 20 Derby offers Robes: Chatsworth MS uncatalogued, letter of 23 February 1858.

p. 20 Queen Victoria on Louise: Roger Fulford (ed.), *Dearest Child*, 1964, Vol. 1, letters of 27 February 1858 and 1 August 1859 (other ref. Vol. 4, letter of 18 April 1877).

p. 20 Granville to Louise: A.L. Kennedy, *My Dear Duchess*, 1956, p. 24 (other refs. pp. 4, 63, 70, 80, 81, 102, 117, 153, 155, 172, 196, 217, 218).

p. 21 Louise to Queen Victoria: A.C Benson and Viscount Esher (ed.), *The Letters of Queen Victoria 1837–61*, 1907, Vol. 3, pp. 383–4.

p. 23 Lord Cowper and Louise: Lady Cowper, *Earl Cowper K.G.: A Memoir*, 1913, p. 86: 'He admired her extremely, and the friendship became a very intimate one.' Lady Cowper could not have written thus of a woman of Louise's reputation without knowing that an affair would be understood (other refs pp. 316, 354).

p. 24 Stillbirth: Huntingdon County Record Office, Manchester Papers C, Diary of 7th Duke of Manchester, 1860–90; an uninformative source.

pp. 24–5 Huntly on the Duke: Marquis of Huntly, *Milestones*, 1926, p. 194.

p. 25 Louise falls over stile: Anita Leslie, *Edwardians in Love*, 1972, pp. 73–82 (other refs pp. 147, 223, 282).

CHAPTER 2: WHIG INHERITANCE

John Pearson provides in *Stags and Serpents*, 1983, a lively general history of the Cavendish family, although giving too free a rein to his imagination on the character of the 8th Duke. Of the two contemporary biographies, H. Leach, *The Duke of Devonshire*, 1904, is compiled from newspapers, *Hansard*, etc., with some dubious anecdotes thrown in, but is useful and accurate within its limits; Bernard Holland, *The Life of the Eighth Duke of Devonshire*, 2 vols, 1911, is fuller and better informed, the author having been on the Duke's secretarial staff from 1892 to 1894. Patrick Jackson, *The Last of the Whigs*, 1994, as a political biography is adequate only for the years 1879–1903; it does not study the Whig background, as the title might suggest.

pp. 31–4 6th Duke of Devonshire: biography by James Lees-Milne, *The Bachelor Duke*, 1991 (refs pp. 90, 203).

pp. 35–8 Cavendish's letters: Chatsworth MSS 340.29 and fol.

pp. 38–9 Lady Louisa Hamilton: *Earl Cowper K.G.*, pp. 42 and 89; G.W.E. Russell's obituary in *The Times*, collected in *Half-Lengths*, 1911, pp. 96–9.

pp. 339–40 Devonshire House is described in A. Beresford Chancellor, *The Private Palaces of London*, 1908, in Christopher Sykes, *Private Palaces*, 1985, and in John Cornforth's article in *Country Life*, November 1980.

p. 40 Lady Eastlake's description: C. Eastlake Smith (ed.), *Journals and Correspondence of Lady Eastlake*, 1895, Vol. 1, pp. 245–6.

p. 40 Dislike of Chesterfield: various letters of Cavendish's in Chatsworth MSS including 340.3364 to Skittles: 'This place looks more black and dirty & beastly & dull than ever.' Neither this nor the address 'Chesterfield' refers to Chatsworth, as interpreted by Patrick Jackson in 'Skittles and the Marquis' in *History Today*, December 1995.

p. 41 Cavendish's letters from Ireland: Chatsworth MSS 340.8, 78, 79. The first of these has been assigned in the archive to 1849, without good reason.

pp. 41–2 Russian embassy: Lord Edmond Fitzgerald, *Life of the Second Earl Granville*, 1905, Vol. 1, pp. 182–208 (other refs pp. 111, 237 and Vol. 2, pp. 71, 390, 461); also Hon. Frederick Leveson Gower (Granville's brother), *Bygone Years*, 1905, pp. 212–36.

p. 44 'breed of spaniels': Donald Southgate, *The Passing of the Whigs*, 1962, p. 282 (other refs pp. 284, 302, 327–8, 410, 417). The book is a comprehensive study of the Whig scene in the period before 1886.

p. 44 Yawn in maiden speech: the story is first told in Leach, p. 61 (1904). For the origin
see note to p. 180.

p. 47 Lady Waldegrave: biography by O.W. Hewett, *Strawberry Fair*, 1956 (other refs
pp. 231, 242–4, 250, 260, 266).

p. 47 Hartington's journal (1857–8, incomplete): Chatsworth MS.

CHAPTER 3: SKITTLES

A useful article is Donald MacAndrew, 'Skittles', in *The Saturday Book*, 1948. Henry
Blyth, *Skittles*, 1970, is said to have dispelled earlier legends regarding her life but
gets the affair with Hartington badly wrong. Lady Longford's biography of W.S.
Blunt, *A Pilgrimage of Passion*, 1979, using the Blunt papers in the Fitzwilliam
Museum, marks a great step forward. The article by Patrick Jackson, 'Skittles and
the Marquis', in *History Today*, December 1995, is written in ignorance of the Blunt
archive (and of Lady Longford's use of it); it tells only half the story and is full of
errors. The entire correspondence of Hartington to Skittles is preserved in two
collections: 236 letters bequeathed to Gerald de Saumarez and now at Chatsworth
(MSS 340. 3321 to 3530), and 21 bequeathed to Blunt (Fitzwilliam MSS 717 to 737-
1976); other Fitzwilliam MSS, e.g. 646, 655 and 656-1976 and 9-1975 (Blunt's
Memoirs, under 7 February and 5 March 1909), also shed light on the affair. Both
collections are in a hopeless jumble, to the extent that Fitzwilliam MS 737-1976 is
the continuation of Chatsworth MS 340.3416, as two halves of the same letter.

p. 51 Blunt's poem: *Esther*, 1892.

p. 52 Chichester Fortescue: biography by O.W. Hewett, . . . *And Mr Fortescue*, 1958, p. 161.

p. 54 G.A. Sala: as article in *The Welcome Guest*, Summer 1858, and published in *Twice
Round the Clock*, 1858.

p. 55 Landseer picture: details and reproduction in Campbell Lennie, *Landseer*, 1976.

p. 60 *Persia*: Chatsworth MSS 340.175, 177, 3413B and 7th Duke's diary for 16 and 20
August 1862. Not the *Great Eastern* as stated by Leach who also wrongly states that
the Duke also went to America.

p. 64 Belmont's ball: George Templeton Strong, *Diary of the Civil War*, New York,
1962, pp. 300–1. According to Strong, Hartington actually spoke to General
McClellan, but this is denied in the account by Belmont's son: Perry Belmont, *An
American Democrat*, New York, 1940, p. 123. See also Sir Shane Leslie, *The End of
a Chapter*, 1916, p. 18.

p. 69 'venial escapade': *Society in London, by a Foreign Resident*, 1885, p. 103 (other refs
pp. 46, 100–2, 114). The author was in fact T.H.S. Escott (compare note to p. 163).

CHAPTER 4: THE PRINCE OF WALES AND FRIENDS

p. 73 Hartington's parliamentary performance: William White, *The Inner Life of the
House of Commons*, 1897, Vol. 2, pp. 11–12 and 21–4.

p. 75 G.W.E. Russell: *Portraits of the Seventies*, 1916, Chapter 6, 'Lord Hartington'. Russell, a cousin of the Duke of Bedford, was a journalist whose works are of special interest for the aristocratic and Whig life of the period. See also his *Collections and Recollections*, 1898, *Social Silhouettes*, 1906, and *Sketches and Snapshots*, 1910.

p. 77 Hartington a Palmerstonian: Holland, Vol. 1, p. 30.

pp. 77–8 Lady Frederick: J. Bailey (ed.), *The Diary of Lady Frederick Cavendish*, 1927, refs Vol. 1, pp. 166, 220, 231, 238, 271, 285, 297, 303, and Vol. 2, pp. 10, 21, 48, 105, 143–6, 172, 186, 204, 237, 278–9, 317–31.

p. 80 Sir George Leveson Gower: *Mixed Grill*, 1948, p. 58 (other refs pp. 22, 40–1, 43).

p. 80 Lord Ronald Gower: *My Reminiscences*, 1895, p. 137 (other ref. p. 318).

p. 83 Daisy Maynard: Countess of Warwick, *Life's Ebb and Flow*, 1929, p. 176.

CHAPTER 5: THE FIRST GLADSTONE MINISTRY

p. 88 'pitchforked' into War Office: Granville to Gladstone 18 August 1873 in Agatha Ramm (ed.), *The Gladstone–Granville Correspondence*, 1952.

p. 89 Queen Victoria on Louise to Gladstone: M.R.D. Foot and H.C.G. Matthew, *The Gladstone Diaries*, 1968–94, entry of 6 December 1868.

p. 89 Queen Victoria to Princess Alexandra: Georgina Battiscombe, *Queen Alexandra*, 1969, and Philip Magnus, *King Edward VII*, 1964, p. 109.

p. 90 Louise at Downing Street: Peter Gordon, *The Red Earl*, 1981 (Diaries of Earl Spencer), Vol. 1, p. 83 (other refs pp. 13, 87, 89, 122, 127, 233 and Vol. 2, pp. 5, 14, 82). There is a story that Hartington received the news of the outbreak of the Franco-Prussian War while grouse-shooting and put the telegram in his pocket with the remark 'These foreigners are always up to something.' As grouse are not shot in mid-July the story falls under suspicion; it has been elaborated from the fact that he received the news of the abdication of Napoleon III (6 September) while on the grouse moors at Bolton.

p. 91 Louise in Ireland: A. Hayward, *Sketches of Eminent Statesmen and Writers*, 1880, Vol. 2, p. 303.

p. 91 Ponsonby on Hartington: Henry Ponsonby, *Lord Ponsonby of Shulbrede*, 1943, p. 265 (other refs. pp. 116, 120, 118).

p. 94 Hartington's racing career: 'Spencer, Eighth Duke of Devonshire', in *British Sports and Sportsmen*, Vol. 2, 1908, ed. by *The Sportsman*.

p. 95 Disraeli's attack on Hartington: Lord George Hamilton, *Parliamentary Reminiscences and Reflections*, 1916, pp. 42–4 (other refs. pp. 41, 87).

p. 95 Duke writes to Hartington at Sandringham: C. Hibbert, *Edward VII*, 1976, p. 228.

p. 99 Duke of Hamilton: Walburga Lady Paget, *The Linings of Life*, 1928, Vol. 1, p. 296 (other refs. pp. 289 and Vol. 2, pp. 331–2, 520, 552).

p. 99 Hartington to Louise: Chatsworth MSS uncatalogued.

p. 101 Mrs Adair: quoted in Gail MacColl and Carol Wallace, *To Marry an English Lord*, 1989, pp. 43–4 (other refs. pp. 87, 89, 167, 289, 356).

p. 101 Lady Randolph Churchill: Anita Leslie, *Jennie*, 1969, p. 67.

p. 101 and fol. Disraeli's letters: Marquis of Zetland, *The Letters of Disraeli to Lady Bradford and Lady Chesterfield*, 1927, refs. letters of 19 July 1874, 2 February 1875, 9 July and 11 October and 23 October 1876, 22 March 1877, 18 July and 6 August 1879, 1 February 1881.

p. 104 'I would marry at once': quoted in *Edwardians in Love*, pp. 80–1; the anecdote was told to Bernard Holland in 1920 by Lady Greville, the widow of Hartington's confidant.

p. 105 Lillie Langtry, *The Days I Knew*, 1925, pp. 42 and 233 (other ref. p. 51).

pp. 106–7 Hartington at Devonshire House: Viscount Esher, *Cloud-Capp'd Towers*, 1927, p. 176.

CHAPTER 6: THE LIBERAL LEADERSHIP

Hartington's leadership, 1875–80, is fully described by John Rossi in *The Transformation of the British Liberal Party: Transactions of the American Philosophical Society*, December 1978, Vol. 68, Part 8, from a Gladstonian and Chamberlainian point of view. T.A. Jenkins, *Gladstone, Whiggery and the Liberal Party 1874–1886*, 1988, provides some corrections to Rossi and a useful view of affairs outside Parliament. The treatment in *The Last of the Whigs*, Chapter 3, is surprisingly weak, beginning with the apology that the period 'is difficult to interpret', but improves with Chapter 4 on events from 1879.

p. 111 Forster on Louise: Lady St Helier, *Memories of Fifty Years*, 1909, p. 172 (other ref. p. 253).

p. 111 Queen Victoria to Louise: Chatsworth MSS uncatalogued.

p. 114 'ablest Whig': A.B. Cooke and John Vincent, *The Governing Passion*, 1974, p. 24.

p. 114 'greatest leader': Jonathan Parry, *The Rise and Fall of Liberal Government in Victorian Britain*, 1993, p. 260.

p. 115 and fol. Disraeli's letters: W.F. Monypenny and G.E. Buckle, *Life of Disraeli* (refs. Vol. 4, pp. 87, 386, Vol. 5, pp. 361, 392, 430, 480, Vol. 6, pp. 69, 79–80, 128, 362, 438).

p. 115 Austrian ambassador: Sarah Bradford, *Disraeli*, 1982, p. 320.

p. 118 Hartington to Spencer: *The Red Earl*, Vol. 1, p. 127.

p. 118 Granville to Louise: Chatsworth MS uncatalogued.

p. 121 Lord Esher: biography by James Lees-Milne, *The Enigmatic Edwardian*, 1986 (other refs. pp. 45, 47, 49, 60, 68, 77).

p. 122 Dilke on Hartington: *The Last of the Whigs*, p. 83.

p. 123 Hartington on Gladstone taking the lead: Philip Magnus, *Gladstone*, 1954, p. 248 (letter of 25 May 1877) (other refs. pp. 292, 348, 381, 391).

p. 124 Gladstone absent from Hartington dinner: A. Ramm (ed.), *The Political Correspondence of Mr Gladstone and Lord Granville 1876–1886*, 1962, Vol. 1, p. 46.

p. 128 Hartington to Granville: quoted in *The Transformation of the British Liberal Party*, p. 105.

p. 129 Forster from Kimbolton: Chatsworth MS 340.886–7.

CHAPTER 7: THE PHOENIX PARK TRAGEDY

p. 123 Lytton: Lady Dorothy Nevill, *Life and Letters*, 1919, p. 255.

p. 124 Lord Ribblesdale, *Impressions and Memories*, 1927, p. 119.

p. 136 Hartington's railway nationalization policy: *The Passing of the Whigs*, p. 348.

p. 136 County boards policy: Holland, Vol. 1, pp. 124, 243, and Hartington's speech at Sheffield on 28 June 1886.

p. 138 Hartington revises Irish Land Bill: Holland, Vol. 1, p. 336; *Earl Cowper K.G.*, p. 468.

p. 139 Hartington and Forster: T.W. Moody and R. Hawkins (ed.), *Florence Arnold-Forster's Irish Journal*, 1988, under 11 March 1882.

CHAPTER 8: GORDON AND KHARTOUM

p. 146 Hartington to Granville: A.B. Cooke and John Vincent, *The Governing Passion*, 1974, p. 246. This book provides an intensive study of Cabinet politics from the beginning of 1885 to the fall of Gladstone's third administration in 1886 (other refs. pp. 24–8, 115, 331).

p. 149 Rosebery: Robert Rhodes James, *Rosebery*, 1963.

p. 151 Incoherence over Gordon: Lord Morley, *Life of Gladstone*, 1903, Book VIII, Chapter 9, Section 5.

p. 152 Hartington to Queen Victoria: A.C. Benson and Viscount Esher (eds), *The Letters of Queen Victoria*, 1879–85, Vol. 3, pp. 486–7.

pp. 152–3 Hartington coming out of War Office: Sir Almeric Fitzroy, *Memoirs*, under 2 March 1907.

p. 157 Speech makes Hartington sick: Sir George Leveson Gower, *Years of Content*, 1940, p. 231.

CHAPTER 9: THE PASSING OF THE WHIGS

p. 161 Hartington's speech at Sheffield, 28 June 1886: reported in *The Times*; compare *The Gladstone Diaries*, 17 August 1886, for Gladstone's reaction.

p. 162 Harcourt proposes Devonshire House meeting: A.S. Gardiner, *Sir William Harcourt*, 1923, Vol. 1, p. 556 (other refs pp. 473 and Vol. 2, p. 4). Jackson, *The Last of the Whigs*, p. 212, states that Chamberlain proposed it but does not cite evidence.

p. 163 Reconciliation with Churchill: T.H.S. Escott, *Society in the Country House*, 1907, pp. 55–6 and 470.

p. 163 Hartington and Lady Randolph: Mrs George Cornwallis-West, *The Reminiscences of Lady Randolph Churchill*, 1908, p. 133.

p. 165 County boards policy: see notes to pp. 136–61.

p. 165 Hartington advocates Irish land purchase (January–March 1886): *The Governing Passion*, p. 90, and Holland, Vol. 2, p. 204, for his support of the 1890 measure.

p. 167 Gladstone prepares his joke: Margot Asquith, *Autobiography*, 1920, Vol. 1, p. 152; compare John Vincent, *The Later Derby Diaries*, 1981, p. 68.

p. 167 Lady Harcourt to Hartington: Leach (1904), p. 249, puts this anecdote in 1886. Later tellings of the story link it more obviously, to Harcourt's 1894 Budget but contain suspicious features, such as the absurdity of Devonshire (as he then was) and Lady Harcourt addressing each other as 'Madam' and 'Your Grace'.

pp. 167–8 Waddesdon party and Chamberlain on Gladstone's malevolence: Robin Harcourt Williams (ed.), *Salisbury–Balfour Correspondence*, 1988, letters of 15 June and 24 July 1886.

p. 169 Gladstone impugns Hartington's conduct in 1880: *The Last of the Whigs*, pp. 121–2.

p. 170 David Cannadine: *The Decline and Fall of the British Aristocracy*, 1990, p. 4, etc.

CHAPTER 10: A TIME TO CANCAN

p. 173 Florence Williams: Mrs Hwfa Williams, *It Was Such Fun*, 1935, pp. 27–8 (other refs. pp. 44, 48–9, 75, 86, 202–3, 223).

p. 174 Louise's stock-jobbing: *The Later Derby Diaries*, p. 112.

p. 175 Louise and Margot Tennant: told in Margot Asquith, *Autobiography*, p. 58, and *More Memories*, 1933, p. 174.

p. 179 Prince dances cancan: Philippe Jullian, *Edward and the Edwardians*, 1967, p. 133.

p. 179 Marsh as Hartington's trainer: Richard Marsh, *A Trainer to Two Kings*, 1925, pp. 84–117, 229–30.

p. 180 Hartington's insomnia: George Smalley, *Anglo-American Memories*, 2nd Series, 1912, pp. 29–30 (other refs. pp. 35, 43 and Series 1, p. 363).

p. 180 Hartington yawns in speech: Henry Lucy, *Memories of Eight Parliaments*, 1908, p. 136.

p. 181 Hartington shoots high partridge: Duke of Portland, *Men, Women and Things*, 1937, p. 247 (other refs. pp. 42, 68, 186–8, 251).

p. 182 Hats given as presents: Holland, Vol. 2, p. 234; Lady Randolph Churchill, *Reminiscences*, p. 154; Duke of Manchester, *My Candid Recollections*, p. 237.

p. 183 'quadruped': Jane Ridley and Clayre Percy (eds), *The Letters of Arthur Balfour and Lady Elcho*, 1992, p. 82; the phrase is often misquoted (other refs. pp. 38–9, 116–17, 177–8, 266).

p. 184 'How that man does talk': Viscount Mersey, *A Picture of Life*, 1941, p. 218.

p. 184 Chamberlain at Chatsworth: Lady Warwick, *Afterthoughts*, 1931, p. 46 (other refs. pp. 51, 76–7, 81, 105, 257).

p. 186 Bessie Bellwood: N.T.P. Murphy, *In Search of Blandings*, 1986, p. 17.

p. 187 Consuelo's gaffe: Duke of Manchester, *My Candid Recollections*, p. 62 (other refs. pp. 47, 49, 57, 128).

CHAPTER 11: DOUBLE DUCHESS

p. 192 Louise to Chaplin: Lady Londonderry, *Henry Chaplin: A Memoir*, 1926, p. 139 (other refs. pp. 297, 340).

pp. 192–4 The Devonshire finances are fully described in David Cannadine, *Aspects of Aristocracy*, 1994: 'The Landowner as Millionaire'.

p. 194 'Clapham Junction': E.F. Benson, *As We Were*, 1930, p. 177 (other refs. pp. 174–7).

p. 201 Ulster's right of resistance: speech at Dalkeith (in Gladstone's constituency) 15 April 1893.

CHAPTER 12: ELDER STATESMAN

p. 204 The Duke at Windsor: Frederick Ponsonby, *Recollections of Three Reigns*, 1951, p. 28 (other refs. pp. 199–205).

p. 204 Duke's hands shake: Kenneth Rose, *Superior Person*, 1969, p. 293 (other ref. p. 380).

p. 204 'sacred day': Lord Askwith, *Lord James of Hereford*, 1930, pp. 255–6 – a better source, since James was a Cabinet colleague, than the Duke of Portland's version (*op. cit.*, p. 189), which is the one often quoted.

pp. 204–5 Salisbury on learning bridge: Fitzroy, *Memoirs*, Vol. 1, pp. 56–7 (entry of 16 July 1901).

p. 205 Victor Cavendish: Harold Macmillan, *The Past Masters*, 1975, pp. 194–5.

p. 208–9 Lady Angela Forbes, *Memories and Base Details*, 1921, p. 97

p. 209 and fol. Chatsworth is described by the Duchess of Devonshire in *The House*, 1982.

p. 210 and fol. Princess Daisy of Pless: *Daisy Princess of Pless, By Herself*, 1928, pp. 83–4, 94, 102, 113, 125, 127, and *From My Private Diary*, 1931, pp. 82–7, 126–7, 180, has numerous descriptions of the Chatsworth house-parties.

p. 213 Louise presents ladies: *The Queen* for May 1897.

p. 213 The ball is splendidly described in Lady Sophia Murphy, *The Duchess of Devonshire's Ball*, 1984.

p. 214 Lord Charles Beresford at Ascot: Giles St Aubyn, *Edward VII: Prince and King*, 1979, p. 192, and Christopher Hibbert, *Edward VII*, 1976, pp. 164–5.

p. 214 Lady Fingall, *Seventy Years Young*, 1937, p. 257. She appears to put this incident in 1896, although she refers to the Prince as the King.

pp. 220–3 German negotiations: Baron Eckardstein, *Ten Years at the Court of St James*, 1921, pp. 93–4, 106, 123, 176, 184, 194–5.

p. 223 Consuelo Marlborough: Consuelo Vanderbilt Balsan, *The Glitter and the Gold*, 1953, p. 107 (other refs. pp. 57, 96).

p. 225 Duke forgets King's dinner: J. Vincent (ed.), *The Crawford Papers*, 1986, p. 66 (other refs. pp. 73, 93, 96, 98, 547, 603).

CHAPTER 13: RESIGNATION

p. 227 Louise at Windsor, 1902: Sir Lionel Cust, *King Edward VII and His Court*, 1930, pp. 42–3.

p. 227 Duchess of Sermoneta, *Things Past*, 1929, p. 75.

p. 227 George Lambton, *Men and Horses I Have Known*, 1924, p. 53.

pp. 229–30 'We don't want to lose a colony': Leach p. 298; compare *The Last of the Whigs*, p. 312, for ministers' efforts to sideline Gorst.

pp. 230–1 Balfour tells the Duke of his appointment: Lord Askwith, *Lord James of Hereford*, 1930, pp. 268–9 (other refs. pp. 94–5, 277, 281). Jackson (*The Last of the Whigs*, p. 322) sees a discrepancy with the Duke's account in Lord Newton, *Lord Lansdowne*, 1929, p. 241.

pp. 231–2 Louise at Coronation: Fitzroy, *Memoirs*, Vol. 1, p. 71.

p. 235 Stanley visits Duke: Randolph Churchill, *Lord Derby, King of Lancashire*, 1959, pp. 79–81.

p. 237 'A lot of damned fools': Randolph Churchill, *Fifteen Famous English Houses*, 1954, p. 105.

p. 238 'The defection of the Duke of Devonshire': A. Adonis, *Making Aristocracy Work*, 1993, p. 181 (other refs. pp. 28, 30, 122, 124).

CHAPTER 14: THE CLOSING YEARS

p. 239–40 Beerbohm: Rupert Hart-Davis, *The Letters of Max Beerbohm*, 1972, p. 231.

p. 242 Lady Gosford on Daisy Pless: Chatsworth MS uncatalogued.

p. 244 King pig-sticking: Lady Maud Warrender, *My First Sixty Years*, 1933, pp. 78–9; 1907 seems to be the only year that fits this account.

BIBLIOGRAPHY

Books relating to the 8th Duke of Devonshire and the Duchess are:

Albedyll, Julie von, *Lebenserinnerungen aus Hannover und Preussen*, Potsdam, 1914

Bernstorff, Count Albrecht von, *Im Kampfe für Preussens Ehre*, Berlin, 1906

Holland, Bernard, *The Life of the Eighth Duke of Devonshire*, Longmans Green, London, 2 vols, 1911

Jackson, Patrick, *The Last of the Whigs*, Associated University Presses, London and Toronto, 1994

Kennedy, A.L., *My Dear Duchess*, John Murray, London, 1956

Leach, Henry, *The Duke of Devonshire*, Methuen, London, 1904

Scholarly studies of the Liberal politics of the period include:

Cooke, A.B. and John Vincent, *The Governing Passion*, Harvester Press, Hassocks, 1974

Jenkins, T.A., *Gladstone, Whiggery and the Liberal Party 1874–1886*, Clarendon Press, London, 1988

Parry, Jonathan, *The Rise and Fall of Liberal Government in Victorian Britain*, Yale University Press, New Haven and London, 1993

Rossi, John, *The Transformation of the British Liberal Party* in *Transactions of the American Philosophical Society*, American Philosophical Society, Philadelphia, 1978

Southgate, Donald, *The Passing of the Whigs*, Macmillan, London, 1962

Works on the social life of the period include:

Leslie, Anita, *Edwardians in Love*, Hutchinson, London, 1972

Russell, G.W.E., *Collections and Recollections,* Thomas Nelson and Sons, London, 1898

Russell, G.W.E., *Portraits of the Seventies*, T. Fisher Unwin, London, 1916

Russell, G.W.E. *Sketches and Snapshots*, Smith, Elder and Co., London, 1910

Russell, G.W.E., *Social Silhouettes*, Smith, Elder and Co., London, 1906

Biographies include:

Battiscombe, Georgina, *Queen Alexandra*, Constable, London, 1969

Fitzgerald, Lord Edmond, *Life of the Second Earl Granville*, Longmans Green, London, 1905

Gardiner, A.S., *Sir William Harcourt*, Constable, London, 1923
Hewett, O.W., *... And Mr Fortescue*, John Murray, London, 1958
Hewett, O.W., *Strawberry Fair*, John Murray, London, 1956
Hibbert, Christopher, *Edward VII*, Allen Lane, London, 1976
Leslie, Anita, *Jennie*, Hutchinson, London, 1969
Magnus, Philip, *Gladstone*, John Murray, London, 1954
Magnus, Philip, *King Edward VII*, John Murray, London, 1964
Monypenny, W. and G. Buckle, *Life of Disraeli*, John Murray, London, 1920
Morley, Lord, *Life of Gladstone*, Macmillan, London, 1903
Ponsonby, Henry, *Lord Ponsonby of Shulbrede*, Macmillan, London, 1943
St Aubyn, Giles, *Edward VII, Prince and King*, Collins, London, 1979

General memoirs, collections of letters and original diaries include:
Asquith, Margot, *Autobiography*, Thornton Butterworth, London, 1920
Asquith, Margot, *More Memories*, Cassell and Co., London, 1933
Bailey, J. (ed.), *The Diary of Lady Frederick Cavendish*, 2 vols, John Murray, London, 1927
Benson, A.C. and Viscount Esher (eds), Victoria, Queen, *The Letters of Queen Victoria*, 1907
Benson, E.F., *As We Were*, Longman, London, 1930
Blyth, Henry, *Skittles*, Rupert Hart-Davis, London, 1970
Cavendish, F.W.H., *Society, Politics and Diplomacy*, T. Fisher Unwin, London, 1913
Churchill, Lady Randolph, *Reminiscences*, Edward Arnold, London, 1908
Cowley, Earl, *The Paris Embassy During the Second Empire*, Thornton Butterworth, London, 1928
Cowper, Lady, *Earl Cowper K.G.: A Memoir*, privately printed, 1913
Disraeli, Benjamin, *The Letters of Disraeli to Lady Bradford and Lady Chesterfield*, Ernest Benn, London, 1927
Eckardstein, Baron, *Ten Years at the Court of St James*, Thornton Butterworth, London, 1921
Esher, Viscount, *Cloud-Capp'd Towers*, John Murray, London, 1927
Fane, Lady Augusta, *Chit-Chat*, Thornton Butterworth, London, 1926
Fingall, Lady, *Seventy Years Young*, Collins, London, 1937
Fitzroy, Sir Almeric, *Memoirs*, Hutchinson, London, 1910
Foot, M. and H. Matthew (eds), Gladstone, W.E., *The Gladstone Diaries*, Clarendon Press, Oxford, 1968–94
Forbes, Lady Angela, *Memories and Base Details*, Hutchinson, London, 1921
Fulford, Roger (ed.), *Dearest Child: Letters Between Queen Victoria and the Princess Royal, 1858–1861*, Evans Brothers, London, 1964
Gordon, Peter (ed.), Spencer, Earl, diaries, in *The Red Earl*, Northamptonshire Record Society, Northampton, 1981

Gower, Lord Ronald, *My Reminiscences*, Kegan Paul, London, 1895

Hamilton, Lord George, *Parliamentary Reminiscences and Reflections*, John Murray, London, 1916

Harcourt-Williams, Robin, *Salisbury–Balfour Correspondence*, Hertfordshire Record Society, Ware, 1988

Langtry, Lillie *The Days I Knew*, Hutchinson, London, 1925

Leveson Gower, Hon. Frederick, *Bygone Years*, John Murray, London, 1905

Leveson Gower, Sir George, *Mixed Grill*, Frederick Muller, London, 1948

Leveson Gower, Sir George, *Years of Content*, John Murray, London, 1940

Lucy, Henry, *Memories of Eight Parliaments*, William Heinemann, London, 1908

Manchester, Duke of, *My Candid Recollections*, Grayson and Grayson, London, *c.* 1930

Marlborough, Consuelo, Duchess of, *The Glitter and the Gold*, George Mann, Maidstone, 1953

Nevill, Lady Dorothy, *Life and Letters*, Methuen and Co., London, 1919

Paget, Walburga, Lady, *The Linings of Life*, Hurst and Blackett, London, 1928

Pless, Daisy, Princess of, *Princess Daisy of Pless, By Herself*, John Murray, London, 1928

Pless, Daisy, Princess of, *From My Private Diary*, John Murray, London, 1931

Ponsonby, Frederick, *Recollections of Three Reigns*, Eyre and Spottiswoode, London, 1951

Portland, Duke of, *Men, Women and Things*, Faber and Faber, London, 1937

Radziwill, Princess, *My Recollections*, Isbister and Co., London, 1904

Ramm, Agatha (ed.), Gladstone, W.E., *The Gladstone–Granville Correspondence*, Royal Historical Society, London, 1952

Ramm, Agatha (ed.), Gladstone, W.E., *The Political Correspondence of Mr Gladstone and Lord Granville*, Clarendon Press, Oxford, 1962

Ridley, J. and C. Percy (eds), *The Letters of Arthur Balfour and Lady Elcho*, Hamish Hamilton, London, 1992

St Helier, Lady, *Memories of Fifty Years*, Edward Arnold, London, 1909

Sermoneta, Duchess of, *Things Past*, Hutchinson, London, 1929

Vincent, John (ed.), *The Crawford Papers*, Manchester University Press, Manchester, 1986

Vincent, John (ed.), *The Later Derby Diaries*, University of Bristol, Bristol, 1981

Warrender, Lady Maud, *My First Sixty Years*, Cassell and Co., London, 1933

Warwick, Countess of, *Life's Ebb and Flow*, Hutchinson, London, 1929

Warwick, Countess of, *Afterthoughts*, Cassell and Co., London, 1931

Williams, Mrs Hwfa, *It Was Such Fun*, Hutchinson, London, 1935

John Pearson gives in *Stags and Serpents*, Macmillan, London, 1983, a general history of the Cavendish family. The present Duchess of Devonshire describes Chatsworth in

The House, Frances Lincoln, London, 1982. Her daughter Lady Sophia Murphy gives an account of the 1897 ball in *The Duchess of Devonshire's Ball*, Sidgwick and Jackson, London, 1984.

The Duke of Devonshire's career as a racing owner is described in:
The Sportsman (ed.), *British Sports and Sportsmen*, London, 1908
Lambton, George, *Men and Horses I Have Known,* Thornton Butterworth, London, 1924
Marsh, Richard, *A Trainer to Two Kings*, Cassell and Co., London, 1925

INDEX